1 Henry IV

Continuum Renaissance Drama

Series Editors: Andrew Hiscock, University of Wales Bangor, UK, and Lisa Hopkins, Sheffield Hallam University, UK

Continuum Renaissance Drama offers practical and accessible introductions to the critical and performative contexts of key Elizabethan and Jacobean plays. Each guide introduces the text's critical and performance history but also provides students with an invaluable insight into the landscape of current scholarly research through a keynote essay on the state of the art and newly commissioned essays of fresh research from different critical perspectives.

A Midsummer Night's Dream: A Critical Guide
edited by Regina Buccola
Doctor Faustus: A Critical Guide
edited by Sarah Munson Deats
Duchess of Malfi: A Critical Guide
edited by Christina Luckyj
King Lear: A Critical Guide
edited by Andrew Hiscock and Lisa Hopkins
The Jew of Malta: A Critical Guide
edited by Robert A. Logan
Volpone: A Critical Guide
edited by Matthew Steggle
Women Beware Women: A Critical Guide
edited by Andrew Hiscock

1 HENRY IV

A Critical Guide

Edited by Stephen Longstaffe

continuum

Continuum International Publishing Group
The Tower Building   80 Maiden Lane,
11 York Road   Suite 704
London SE1 7NX   New York NY 10038

© Stephen Longstaffe and contributors 2011

British Library Cataloguing-in-Publication Data
A catalogue record for this book is available from the British Library.

ISBN: 978-0-8264-4196-6 (Paperback)
         978-0-8264-2331-3 (Hardback)

Library of Congress Cataloguing-in-Publication Data
A catalog record for this book is available from the Library of Congress.

Typeset by Newgen Imaging Systems Pvt Ltd, Chennai, India
Printed and bound in India

Contents

Series Introduction

The drama of Shakespeare and his contemporaries has remained at the very heart of English curricula internationally and the pedagogic needs surrounding this body of literature have grown increasingly complex as more sophisticated resources become available to scholars, tutors and students. This series aims to offer a clear picture of the critical and performative contexts of a range of chosen texts. In addition, each volume furnishes readers with invaluable insights into the landscape of current scholarly research as well as including new pieces of research by leading critics.

This series is designed to respond to the clearly identified needs of scholars, tutors and students for volumes which will bridge the gap between accounts of previous critical developments and performance history and an acquaintance with new research initiatives related to the chosen plays. Thus, our ambition is to offer innovative and challenging Guides which will provide practical, accessible and thought-provoking analyses of Renaissance drama. Each volume is organised according to a progressive reading strategy involving introductory discussion, critical review and cutting-edge scholarly debate. It has been an enormous pleasure to work with so many dedicated scholars of Renaissance drama and we are sure that this series will encourage to you read 400-year old playtexts with fresh eyes.

Andrew Hiscock and Lisa Hopkins

Timeline

1399   Henry IV becomes king of England following the deposition of Richard II.

1400   Richard II dies.

1403   The battle of Shrewsbury, first battle on English soil to make massed use of the longbow.

1413   Henry IV dies; his son, the Hal of *1 Henry IV*, becomes King Henry V and has Richard II's body reburied in Westminster Abbey.

1417   Sir John Oldcastle executed for heresy.

1422   Henry V dies.

1564   Shakespeare born.

1587   Publication of the second edition of Raphael Holinshed's *Chronicles*, one of Shakespeare's major sources for *1 Henry IV*.

1595   Publication of Samuel Daniel's poem sequence *The Civil Wars*, one of Shakespeare's major sources for *1 Henry IV*.

1598   Frances Meres' *Palladis Tamia* mentions Shakespeare's 'Henry the 4'. Publication of *The History of Henry the Fourth* in Quarto format. Often referred to as Q1. Publication of *The Famous Victories of Henry V*, one of Shakespeare's sources for *1 Henry IV*, which was certainly on the stage 1588 or earlier.

1599   Publication of second edition of *The History of Henry the Fourth* in Quarto format (Q2).

1600	First record of performance of *1 Henry IV*, at Lord Hunsdon's house in London. The Flemish ambassador attended a performance of 'Sir John Oldcastle'. Hunsdon was the patron of Shakespeare's theatre company, then called the Lord Chamberlain's Men. Publication of first edition of *2 Henry IV*, at the end of which Hal becomes king and rejects Falstaff. Publication of first edition of *Henry V*, which shares some characters with *1 Henry IV*, and which describes Falstaff's death.
1602	Publication of first edition of *The Merry Wives of Windsor*, a comedy set in contemporary England featuring Falstaff and companions.
1604	Publication of third edition of *The History of Henry the Fourth* in Quarto format (Q3).
1608	Publication of fourth edition of *The History of Henry the Fourth* in Quarto format (Q4).
1612–1613	First recorded performance of *1 Henry IV* at court, as part of the wedding celebrations of James I/VI's daughter Elizabeth. Play referred to in records as 'the Hotspur'.
1613	Shakespeare dies. Publication of fifth edition of *The History of Henry the Fourth* in Quarto format (Q5).
1616	Shakespeare dies.
1622	Publication of sixth edition of *The History of Henry the Fourth* in Quarto format (Q6).
1623	First publication of Shakespeare's collected works in Folio format, *Comedies, Histories and Tragedies*. Now often referred to as *The First Folio*, or *F* for short.
1624–1625	Another court performance of *1 Henry IV*, on New Year's night 1624/1625. Play referred to as 'the first part of Sir John Falstaff'. Further court performances of 'Oldcastle' recorded in 1631 and 1638.
1700	First performance of Thomas Betterton's *King Henry IV with the Humours of Sir John Falstaff: A Tragicomedy*. Betterton played Falstaff.
1746	Production of *1 Henry IV* at Covent Garden, with James Quin as Falstaff and David Garrick as Hotspur.

1777   Publication of Maurice Morgann's 'An Essay on the Dramatic Character of Sir John Falstaff'.

1788   Publication of William Richardson's *Essay on Shakespeare's Dramatic Character of Sir John Falstaff*.

1817   Publication of William Hazlitt's *Characters of Shakespeare's Plays*.

1874   Publication of Richard Simpson's 'The Politics of Shakespeare's Historical Plays'.

1876   Publication of Hermann Ulrici's *Shakespeare's Dramatic Art*; original German version published 1839.

1893   First performance in Milan of Guiseppe Verdi's opera *Falstaff*.

1909   First publication of 'The Rejection of Falstaff' in A. C. Bradley's *Oxford Lectures on English Poetry*.

1929   First performance of Ralph Vaughan Williams's opera *Sir John in Love*, based on *The Merry Wives of Windsor*.

1943   Publication of John Dover Wilson's *The Fortunes of Falstaff*.

1944   Publication of E. M. W. Tillyard's *Shakespeare's History Plays*.

1945   Old Vic production of *1 Henry IV* with Ralph Richardson as Falstaff and Laurence Olivier as Hotspur. Richardson had played Hal in 1930 against John Gielgud's Hotspur.

1951   Stratford production of *1 Henry IV* with Anthony Quayle as Falstaff, Michael Redgrave as Hotspur and Richard Burton as Hal; excerpts broadcast on BBC children's television in the same year.

1959   *The Life and Death of Sir John Falstaff* (a seven-part adaptation from all the Falstaff plays) broadcast on BBC children's television, with Roger Livesey as Falstaff. Publication of C. L. Barber's *Shakespeare's Festive Comedy*.

1960   *1 Henry IV* broadcast virtually uncut as part of BBC adaptation of all Shakespeare's histories called *An Age of Kings*. Sean Connery played Hotspur.

1965   Orson Welles's *Chimes at Midnight* released. The film is a collage of several Shakespeare plays, with a focus on Falstaff.

1979   First transmission of David Giles's *1 Henry IV* for the BBC Shakespeare.

1985   First publication of Stephen Greenblatt's essay 'Invisible bullets: Renaissance authority and its subversion, *Henry IV* and *Henry V*'.

1991   Gus Van Sant's *My Own Private Idaho* released. The film is a contemporary story drawing explicitly on elements from the *Henry IV* plays.

1995   Three-hour compression of both *Henry IV* plays broadcast by BBC, with Rufus Sewell as Hotspur, Ronald Pickup as Henry IV, and David Calder as Falstaff.

1997   First publication of *Engendering a Nation: A Feminist Account of Shakespeare's English Histories* by Jean E. Howard and Phyllis Rackin.

2002   Publication of Tom McAlindon's *Shakespeare's Tudor History: A Study of Henry IV, Parts One and Two*.

2010   First production of *1 Henry IV* at Shakespeare's Globe, London, with Roger Allam as Falstaff and Jamie Parker as Hal.

Introduction

Stephen Longstaffe

When they have had enough of serious matters, Shakespeare scholars sometimes play, extempore, a party game. What if? What would we think of Shakespeare if the First Folio had not made it into print, and we did not have *As You Like It, Macbeth, Twelfth Night, Antony and Cleopatra, The Tempest, The Winter's Tale, Julius Caesar*? What would we think of Shakespeare if we only had five comedies and six tragedies to go on? How would we then feel about Shakespeare's extant sequence of *seven* history plays, beginning with the reign of Richard II and ending with the death of Richard III? And what would we think about Falstaff, who dominates 3 of those 18 plays, giving his name to one of them, and whose death is movingly described in a fourth?[1] We might then still have had a Shakespeare who is pre-eminent in the creation of character – but with an achievement weighted rather more towards comic character than currently is the case. We might then still have had a Shakespeare with some claim to be a 'national poet' – but with rather more of an interest in the actual history of that nation, as understood in his own place and time, than in 'human nature'. And, in *1 Henry IV*, we would still have plenty of evidence that Shakespeare was a theatrical genius.

Shakespeare's four most instantly popular plays – going through four cheap editions each in their first ten years in print – were *Pericles, Richard II, Richard III* – and *1 Henry IV*. In other words, to his early readers, Shakespeare the playwright was first and foremost a historian. These three popular histories were all produced, so far as we can tell, during the 1590s, and form the beginning-, mid- and end-point of Shakespeare's eight-play sequence on the Wars of the Roses. *Richard III*, the final play in the historical sequence, was the first of these three to be performed, to be followed by the equally tragic *Richard II*, chronologically the start of the sequence. Both plays share common sources in the chronicles of Hall (1548) and Holinshed (1587), and are indebted to the mid-century compilation of first-person narrated verse 'tragedies' in which historical persons lament their eventual fates, *The Mirror for Magistrates* (1559, and subsequent editions), as well as to a range of prior tragic dramas on these and other English kings' reigns. They share a narrative arc too, focusing on the downfall (or in Richard III's case, the rise and fall) of their principal characters, who get far and away the lion's share of the lines spoken.

1 Henry IV deals, as the two others do, with civil war, and ends, as *Richard III* does, with a climactic battle. It too draws on Holinshed, and shares with *Richard II* an important source in Samuel Daniel's verse retelling of *The Civil Wars* (1595). Yet it presents a very different version of the historical past both tonally and in terms of narrative. The play does present a 'fall', that of Harry Percy ('Hotspur'), killed at Shrewsbury. But Shakespeare alters his historical sources, following Daniel's lead, to make Hotspur the contemporary of Henry IV's son (though he was actually three years older than the king himself). Hotspur's fall is bound up with Prince Hal's rise, and, to reinforce the point, Shakespeare gives the two characters almost the same number of lines. Indeed, in its distribution of lines, the play resembles a comedy rather than a tragedy focused on one protagonist, with Hal, Falstaff and Hotspur all speaking between 18 per cent and 20 per cent of the lines. As for the king the play is named after, he speaks only 12 per cent of the lines. Apart from anything else, this even distribution of parts has ensured that the play has remained a steady attraction on the English stage, especially in the eighteenth and nineteenth centuries, and it was common for actors to play (usually) Hotspur while young and Falstaff when they were older. But in its overlapping spheres – court, tavern, rival court, each with their 'star' – it also helps to construct an idea of the nation which is not simply dependent on the (tragic) fate of one notable individual. *1 Henry IV* is thus a 'comical history' (to coin a Polonian phrase), ending with a 'resurrection' rather than a marriage, and furthermore takes its place as part of a 'tetralogy', a sequence of four plays, dealing with the reigns of Richard II, Henry IV and Henry V. All of its main characters appear in more than one play, though Hotspur has only a walk-on part in *Richard II* and really lives (and dies) in *1 Henry IV*.

By the time Shakespeare wrote this play, the vogue for plays on post-Conquest English history was well-established on the London stage. The 1590s was a particularly stressful decade, both at home and abroad, with a court growing increasingly skittish about the succession question, recurrent fears of invasion and economic and social dislocation as a result of Elizabeth's wars. English history plays came in many shapes and sizes – comical histories featuring disguised kings and feisty common-ers, *Mirror for Magistrates*-style tragic discourses, and plenty of plays on civil war. The century up to the 1590s (especially its religious element) was fairly lightly touched upon. One reason for this is that history was a family affair, and late-Elizabethan society was full of families who, not-withstanding the Henrician and Elizabethan purges of the major nobil-ity, could trace their lines back to the houses represented in the histories themselves. Many of the characters in Shakespeare's histories had living descendants of one kind or another, and many scholars have detected in the representation of these historical figures a knowing engagement with the family's current status and reputation.[2] The London stage was in normal circumstances relatively lightly policed, but one thing which consistently caused trouble for companies was displeasing powerful people, who were well capable of having theatre companies shut down and actors imprisoned.

And it appears that, sometime in 1597, Shakespeare's company ran into one of these powerful people. The family in question was the Brookes, whose family name does not appear in *1 Henry IV*. It would be more to the point to say that their family name no longer appears in *1 Henry IV*, though traces of its removal from both *1* and *2 Henry IV* remain. Shakespeare's first choice of name for the prince's larger-than-life companion in both plays was that of a historical contemporary, Sir John Oldcastle, who had already appeared onstage in a play covering *The Famous Victories of Henry V* for the queen's own company, the Queen's Men. Indeed, it is generally agreed that Shakespeare's own play is 'dependent' upon the earlier one for plot and characterization, and a line from it recurs in *Henry V*. However innocuous it may have been in the past to portray Oldcastle, Shakespeare's particular take on the char-acter was quickly linked to his contemporary, if remote, descendants, the Brookes.[3] William Brooke, Lord Cobham, was an unfortunate man for a theatre company to annoy; a Privy Councillor and father-in-law to Robert Cecil, between August 1596 and his death in March 1597 he held the post of Lord Chamberlain of the royal household, a post involving (among other things) oversight of court entertainments. Shakespeare's own company for much of the 1590s was under the patronage of two other Lord Chamberlains, the Hunsdons, during which time it was known as the Lord Chamberlain's Men.

By February 1598 – before the play was printed – the Earl of Essex referred to William Brooke as Falstaff in a private letter. Clearly, by then, Shakespeare had replaced the original 'Oldcastle' with 'Falstaff', a name he had already used in *1 Henry VI*, and attempted to dissociate Falstaff from Oldcastle in the epilogue to *2 Henry IV*, which states that 'Oldcastle died a martyr, and this is not the man'. Two other families were also, presumably to their satisfaction, written out of the plays, as 'Sir John Russell' and 'Harvey' were replaced by Bardolph and Peto respectively.

We have no way of knowing whether Shakespeare voluntarily acquiesced to the changes, or how often this kind of negotiation took place. To complicate matters, the first printing of *Merry Wives* in 1602 (a play built around Falstaff and friends in present-day Windsor) *does* have a character called 'Brooke', though the name was changed to 'Broom' in the First Folio. Giorgio Melchiori, the most recent Arden editor of the play, sees this as 'revenge on the censorship of *Henry IV* suffered at the hand of William Brooke, Baron Cobham.'[4]

'Oldcastle' was clearly a different transgression to 'Brooke'. The reason for this is probably that 'Oldcastle' was not any old ancestor. He was executed for heresy in the reign of Henry V, something which, after the triumph of Protestantism in sixteenth-century England, gave him the status of a martyr for the true faith. And yet, the loss of the name 'Oldcastle' from the play did not prevent it from being interchangeable with 'Falstaff' for many years.[5] Ben Jonson and Thomas Nashe also got into trouble in 1597 over a play called *The Isle of Dogs* – Jonson was imprisoned with two other actors and was spied on in jail and Nashe's house was raided and his manuscripts seized. We know nothing about the play. However, it has been plausibly suggested in the light of Jonson's and Nashe's continuing animus in print against the Brookes/Cobhams (including Jonson's portrait in *Every Man In His Humour* (1599) of a watercarrier called 'Cob' who is overly proud of his ancestry) that they played a role in the affair.[6] These two plays experienced very different fates, for while Jonson's and Nashe's play has disappeared, *1 Henry IV* remains one of Shakespeare's crowning achievements.

This collection of essays testifies to the historic hold the play and its characters have had on stage and in study. Edel Lamb's chapter on the play's critical backstory shows how the play immediately made an impact on contemporaries, not least because of the Oldcastle affair, and many references to its theatrical popularity survive. Falstaff's popularity was worried over, particularly in the eighteenth century, by critics thinking through the implications of such an 'immoral' character being so attractive. Romantic-era critics were more sanguine about Falstaff's 'Vices' which were, after all, social and secular; critics with democratic leanings (such as Hazlitt) even contrasted him favourably with the squalid doings of the play's higher nobles. Indeed, some famous 'defences' of the fat knight's character, up to and including A. C. Bradley's early twentieth-century piece on 'the rejection of Falstaff', display considerable, if sentimental, ingenuity in their attempt to forestall any hint of moral judgement. A post-Pax-Britannica twentieth century was, initially at least, to be much more open to the idea of territory folks sticking together, and the attractions of the strong arm defending existing order against chaos. Falstaff, the witty freeloader, and Hotspur, the charismatic boy warrior, had to wait a while to have their moment. But the tide turned once again; power, whether located in the male body or the state's gaze, came under suspicion, and the chimes at midnight did not seem so bad when the alternative might be the clocks striking thirteen. Lamb's essay takes us up to a quarter century ago, with feminism and historicism established as dominant approaches; but as Jonathan Hart's chapter on the 'the state of the art' shows, the play, like Falstaff, is never comprehensively pinned down for long. Ranging far more widely than is usual in such overviews, and respectful of criticism from beyond the Anglosphere, Hart stresses the *copiousness* of criticism that this ever-fertile play continues to produce. It is certainly possible to isolate some key themes – theatricality, the education of the ruler, Falstaff, festivity and Englishness, the matter of 'Britain', rhetoric, gender, economics – some of which already have a long history. But Hart's comprehensive, multilingual overview stresses that, though it has been much worked over, this play shows no signs of being worked out, and looks set to remain, in his resonant phrase, a 'renewable resource'.

The play does not merely live on the page: it exists for and in performance, on stage and in other media, and in the classroom. Graham Atkin's history of the play in production begins by quoting an actor, the great Falstaff, Anthony Quayle, and moves quickly on to an appreciative early 'review' from Samuel Pepys. Acting is based on reading, an interpretation of a part. Theatre directors, with their concern for the 'whole' play rather than the 'part', arrive late on the scene, historically speaking, and more or less up until the twentieth century the stage was the local habitation of the actor–manager–impresario. Stage history is the history of creative–critical, rather than simply critical, readings. Samuel Johnson famously said of *Lear* that it was unactable (and, indeed, there was very little unadapted Shakespeare around in the theatres of the eighteenth and nineteenth centuries), and though *1 Henry IV* survived better than most on stage (usually minus, inexplicably to modern audiences, the play extempore), critics sometimes complained that actors simply were not up to producing the Falstaff of their mind's eye. But as the evidence accumulates, particularly in the twentieth century, the sheer imaginative range of engagement with the play becomes clear. It is too easy to see productions as 'mirroring' the times in which they are produced – something most obvious, perhaps, in the common critical comparison between Olivier's 'D-Day' film of *Henry V* and Branagh's 'Falklands' version of the same play. In fact, as Atkin makes clear, great productions are *ahead* of their times. Richardson's Falstaff, seen at the age of 15, inspired the critic Harold Bloom to a lifetime of thinking through what he came to see as Shakespeare's 'invention of the human'. Welles's *Chimes at Midnight* joins film-making and acting genius to create a wholly new masterpiece.

Brian Walsh's chapter '"'By Shrewsbury Clock": The Time of Day and the Death of Hotspur in *1 Henry IV*' reminds us that Shakespeare (and his first audiences for the play) began from its predecessor, *The Famous Victories of Henry V*, a play whose action Shakespeare extends throughout the two parts of *Henry IV* and into *Henry V*. Perhaps Shakespeare's major innovation was – inspired by Samuel Daniel – to include Hotspur as a foil for the young prince in addition to his disreputable companions in the tavern. Apart from anything else, Hotspur slows the action down by his sheer wordiness. Walsh suggests that, in context, Shakespeare's remaking of the shape of history available in *The Famous Victories* – from reprobate prince to Agincourt victor in a couple of hours – shows historical action as a continuum, to be shaped according to the particular agenda of the writer and theatre company. The aftermath of the battle of Shrewsbury makes this clear. Not only does Falstaff claim, ridiculously, that he fought a 'long hour by Shrewsbury clock' (the audience sees exactly how long he fought, which is presented in real time to them), but the prince agrees to 'gild' the truth, to support the lie that Falstaff killed Percy. This is history-making in action, and it lays bare Shakespeare's own project as a history-maker (e.g., inventing the death of Hotspur at the hands of the prince).

Alison Findlay's essay 'The Madcap and Politic Prince of Wales: Ceremony and Courtly Performance in *Henry IV*' focuses on courtly ceremony in the play. Notwithstanding the clearly fictional representation of ceremony, she argues that the play complicates such representations further by including Falstaff's parodic interview with the prince before we see him meet his father for real. For a performance in a public playhouse, perhaps to a predominantly plebeian audience, she suggests a subversive momentum to the pair's easy and, it appears, practised appropriation of forms supposedly reserved for 'sacred' majesty. But Findlay does not stop at suggesting 'subversion' in such circumstances. Rather, she goes on to consider how these scenes might have functioned in an opposite context – performance at court. The parody of Falstaff in state now takes place within a real palace, offering the court a glimpse of itself 'from the outside'. In addition, the first recorded court performance took place, as part of the marriage celebrations of the king's daughter, just after James' heir, prince Henry, died suddenly. In such a circumstance, the play's concern with the education of the prince, with true chivalry, and the responsibilities of rule (and its location of all of these in relation to *three* main characters named Henry) took on new resonances. In particular, given the dead prince's well-known chivalric persona, the relationship between Hotspur's 'honour community' and rebellion raised interesting questions – as did the parallel between James's public fondness for his new son-in-law rather than his own son, with Henry IV's open admiration for Hotspur. The play had further court performances in the year of Charles's accession to the throne, and on the ninth birthday of *his* son, perhaps, as Findlay suggests, because the play's concern with the making of a prince continued to generate fresh meanings in new contexts. Finally, Findlay suggests that the 1620s conflation of both *Henry IV* plays in the Dering manuscript for amateur performance may have been prepared to entertain Charles (then Prince of Wales) as he passed through en route to Dover and Madrid.

Chris Fitter's ' "The Devil Take Such Cozeners!" ': Radical Shakespeare in *1 Henry IV*' situates the play in one powerfully imagined moment – that of its composition and first performance in the crisis-hit London of late 1596 and early 1597. The frequent notes of paranoia struck by conspirators and king alike speak of the situation of early audiences, for the plebeians of the capital were 'between malnutrition and martial law' as dearth-driven rioting had in turn produced savage reprisals and a regime of close surveillance and brutal punishment. In such circumstances, the late-night knock on the door which disturbs the princely play extempore is significantly located, for in the London of the mid-1590s, in particular, the alehouse was the plebeian locus of solidarity, fellowship and food. The alehouse and its customers were also subject to a disciplinary crackdown, with licences under review and virtual curfews imposed on apprentices. In such a context, the play's 'delighting central scenes of boozy anti-establishment bonhomie', its bawds, drinking games, fecklessness, subcultures and slang are not too difficult to read as offering to playgoers the spectacle of their own 'imagined community'. This community was under threat outside the theatres – in the theatre, in the person of the counterfeiting outsider, who says directly 'I know you all . . . and will a while uphold the unyoked humour of your idleness', attacks 'playing holidays', bullies Francis, searches Falstaff's pockets when he is asleep, and includes riffs on hanging in his many gags and comebacks.

The prince's 'puritan' project of self-improvement, of which his time in the tavern forms a part, is, of course, mercilessly mocked from the inside by Falstaff. But Falstaff – always an ambivalent figure in a time of dearth, focused on feeding himself to excess – turns out, once he goes to war, to be a similarly ambivalent figure, for all his sympathetic appeal for sixteenth-century 'youth culture'. By this time, however, the audience has itself gazed, undetected, upon the inner workings of royalty as it eavesdrops on the prince's interview with his father, in an empowering moment in which they, via the theatre, conduct some surveillance of their own.

Robert Hornback's 'Falstaffian "Gross Indecorum", "Contrarietie", and Arrested Prodigality: Anachronism and Colliding Generational Sensibilities in *1 Henry IV*' also historicizes Falstaff and the prince, focusing on the clashes between them. Falstaff is, in the fullest sense, 'indecorous' – everything he does goes against place, time, and/or persons, whether that be invoking scripture in a tavern or stabbing Hotspur's corpse. He shares this with his theatrical (not-too-distant) ancestor, the Vice. One of his most 'contrary' characteristics is his identification with youth; an old Falstaff 'in' the 1590s would have been young in the 1550s, which places him as part of the same generation as the Edwardian evangelicals who deployed carnivalesque mockery and misrule against perceived Popery. Falstaff's attachment to misrule is generational, in other words, placing him as a by now elderly sixteenth-century *soixante-huitard*. Like twenty-first-century evangelicals, this prankster generation was not afraid to fight the good fight in the tavern. But, Hornback suggests, such figures would seem decidedly old-fashioned against the 'new' puritan generations succeeding them, for whom scripturally backed disputation in the alehouse would have been profanation. Old-fashioned too is Falstaff's theatricality, 'in King Cambyses' vein'; the radical Protestants succeeding the evangelical generation wanted, at least in their rhetoric, to have nothing to do with the theatre. And the prince is in need of no help; at the very opening of the play he has planned the public arc of his 'reformation'. In this he is not at all the prodigal son of some critical accounts – it is Falstaff who uses the language of repentance, who is something of an 'arrested Prodigal', stuck among the wicked with no direction home. It is Hal who presents, paradoxically, as the Vice, the hoodwinker of the pious father-figure (his father presents as a similarly old-fashioned Catholic with his talk of penance and crusades). The play, in fact, layers elements of the sixteenth-century morality play so as to produce rich and complex ironies potentially unsettling to some of the major (and still influential) paradigms through which the play has been read.

Martha Tuck Rozett's chapter on resources offers yet another way in to the play, this time from the perspective of the professional critic–educator using it as part of an undergraduate university degree. She provides an overview of how classic critical pieces can work as part of a syllabus, usefully overlapping in places with Lamb, and providing helpful key quotations, before moving on to a survey of the contents of key 'critical editions'. These variously provide a text of the play alongside a selection of relevant criticism and contemporary documents for pedagogic use and private study, those part of one-volume complete Shakespeares, and 'single-volume' editions of the play. Practical pedagogical guides are described, and their distinctive natures distinguished.

The chapter ends by drawing on the writer's own research-informed practice with film and TV resources, and her innovative pedagogical use of historical fiction set in the world of the play (sometimes even using the characters as part of a 'metafictional commentary', as with Robert Nye's *Falstaff*).

Each of these essays challenges us to think afresh about the play. They challenge each other as well, asking the reader whether it is possible to square radically different (or differently radical) understandings of Falstaff, of genre, of historical context and meaning. In doing so they demonstrate, once more, the continuing rewards of engaging imaginatively with this most vital of plays.

Notes

1. Apart from *1* and *2 Henry IV*, in which Falstaff appears, and *Henry V*, in which his death is described, there is what its first quarto printing called 'a Most pleasaunt and excellent conceited Comedie, of Syr *Iohn Falstaffe* and the merrie Wives of *Windsor*'. Readers of the First Folio of 1623 would have been able to encounter yet another Falstaff, the Sir John Falstaff who betrays Talbot in *1 Henry VI*, a play probably written at least half a decade before *1 Henry IV*. The historical person is recorded in the chronicle as 'Sir John Fastolfe'. The change to Falstaff, so far as we can tell, was Shakespeare's own.

2. One of the most common examples is Shakespeare's expanding the role historically played by the Stanley family in his *Richard III*, for which see Richard Wilson's 'A sea of troubles: the thought of the outside in Shakespeare's histories', in *Shakespeare's Histories and Counter-Histories*, ed. by Dermot Cavanagh et al. (Manchester: Manchester University Press, 2006), pp. 101–34. Catherine Grace Canino's *Shakespeare and the Nobility: The Negotiation of Lineage* (Cambridge: Cambridge University Press, 2007) investigates many of the major families represented in Shakespeare's early histories, including the Stanleys.

3. Oldcastle was, as Lord Cobham by marriage, a predecessor of Brooke's in the title, though not a direct ancestor (he had a childless marriage to Brooke's great-great-great-great-great grandmother Joan).

4. *The Merry Wives of Windsor*, ed. by Giorgio Melchiori (Walton-on-Thames: Thomas Nelson and Son, 2000), p. 51.

5. Early responses are contextualized and analyzed in Charles Whitney's *Early Responses to Renaissance Drama* (Cambridge: Cambridge University Press, 2006), pp. 70–112.

6. Gustav Ungerer, 'Prostitution in Late Elizabethan London: The Case of Mary Newborough', *Medieval and Renaissance Drama in England*, 15 (2002), 138–223 (174–75).

CHAPTER ONE

The Critical Backstory

Edel Lamb

The critical history of *1 Henry IV* dates back to the year in which the play was first published. In 1598 Francis Meres named it alongside other Shakespeare plays as exemplary of the diversity and sophistication of drama produced within the English nation.[1] Meres's brief invocation of this relatively new play as an example of tragedy immediately established two areas for critical enquiry: the play's generic classification and issues of national identity. These topics have remained crucial to interpretations of *1 Henry IV* to the present day and have been complemented by investigations into character, history, structure and gender. But the play has not only been of interest to critics. In 1765, Samuel Johnson commented on the extent to which readers, with and without scholarly interests, were engaging with this play and *2 Henry IV*, noting that 'none of Shakespeare's plays are read more than the *First* and *Second Parts* of *Henry the Fourth*' and that 'perhaps no author has ever in two plays afforded so much delight'.[2] Enjoyment of the play has been at the forefront of responses, many proclaiming it the best of Shakespeare's plays, and even the epitome of historical dramatic form and linguistic excellence.[3] Others have struggled to reconcile the pleasurable elements of the play with its representations of morality and power, resulting in extended debates on the characters of Falstaff and Hal, as well as on the relationship between them. Critics have been further divided over the decision to read the play as an independent dramatic text or, like Johnson, to analyse it in conjunction with *2 Henry IV*, or to interpret it as part of the larger sequence of Shakespeare's history plays. *1 Henry IV* has also held a central position in major scholarly movements from the male- and female-authored character criticism of the eighteenth century to debates on history and ideology in the nineteenth and twentieth centuries to the revised methodological approaches to these topics during the last decades of the twentieth century. This chapter provides an overview of this rich and varied critical backstory.

Early Critical Contexts

1 Henry IV is unusual among Shakespeare's plays in that allusions to it began early and have continued in profusion. It was frequently cited, performed and commented on during the seventeenth century, and it also gave rise to a number of derivative performances on the public, court and interregnum stages.[4] The play was subject to critical commentary almost from the moment of its origin. In addition to citing the play as an example of a tragedy in *Palladis Tamia*, Meres quoted from Act II to praise Michael Drayton.[5] Numerous early modern plays, pamphlets and scholarly essays contain similar echoes of the play's language and allusions to its characters. Sir John Harrington's commentary on *The Aeneid* (1604) for the young Prince Henry arraigned Shakespeare's knight; Thomas Randolph's *Hey for Honesty, Down with Knavery* (printed 1651) evoked the 'incomparable carbuncles of Sir John Oldcastle's nose'; and, Nathan Field alluded to *1 Henry IV* in his *Amends for Ladies* (performed *c.* 1611 and first published in 1618) by asking:

> Did you never see
> The Play, where the fat Knight hight *Old-castle*,
> Did tell you truly what his honour was?[6]

Evidently the play, and particularly the character of Falstaff, quickly entered the consciousness of the critical and theatrical cultures of seventeenth-century England.

These allusions to Falstaff as the 'fat Knight' Oldcastle constitute early contributions to a longstanding commentary on the associations between Shakespeare's character and the historical proto-Puritan martyr, Sir John Oldcastle. A variety of seventeenth-century texts, including Thomas Middleton's *A Mad World, My Masters* (performed *c.* 1604–1606 and first published in 1608) and the anonymously authored *The Wandering Jew Telling Fortunes to Englishmen* (1628), referred to the historical character of Oldcastle using the language of *1 Henry IV*. Others, such as Peter Heylyn and Thomas Fuller's *The Appeal of Injured Innocence* (1659) and Fuller's *Worthies of England* (1662), bemoaned the abuse of Falstaff in Shakespeare's plays via references to the historical character.[7] Richard James posited a direct connection between Shakespeare's character and the Oldcastle in his 1625 'Legend and

Defence of the Noble Knight and Martyr, Sir John Oldcastle', writing 'In Shakespeare's first shew of Harrie the Fift the person with which he undertook to play a buffone was not Falstaffe, but Sir John Oldcastle'.[8] According to many critics these references are of utmost significance as they provide proof that Falstaff was a direct and deliberate representation of the famous Lollard, and that the character was originally written with the same name as the historical knight.[9] This Falstaff-Oldcastle scholarship has influenced late-twentieth-century editorial practices, most notably resulting in the decision of the Oxford editors to revert to the use of the name 'Oldcastle' in the 1986 edition of Shakespeare's works.[10] Debates on the relationship between the theatrical and historical figures continue to impact on current work on the play, as Robert Hornback's essay in this collection (Chapter 6) demonstrates.

Falstaff also appeared in early commentaries on the play's popularity, frequently invoked to gesture towards the play's commercial successes. Leonard Digges used the image of Falstaff as a signifier of full playhouses in 1640 when he wrote in his commendatory verse on Shakespeare: 'let but *Falstaffe* come, | *Hall*, *Poines*, the rest, you scarce shall have a room'.[11] T. Palmer similarly associated Falstaff with attentive playhouse audiences to emphasize the talent of another playwright, John Fletcher, by suggesting that a description of this playwright's talent would exceed even a description of 'how long, | *Falstaffe* from cracking Nuts hath kept the throng'.[12] Falstaff was also called upon to demonstrate Shakespeare's talents. In her *Sociable Letters* (1664), Margaret Cavendish defended the playwright's range of abilities with the claim that he 'hath Express'd in his Playes all Sorts of Persons, as one would think he had been Transformed into every one of those Persons he hath Described'. She supported this claim with a list of exceptional transformations that included 'such a man as his *Sir John Falstaffe*' and Mistress Quickly.[13]

Although *1 Henry IV* was, according to William Winstanley's 'The Lives of the Most Famous English Poets' (1687), 'commended by some, as being full of sublime Wit, and as much condemned by others, for making *Sir John Falstaffe*, the property of pleasure for Prince *Henry* to abuse', the seventeenth-century critical contexts for the play were largely favourable.[14] John Dryden praised the 'singular' wit and 'Miscellany of Humours' that made up this 'best of comical Characters', Falstaff.[15] In 1673, Aphra Behn built on earlier representations of the play's popularity and its status as a signifier of Shakespeare's skill in 'An Epistle to the Reader' of her play, *The Dutch Lover*. Proposing that Shakespeare's works had 'better pleas'd the World than Johnson's', she used *Henry IV* as an example, writing:

> I have seen a man the most severe of Johnson's sect, sit with his
> Hat remov'd less than a hairs breadth from one sullen posture for

almost three hours at the Alchymist, who at that excellent Play of Harry the Fourth (which yet I hope is far enough from farce) hath very hardly kept his Doublet whole.[16]

Samuel Pepys claimed in 1667 that he was pleased by the 'speaking of Falstaff's speech "What is Honour?"', a speech also highlighted in Nathan Field's earlier allusion to the play and which formed the subject of numerous later scholarly enquiries.[17] George Daniel's mid-seventeenth-century views on the play were ambiguous – while he admired the 'Comicke Mirth' of Falstaff and the prince, he took issue with the play's moral standing.[18] Indeed, the nature of the play's humour and its morality have been repeatedly debated throughout its critical history.

Reading Character

As Charles Whitney usefully points out, there has been 'an almost continuous tradition from 1598 to the present' of extant response to Falstaff.[19] Analyses of this figure, and of the play's other protagonists, Prince Hal and Hotspur, have constituted a significant portion of scholarship on this play throughout history. This character-focused criticism was at its most intense in eighteenth-century British scholarship. This period witnessed increasing debates on the virtues of Falstaff's character, often as a case study to develop methodological approaches to reading character that extended beyond Shakespeare's play.

The dominant themes of the character critics' reactions to Falstaff had been prefigured in Daniel's ambivalent comments in 1647. The mirth of this character, who according to one observer 'almost singly supports the whole comic plot of the first part of *Henry the Fourth*', was crucial to a range of emotionally-charged readings of the play as commentators focused their attention on this character and on what Samuel Taylor Coleridge later termed his 'complete moral depravity'.[20] While Charles Gildon suggested that 'the Humour of *Falstaffe* be what is most valuable' in the *Henry IV* plays, and better in Part 1 than in Part 2, Samuel Johnson warned against the moral dangers of this character's corrupting wit and seductive 'power to please'.[21] In this often-cited description of 'unimitated, unimitable Falstaff', Johnson emphasized his vices, including thievery, gluttony, cowardice and boasting. Yet, in spite of this, he conceded that his 'licentiousness is not so offensive but that it may be borne for his mirth'.[22] Numerous scholars followed this line of analysis. In his *Essay on Shakespeare's Dramatic Character of Sir John Falstaff* (1788), William Richardson made this his central purpose and attempted to 'explain and account for the pleasure we receive from the representation of Shakespeare's dramatic character of Sir John

Falstaff'.[23] Offering an analysis first of Falstaff's 'baser' parts, his sensuality, deceit, presumption, boastful affectation and vainglory, and then of his joviality, good humour and wit, Richardson concluded that the 'general effect is in the highest degree delightful' because his deformities are 'veiled by the pleasantry employed by the poet in their display'.[24] In another moral analysis of the play in 1775, the actress Elizabeth Griffith suggested that this 'extraordinary personage' is the 'only one that ever offended so high a degree of pleasure, without the least pretence to merit of virtue to support it'.[25] Just over a decade later, Richard Cumberland acknowledged that Falstaff's 'lies, his vanity, and his cowardice, too gross to deceive, were to be so ingenious as to give delight'.[26] Despite their emphasis on morality, these critics were repeatedly won over by the play's humour. In a discussion of humour in English comedies, Corbyn Morris also took Falstaff as exemplary. Arguing that this is what is most noteworthy about his character, he suggested in 1744 that 'For the sake of his wit you forgive his cowardice, or rather are fond of his cowardice for the occasions it gives to his wit'.[27] Richard Stack worked out similar conclusions at length in the 1780s.[28] Yet, Morris's evaluation, in particular, offers an insight into the problematic nature of such readings. His suggestion that the 'secret of carrying comedy to the highest pitch of delight' lies in drawing characters 'with such delight and amiable oddities and foibles as you would choose in your own companions in real life' indicates the troubling ways in which readings of Falstaff's moral status interpreted Shakespeare's famous dramatic character as a living person.[29]

This tendency was further reflected in eighteenth-century debates on Shakespeare's originality as a dramatist and his role as an historian. In her nationalistic defence of Shakespeare, 'An Essay on the Writings and Genius of Shakespeare, Compared with the Greek and French Dramatic Poets' in 1769, Elizabeth Montagu offered another analysis of Falstaff's 'finesse of wit' and 'drollery of humour'.[30] Criticizing those who did not 'partake of his merriment' as 'ill-natured as well as dull', she insisted that no matter what individual's personal responses to the character were, it was necessary to 'own it to be perfectly original' and to 'applaud the dexterity of Shakespeare' in the creation of both the prince and Falstaff.[31] Montagu recognized the fictional nature of Shakespeare's characters and commended the playwright's inventiveness. Henry Mackenzie similarly admired Shakespeare's 'luxuriantly fertile' imagination for its production of 'ordinary life characters of such perfect originality that we look on them with no less wonder at his invention', and also named Falstaff as the prime example of this.[32] In *Shakespeare Illustrated* (1754), Charlotte Lennox agreed that 'the extravagant Sallies of the Prince of *Wales*, and the inimitable Humour of *Falstaff* were entirely of the playwright's 'own Invention'.[33] Noting Shakespeare's deviations from history, she contended that the playwright had improved the latter from the historical figure. Despite continuing to read Falstaff as 'the great master-piece of our inimitable writer' and a 'theatrical prodigy', Thomas Davies returned in his *Dramatic Micellanies* (1783) to a comparison of Falstaff and Sir John Oldcastle.[34] In addition, in his analysis of the king, the prince and Hotspur, he insisted that the first two were 'faithful resemblances taken from history' and offered another nationalistic evaluation through a reading of Shakespeare's history plays as 'a valuable treasure to Englishmen'.[35]

In the early nineteenth century, Elizabeth Inchbald reiterated the judgements of many eighteenth-century critics on both history and character in her immense commentary on British theatre. She read *1 Henry IV* as the work of a 'faithful historian, as well as of a great poet' who created every character 'as a complete copy of nature'.[36] Despite her dislike for Falstaff, she suggested that the play nonetheless offered delight as even 'the reader who is too refined to laugh at the wit of Sir John' should enjoy Hotspur's speeches.[37] Inchbald's evaluation provided an insight into a particular category of reader in the late-eighteenth and early-nineteenth centuries: the 'refined' and gendered reader of *1 Henry IV*. Indeed, her comments are almost unique in the play's critical history in outlining gender-specific responses to the play, as she claimed:

> This is a play which all men admire, and which most women dislike. Many revolting expressions in the comic parts, much boisterous courage in some of the graver scenes, together with Falstaff's unwieldy person, offended every female auditor; and whilst a facetious Prince of Wales is employed in taking purses on the highway, a lady would rather see him stealing hearts at a ball, though the event might produce more fatal consequences.[38]

Although most character critics of the eighteenth and nineteenth centuries accounted for the delight offered by Falstaff in spite of his immoral character, Inchbald refuted this element of the character in her re-imagining of responses to the character in gendered terms. Falstaff, Inchbald insisted, offered no pleasure whatsoever to the female auditor or reader.

Falstaff was also at the centre of wider debates about the interpretation of literary characters. Maurice Morgann's frequently discussed piece, 'An Essay on the Dramatic Character of Sir John Falstaff' (1777), is important in relation to both the play's critical history and this scholarly trend. Morgann's explicit aim was to defend Falstaff against the charges of cowardice put forward by critics, such as Johnson, and to set out his alternative views of the 'courage and military character of the dramatic Sir John Falstaff' that 'are so different from those which I find generally to prevail in the world'.[39] He achieved this via detailed readings of key moments in the play, largely the same episodes that had been evoked by his contemporaries to denigrate Falstaff, in particular, the robbery at Gad's Hill. However, this focused evaluation of the character in the context of the play differed from the other critics of the period in more than its empathy for Shakespeare's knight. By highlighting that the play–text was not intended to be interpreted literally and insisting that Falstaff's incongruous and diverse character was one 'made up by Shakespeare' and dependent on his hand, Morgann, as Christy Desmet has pointed out, reflected on the act of analysing Falstaff as much as on the character himself.[40] His essay constituted a commentary on methods of interpretation.

While subsequent scholars questioned Morgann's argument, initially terming it as paradoxical and later rejecting it as over-sentimentalized, this landmark essay signalled a shift in interpretations of the play's characters.[41] In commenting on Shakespeare's originality in producing lively characters, earlier critics had attended, implicitly, to the literary nature of the play. Yet, in 1817, William Hazlitt problematized moral and historical readings of character in his *Characters of Shakespeare's Plays* by bringing this aspect to the fore. He insisted that scholars can 'speak only as dramatic critics', an obvious point that was nonetheless necessary given the tendency of many to treat Falstaff as an historical entity.[42] By clearly differentiating between history and literature, Hazlitt offered an alternative justification for his admiration of this 'most substantial comic character that was ever invented'.[43] It was because of this distinction that he was able to convincingly state that 'whatever terror the French in those days might have of Henry V, yet, to the readers of poetry at present, Falstaff is the better man of the two'.[44]

However, moral evaluations of the play's characters continued, albeit under a new aegis. A. C. Bradley's early-twentieth-century analysis of Falstaff summed up the prevailing earlier view of this character as a comic figure, genius of mirth and devoted companion to the prince. Bradley's work also signalled a further change of direction in the character-focused criticism of the play. His reading of Falstaff depended on an interpretation of the extended narrative from *1 Henry IV* to *2 Henry IV* and focused on the rejection of Falstaff. Addressing once again the reasons for our delight in Falstaff, Bradley argued that a sympathetic response transcended moral judgement. The effect of this, he suggested, was to problematize Henry's rejection of the knight. He moved character criticism forward by focusing instead on what we feel, and are meant to feel, when we witness this, and by asking 'what does our feeling imply as to the characters of Falstaff and the new King?'.[45] While Bradley's overall argument, made (like Morgann's) through an analysis of key scenes, was that Shakespeare must have intended sympathy for Falstaff to weaken gradually, and largely in Part 2, he proposed that the dramatist, in fact, 'overshot his mark' in the Falstaff scenes. Shakespeare, he suggested, 'created so extraordinary a being and fixed him so firmly on his intellectual throne, that when he thought to dethrone him he could not'.[46] Thus, as Robert Langbaum has noted, sympathy rather than moral judgement became the prevailing tone in early twentieth-century interpretations of Falstaff.[47]

Re-reading Falstaff in the Twentieth Century

Towards the mid-twentieth century, scholars quickly and explicitly rejected the traditional character criticism stretching from Morgann to Bradley. John Dover Wilson famously urged for a return to the unsentimentalized characterization of Falstaff by Samuel Johnson. His detailed charting of Falstaff's career through the *Henry IV* plays in *The Fortunes of Falstaff* (1943) admitted that Falstaff is the 'most conspicuous' and 'most fascinating' character in the plays, but insisted that 'not the fat knight but the lean prince' lies at the structural centre of the drama, which according to Wilson is a study of kingship.[48] This study additionally positioned *1 Henry IV* within a history of the theatre and of dramatic performance. A similar approach had earlier been adopted by Elmer Edgar Stoll, who, highlighting flaws in Morgann's analysis, considered Falstaff in relation to the theatrical tradition of the *miles gloriosus* (braggart soldier) stretching back through the Commedia dell'Arte to classical Roman comedy in order to counter his predecessor's conclusions and to 'prove' Falstaff a coward.[49] In contrast, Wilson read Falstaff alongside these traditions in order to argue that 'the growing-up of a madcap prince into the ideal king' is the main theme of the two parts of *Henry IV*.[50] For Wilson, Hal, the admirable Prodigal, and Falstaff, the Riot or Devil, drew on the traditions of morality plays and miracle plays, as well as the *miles gloriosus*. This interpretation suggests that these characters would have embodied 'a miscellaneous congeries of popular notion and associations' for the original Elizabethan audiences and that this would have influenced original responses to the play.[51]

Read in this way, Falstaff is seen to function in the play as a dramatic type: his role shaped by these alternative yet well-known dramatic forms and his purpose to facilitate the development of the character of the prince. W. H. Auden extended this contemplation of Falstaff's theatrical function in 'The Prince's Dog' (1948). Suggesting that he is the 'means by which Hal is revealed to be the Just Ruler', Auden's reading of Falstaff as a comic symbol and Lord of Misrule followed Wilson in placing

Hal at the thematic and structural centres of both *1 Henry IV* and *2 Henry IV*.[52] Similarly, C. L. Barber's landmark study, *Shakespeare's Festive Comedy* (1959), via a reading of Falstaff's function as clown, insisted that both parts focus attention on Hal. The central issue of *1 Henry IV* for Barber was the prince's development through his relationship with Falstaff, the figure of misrule. Barber drew on the earlier considerations of Falstaff as morality Vice and Lord of Misrule, put forward by Northrop Frye (1949), William Empson (1953) and Bernard Spivack (1958), in addition to the scholars already mentioned.[53] He simultaneously offered an original and influential evaluation of Shakespeare's use of another dramatic tradition – the comic accompaniment and counter-statement by the clown – to suggest that Shakespeare fused two saturnalian traditions of stage clowning and the folly of holiday. According to this study, the playwright dramatizes holiday and the need for it through Falstaff's comedy, but similarly presents the necessity of limiting this holiday.[54]

The significance of the rejection or control of Falstaff highlighted by Bradley's essay thus figured centrally in a range of twentieth-century scholarship on the *Henry IV* plays which effectively repositioned the prince at the core of *1 Henry IV* and of critical work on the play. This focus on Hal had surfaced at an earlier stage in the play's critical history in studies such as Lewis Theobald's 1733 defence of his honour, but it increased steadily throughout the nineteenth and twentieth centuries.[55] Edward Dowden, for example, examined Shakespeare's portrayal of the historical figure of the prince in 1875 and defended the character against early critiques of his rejection of Falstaff.[56] This Hal-centred criticism was developed further, in the twentieth century, by applying psychoanalytic criticism to the play. Franz Alexander, reading Falstaff as 'deep infantile layers of the personality', proposed in 1933 that Hal must overcome this self-centred narcissistic libido child and additionally destroy his alter ego by killing Hotspur.[57] Subsequently, Ernst Kris and J. I. M. Stewart viewed Falstaff as a substitute father-figure and interpreted the killing of Hotspur as Hal's displacement activity.[58] More recently, Robert Watson considered Hal's relationship with the pleasure-seeking principle.[59] Many of these readings prioritized another of Hal's relationships in the play: with Hotspur. This was also crucial to Sigurd Burckhardt's and Derek Cohen's evaluations of Hal's development towards kingship. Burckhardt interpreted both Falstaff and Hotspur as foils for the prince in his examination of the play's representation of combat.[60] In Cohen's anthropological analysis of Hal's killing of Hotspur, the latter was interpreted as the heroic figure, ceremoniously slaughtered to enable the prince to strengthen his claim to royal authority.[61]

Despite the increasing tendency of early-twentieth-century scholarship to focus on Hal's rejection of Falstaff and to dismiss the clown, critics have continued to engage extensively with this character. Later twentieth-century psychoanalytic readings of the play shifted the emphasis back to Falstaff by examining the ways in which he is coded in feminine and maternal terms, in spite of being figured as the surrogate father.[62] Earlier twentieth-century scholars also offered more positive analyses of Falstaff's diverse traits. In *Shakespearian Comedy* (1938), H. B. Charlton attempted to ascertain why Shakespeare rejected this character but retained his focus on the knight's more admirable traits (while simultaneously admitting that Falstaff is not the victor of Part 1).[63] Mark Van Doren took an alternative approach in 1939 and read Falstaff as a 'comic actor' and 'universal mimic' to offer a fresh account of the genius of this character in relation to theatrical traditions.[64] Scholars influenced by New Criticism in the middle of the century considered the significant function of Falstaff and his comedy in relation to the play's oppositional patterns. Cleanth Brooks and Robert Heilman argued for the need to reconsider Falstaff's role in the play as a whole in their 1946 essay on *1 Henry IV*. Focusing on Falstaff's witty 'prose poetry', they examined Falstaff's function in defining and enriching the main themes of the play.[65] R. J. Dorius analysed the play's imagery of extremes, specifically the 'lean king of state' versus the 'fat king of revels', to suggest that Falstaff dramatized the gulf between the virtues of the private man and those of the ruler.[66] In his well-known essay, 'Angel with Horns: The Unity of *Richard III*' (1961), A. P. Rossiter considered the play's doubleness via his reading of the comic plot as a commentary on the main plot.[67] After these diverse readings of the play's carnivalesque elements, the comic subplot and the knight as figure of the revels, debates on the relationship between the play's comic aspects and the 'main' 'historical' plot have increased and the former have come to be regarded as having an integral role. Robert Weimann, for instance, read the play's comedy and subplot as crucial elements of the play's form.[68] Derek Traversi also explored Falstaff's dramatic function through an analysis of the two 'worlds' or plots of the play: serious and comic. Reading Falstaff as the connection between these strands, he proposed that this character is uniquely positioned outside the prevailing political spirit of the play to comment on both plots. For Traversi, Falstaff is a figure of imagination, and it is because of this element that he 'habitually transcends his situation'.[69] This incarnation of the figure of misrule, cowardice and *miles gloriosus* provides a (limited) inversion of Puritan values. Robert Hunter also read Falstaff as the anti-embodiment of the Protestant ethic via a reading of the character in terms of appetite, carnival and play. Yet this later critic recognized the limitations of this

alternative figure, suggesting that the ultimate rejection of Falstaff sig-
nals the victory of this ethic.[70] Nonetheless, Falstaff is re-imagined in
such readings as central to the play and to its critical history once
again.

Graham Holderness built on this work in his analysis of Falstaff as a
Bakhtinian carnival figure. Noting that Barber tended towards an official permissive view of saturnalian comedy, Holderness insisted that
further theoretical work on the specific social practices of saturnalian
custom and its passage into drama is necessary and proposed that the
scholarship of Mikhail Bakhtin made this possible. In contrast to Barber,
Holderness offered a 'popular subversive view' of carnival and comedy.
For him, Falstaff 'constitutes a constant focus of opposition to the official and serious tone of authority and power', a perspective that was
clearly influenced by the late-twentieth-century critical schools of new
historicism and cultural materialism.[71] In another materialist reading of
the play in his 1985 monograph, *Shakespeare's History*, Holderness considered the play's invocation of older popular culture and representation
of carnival. In this study, he proposed that Falstaff and the carnivalesque
elements are 'conscious acts of historiography: reconstructions of a feudal society analysed in the process of dissolution, where its characteristic contradictions are most clearly visible'.[72] Via its comic character that
draws together various cultural elements and spaces, the play, according
to this reading, imagines the infinite possibilities of change. For François
Laroque, similarly influenced by the work of Bakhtin and Barber, Falstaff
is located at the centre of *1 Henry IV* because of his body and its function as a metaphor of the body heroic and politic.[73]

Falstaff also figures prominently in later twentieth-century scholarship on the play as a result of the return to earlier debates on the associations between this character and Sir John Oldcastle. Alice-Lyle
Scoufos's detailed examination of the 'Falstaff-Oldcastle Problem' in her
monograph reconsidered Falstaff and his relationship to the play's historical material, proposing that Shakespeare has reached a mature stage
in his thinking about the relationship between drama and history in
1 Henry IV.[74] Following the naming of the character as Oldcastle in the
1986 edition of the play (mentioned above), critics responded, firstly, by
registering their opinion on the editorial decision, and secondly, by
shedding new light on the historical contexts for Shakespeare's character.[75] Kristen Poole's excellent study of Falstaff in relation to the Martin
Marprelate pamphlet war of the 1580s is noteworthy in this respect. It
offered a cogent reading of Falstaff as a parody of the sixteenth-century
Puritan, an element which had been evaluated by Traversi and Hunter,
mentioned above, and which Holderness and Harold Bloom also
attended to in their late twentieth-century evaluations of the play.[76]

The Importance of Form

A large portion of twentieth-century scholarship on Falstaff read character in conjunction with the formal elements of the play, most notably its structure, plot and sub-plot, or as the first part of a two-part play, and its relationship with other traditions of theatre and performance. This is evident in the considerations of Falstaff's 'function' in the play and the extent to which this is dependent upon the critical interpretation of the play's deliberate appropriation of dramatic traditions such as carnival, and of the balance of comic and serious or political action in *1 Henry IV*. Structure has been another significant and enduring subject in the play's critical history. As many of the studies on character indicate, the structural relationship between the two parts of *Henry IV* has been particularly important to interpretations of Part 1. The question of whether the two parts are independent or should be considered together first appeared in eighteenth-century criticism when John Upton declared that the plays were separate pieces and observed that 'To call the two plays *first and second parts* is [. . .] injurious to the author-character of Shakespeare'.[77] However, less than 20 years later Samuel Johnson claimed that the two parts formed one play, and were only separated because it would have be too long for viewing otherwise.[78]

Opinion continues to be divided. Subsequent scholarship offered various reasons for the existence of the two parts. In 1779 Edward Capell claimed that the plays were planned together, while in 1955 Harold Jenkins suggested that Shakespeare began writing one single play but on realizing that it would be too long wrote two parts instead.[79] Matthias Shaaber followed Upton in arguing that *1 Henry IV* constitutes a single and independent play; yet Sherman Hawkins saw *1 Henry IV* and *2 Henry IV* as a single structure.[80] G. K. Hunter suggested a different approach and perceived an alternative form of unity to exist between the two plays. Proposing a unity of theme and repetition of phrasing, scenes and episodes, he claimed that the 'unity of the play is that of a diptych, in which repetition of shape and design focuses attention on what is common to the two parts'.[81] Other critics have observed structural and thematic connections not only between *1 Henry IV* and *2 Henry IV* but also between Shakespeare's other histories. E. M. W. Tillyard, for example, treated the two parts of *Henry IV* as a single unit, but also suggested that all the plays of the second tetralogy are so closely connected that they must be treated as a single organism.[82]

1 Henry IV's generic status has also been a recurrent topic in scholarship. Towards the end of the seventeenth century, Gerard Langbaine noted that the 'play is built upon our English history' but that it also contains a 'Comical part' of 'our Author's own invention'.[83] Eighteenth-century scholars judged this blend more harshly, with Nicholas Rowe writing in his edition of Shakespeare's works in 1709 that the mixing of tragedy and comedy was something that the 'severer Critiques among us cannot bear'.[84] Elizabeth Montagu, however, defended this combination. She admitted that the play was 'liable to those objections which are made to tragicomedy' but suggested that it might in fact 'obtain favour for the species itself'.[85] By the twentieth century, despite the attention lavished on the play's comic elements, it was more commonly defined as a history play, reinforced by H. B. Charlton's insistence that the *Henry IV* plays are 'perfect specimens of a dramatic type', that is, history or political plays, not chronicles, pageants, tragedies or comedies.[86]

The definition of a 'history' play was a recurrent question in early-twentieth-century criticism on Shakespeare's history plays more generally. Felix Schelling's *The English Chronicle Play* (1902) traced the development of this form and identified the continual assertion of national consciousness in Shakespeare's plays of this genre.[87] The generic debate has continued, with critics such as Ronald McDonald stressing the tendency of these plays to overlap with other generic modes – comedy in the case of *1 Henry IV* – though such plays have a common interest in the processes and inner necessities of historical change and mechanisms of transition.[88] More recently, Paul Dean took the *Henry IV* plays as a case study to demonstrate the ways in which two-part Elizabethan history plays force recognition of the limitations of the descriptive categories of chronicle and romance. Dean's suggestion that 'the multi-facetedness of Shakespeare's engagement with the historical mode is everywhere apparent' is evident in the long-standing debate on the generic qualities of *1 Henry IV*, and the diverse scholarship reading the play in relation to various theatrical forms from the morality play to carnival.[89] The implications of generic categorization for topics such as character, narrative and theme have also been considered. A. C. Bradley and Harold Toliver, for instance, both suggested that the play's genre made the rejection of Falstaff necessary.[90] Structure and genre have thus been integral to diverse critical investigations into the play, and particularly to the extensive analyses of Falstaff.

Representations of History

History, as a theme as well as a generic label, has been another recurring element in the critical backstory of *1 Henry IV*. It figured prominently in the seventeenth- and eighteenth-century comments on the playwright's faithfulness to historical representation in terms of characterization. This trend continued with studies such as Thomas Courtenay's analysis of the historical veracity of the play in his *Commentaries on the*

Historical Plays of Shakespeare (1840) through to nineteenth- and early-twentieth-century evaluations of the play's representation of a unified world picture to late-twentieth century New Historicist re-evaluations of history and the representations of the historical moment offered by Shakespeare's plays.[91] This has been a rapidly evolving area of *1 Henry IV*'s critical history from the nineteenth century onwards, as critics became interested in the political significance of Shakespeare's histories.[92]

Study of the play as part of Shakespeare's cycle of history plays flourished in the nineteenth century. In 1811, A. W. Schlegel read the playwright's histories as a sequential unit that functioned as 'an historical heroic poem in the dramatic form'.[93] Hermann Ulrici's two-volume study of *Shakespeare's Dramatic Art*, first published in German in 1839, similarly saw the *Henry IV* plays as the key points in the development of a 'great historical drama of five acts' which begins with *Richard II* and finishes with *Richard III*.[94] This study began by locating Shakespeare's plays in relation to both the state of the nation and the theatre in the playwright's time. Viewing Henry V as the king under whom the history of England reaches a temporary point of stability, Ulrici suggested that Shakespeare gave this figure the role of hero in the *Henry IV* plays in order to direct our attention to this and towards the plays as revealing the 'nature of the feudal state'.[95] In his analysis of Falstaff, he proposed that the comic and non-historical portions of the plays, related to this 'wholly unhistorical person', are not included simply to please an audience or act as a foil to Henry, but instead function as a 'parody on the historical representation'.[96] For Ulrici, therefore, all elements of *1 Henry IV* relate to the depiction of English history.

Tom McAlindon has recently argued that 'critical understanding of *Henry IV* takes a greater leap forward than at any other time before or since' with Ulrici's study.[97] The view put forward by the nineteenth-century critic of Shakespeare as historian and of the play as a study of feudalism, McAlindon suggested, is one that was recycled frequently in the nineteenth and twentieth centuries. In particular, McAlindon noted the influence of Ulrici's *Shakespeare's Dramatic Art* on one of the most widely known and frequently cited studies of the history plays, E. M. W. Tillyard's *Shakespeare's History Plays* (1944), citing the latter's wartime context as the reason he does not acknowledge the influence of the German critic. Indeed Ulrici's approach to the play not only resurfaced in Tillyard's analysis of the second tetralogy as a single unit, but also in his assertion that *1 Henry IV* represents Shakespeare's view of contemporary England. Tillyard was also interested primarily in Shakespeare's use of history and his representation of the ideas of his age. Examining the connections between the history plays and Edward Hall's *The Union of the Two Noble and Illustre Famelies of Lancastre and*

Yorke (1548) and Holinshed's chronicles and chronicle plays, this significant study most famously offered a view of the Elizabethan conception of world order, which, Tillyard claimed, Shakespeare propagated in his plays. In his reading of the *Henry IV* plays, Tillyard made two main assumptions: that the two plays are one, and that it is evident from the start that the prince will become a good king. He read Hal as 'Shakespeare's study of the kingly type' and, like other critics of his time, repositioned him at the centre of the play.[98] The prince's relationship with Falstaff is, according to this analysis, simply evidence that the future king is 'versed in every phase of human nature'.[99] In Tillyard's rendering of the 'Tudor myth' of cosmic order, Falstaff, although a complicated figure and characterized by his sheer vitality, also symbolizes disorder and must be rejected.[100]

Tillyard's influential examination of Tudor history and the representation of the period's sweeping ideals in Shakespeare's plays were quickly refined by subsequent scholarship. While Tillyard read the play as a clear celebration of power, other scholars, as early as John Dover Wilson and A. P. Rossiter, were more interested in the ways in which the play disrupted the unified world picture. Others, such as Irving Ribner, continued with the line of thought that the play used history 'to glorify England and support temporal political doctrine', yet criticized Tillyard's methodology in other ways, questioning the earlier critic's emphasis on the history plays as constituting a cyclic unit, and, in addition, problematizing his reliance on Hall for historical context.[101] In *Shakespeare's Histories: Mirrors of Elizabethan Policy* (1947), Lily Campbell shared many aspects of Tillyard's approach as she viewed the history plays as both interpretations of medieval history and commentaries on Elizabethan politics. However, proposing that 'the chief function of history was considered to be that of acting as a political mirror', she interpreted *1 Henry IV* as simultaneously offering a universalized version of history and refracting the events of the 1569 Northern Rebellion.[102] In this, Campbell followed Richard Simpson's nineteenth-century view of Shakespeare's history plays. In 'The Politics of Shakespeare's Historical Plays' (1874), Simpson had also suggested that both Parts 1 and 2 provided a parallel with the Northern Rebellion.[103] While Simpson's analysis had much in common with Ulrici's, and indeed with Tillyard's later study, particularly in his evaluation of the way in which Shakespeare's history plays chart the changing feudal state, it differed in this close topical analysis. Indeed this method of analysis influenced not only Campbell but also, as she points out, H. B. Charlton's, John Dover Wilson's and Alfred Hart's attention to Shakespeare's representation of history.[104] Hart, for example, was also interested in the political view put forward by

Shakespeare in the play, but he read it in relation to Elizabethan ideals revealed by the period's homilies.[105]

One significant divergence in Campbell's study from both Ulrici's and Tillyard's earlier work lay in her reading of Falstaff's function in this mediation of history. For Campbell, Falstaff does not reflect on the play's political events but simply diverts from the historical plot. The effect of this, she suggested, is that 'the working out of divine justice in the fate of the usurping king is almost forgotten in the delight of the comic episodes'.[106] Falstaff was further re-imagined in later investigations of the play's politics. Sigurd Burckhardt directly countered Tillyard by arguing that Shakespeare actually opposes the Elizabethan world picture. According to Burckhardt, this is demonstrated by the dominating presence of Falstaff, the figure of imagination rather than history, which indicates that disorder is not controlled.[107] Falstaff, therefore, maintains a crucial presence across critical approaches to the play throughout the twentieth century.

A New (Critical) History

Tillyard's seminal consideration of Shakespeare's history plays in relation to their historical and political contexts – in other words, his historicist methodology – has had an enduring influence on approaches to *1 Henry IV*. Studies in the latter half of the twentieth century have refuted, or refined, Tillyard's approach in two main ways: first, in rebalancing the consideration of the plays as history and as art, and secondly, in their analysis of the play's depiction of power structures.

Robert Ornstein's original scholarship on Shakespeare's history plays in *A Kingdom for a Stage: The Achievement of Shakespeare's History Plays* (1972) further refined the processes of reading *1 Henry IV* in terms of its representations of history and alongside its political and social contexts. It similarly insisted on Shakespeare's artistry and the need to consider the aesthetic in conjunction with the historical. Ornstein's work thus interestingly combined a focus on history with an emphasis on character. Like early-twentieth-century critics, he located Hal at the centre of the play; however, he did not read him in the typically positive light of such scholars. Via an exploration of the prince as a politician who has perfected his skills as a performer, he explored the relationship between power and performance. Ornstein's study paved the way for new critical approaches to the play in the final two decades of the twentieth century, approaches which were central to the critical schools of new historicism and cultural materialism. Among these Stephen Greenblatt's seminal essay, 'Invisible Bullets: Renaissance Authority and its Subversion, *Henry IV* and *Henry V*' is noteworthy as it demarcated fresh approaches to the play's ideological structures. Greenblatt critiqued Tillyard's work for its legitimization of the dominant social order and suggested instead that Shakespeare's plays, as sites of institutional and ideological contestation, depict power in more complex ways.[108] Power, he pointed out, is not monolithic, and Shakespeare's plays 'are centrally and repeatedly concerned with the production and containment of subversion and disorder'.[109] *1 Henry IV* was crucial to Greenblatt's demonstration of this thesis. He identified it as a play in which superficially 'authority seems far less problematical'.[110] Yet, he suggested that it is in this idealized image of a king that subversion, and the containment of that subversion, can be identified. Moreover, while the play's alternative, that is, subversive voices can be most clearly seen in Falstaff, their existence, according to Greenblatt, 'proves to be utterly bound up with Hal'.[111] It was thus through an examination of the relationship between these two characters that Greenblatt demonstrated firstly that the play provides a space for subversive voices, and secondly that although they are 'powerfully registered [. . .] they do not undermine that order'.[112]

In this politically conservative reading of Shakespeare's complicity in the Elizabethan world order, Michael Taylor has suggested that Greenblatt echoed some of Tillyard's ideas, despite his critique of his predecessor's approach to the play's political connotations.[113] The same might be said of numerous New Historicist readings of the play reaching the same conclusions. Yet Greenblatt's approach was equally influenced by Ornstein's examination of the relationship between theatre and power. His contentions were made possible by his alignment of the theatricality of power with the theatre itself. In other words, he dissolved the boundaries between art and social contexts to argue the now widely accepted maxim that

> theatrical values do not exist in a realm of privileged literariness, of textual or even institutional self-referentiality [. . .] rather the Elizabethan and Jacobean theatre was itself a *social event*.[114]

Greenblatt demonstrated this by aligning dramatic and political documents and reading *1 Henry IV* in the context of Thomas Harriot's *A Brief and True Report of the New Found Land of Virginia* (1588).

In 1991, David Scott Kastan problematized Greenblatt's methodology to offer a more radical reading of the subversive tendencies of *1 Henry IV*. In ' "The King hath many marching in his coats," or, What did you do in the war, Daddy?' he agreed that if the play can be said to be about anything it is about the production of power, an issue as acute in the final years of the reign of Henry IV as in the final years of the aging Elizabeth when the play was written.[115]

Yet he proposed that although 'we need to recognize the relationship between Shakespeare's dramatic practices and Elizabethan political conditions', it is necessary to 'distinguish between the theatricalized world of Elizabethan politics and the politicized world of the Elizabethan theatre' if we are to accurately historicize the plays.[116] Noting that previous scholarship had proven aesthetic unity by imposing the 'hierarchies of privilege and power that exist in the state upon the play' to prioritize the historical plot over the comic subplot, Kastan read the play and the theatrical context in which it was produced as 'less willing to organize its disparate voices into hierarchies'.[117] On the popular stage, he argued, kings and clowns did mix and disparate voices and conventions competed for control. In this reading, Falstaff's resistance to power cannot be incorporated on this stage into the hierarchical logic of the unified state or of the unified play. He occupies an oppositional role, a point also emphasized in Graham Holderness's reading of Falstaff as a Bakhtinian figure of carnival, discussed above. Kastan additionally suggested that Henry's understanding of power as constituted by theatricality, analysed by Ornstein and Greenblatt, and the exclusive presentation of royal power as representation in the play, also subverts authority in a Derridean 'risk of mimesis'.[118] This reading of *1 Henry IV* took Greenblatt's acknowledgement of the play's subversive elements to the next level by suggesting that these elements were not contained. This issue was also explored by Barbara Hodgdon. Hodgdon attended to the split between Falstaffian economy and royal legitimation in her analysis of twentieth-century appropriations of the play and pointed out that it is Falstaff, the 'kingly other' who rises in Part 1, in spite of the tendency of critical narratives to link 'the two parts of the play so consistently that Falstaff's banishment becomes the "end that crowns all"'.[119]

Issues pertaining to nation and national identity emerged from such analyses of power and its potential subversion as a significant issue in criticism on the play in the 1990s, and in the early twenty-first century. For Kastan, the play's inability to contain opposition pertained specifically to the play's representation of the nation, and he proposed that the England of the play is a fantasy of political incorporation.[120] Richard Helgerson directly engaged with Kastan's interpretation of the play in his 1992 study, *Forms of Nationhood: The Elizabethan Writing of England*. While Helgerson agreed with Kastan's reading to a certain extent, reiterating that the play doesn't wholly banish Falstaff, he was simultaneously persuaded by Greenblatt's model of containment and argued that the 'play participates with Hal in a rite of exclusion that breaks the rhythmic alteration of carnival and Lent; it shares the total-ising fantasy of power'.[121] Like Kastan, Helgerson turned to the play's performance context to support his argument. Nonetheless his inter-pretation of the mingling of kings and clowns in the popular theatre was vastly different. He suggested that the play's inclusion of Falstaff does share this social heterogeneity, but that in banishing him it dis-solves the dream of inclusion.[122]

Christopher Highley also took the historical context of national identity to be crucial to the interpretation of *1 Henry IV* in his late-twentieth-century monograph, *Shakespeare, Spenser, and the Crisis in Ireland* (1997). Highley's study addressed the ways in which early mod-ern writers, particularly Shakespeare, engaged with contemporary Anglo-Irish affairs, and he identified a reorientation of this engagement in *1 Henry IV*. Locating the play in the context of a nation-wide increase in Irish resistance to English rule, Highley interpreted a cluster of top-ical references in the play about the Earl of Tyrone, the Irish rebellion and the politics of English–Irish conflict via an examination of Mortimer and Glendower and the seductive power of the play's Welsh women. The play, he suggested, works at a topical level in its engagement with Ireland, 'encoding and exploring historical figures, events and patterns', yet it simultaneously 'maps local concerns onto perennial sources of English anxiety, especially anxieties of gender'.[123] He proposed that the play struggles to contain the multiple dangers of Ireland. Despite his interest in different issues from Kastan, Highley shared the earlier crit-ic's overarching view of the play and read *1 Henry IV* as providing a space for oppositional voices and alternative histories.

The context of early modern Wales underpinned Jean E. Howard and Phyllis Rackin's reading of nationhood in the *Henry IV* plays in their groundbreaking study, *Engendering a Nation: A Feminist Account of Shakespeare's English Histories* (1997). This innovative monograph attended to both gender and nation in Shakespeare's history plays, yet it treated the former topic in a more sustained manner than Highley's study. A consideration of the play's female characters or of its representa-tion of gender had been, until this point, noticeably absent from the crit-ical history of *1 Henry IV*. While Elizabeth Montagu admired Falstaff, she dismissed Mistress Quickly as sinking from 'comedy to farce' and Doll Tearsheet as 'indefensible and inexcusable' in her commentary on Part 2 in 1769.[124] Henrietta Lee Palmer included a chapter on Lady Percy in her nineteenth-century study of the 'Shakespeare Sisterhood'. Yet she admitted that this character 'can scarcely be denominated the heroine of *King Henry IV*, because properly speaking, that play is constructed without one.[125] Beyond admiring Lady Percy's marriage, Palmer offered limited comments on her character, suggesting that she has 'no peculiar traits, mental or moral'.[126] Howard and Rackin also pointed to the limited presence of women in the *Henry IV* plays. However, their focus was not the images of women, but on the impact that Shakespeare's historical drama has had on the way that we imagine gender and sexual difference, the institution of marriage and concepts of public and private.[127] In other words, they proposed that the history plays shed light on the gendering of social life in the 1590s and in the present day. They built on earlier analyses of the characterization of Falstaff in feminine terms, by critics such as Valerie Traub, to suggest that he 'threatens the virility of other men'.[128] Their main focus, however, was on the marginal spaces of the play's female characters, Wales and the Eastcheap tavern, and the impact of these on masculine national identity. They read depictions of geographical space in gendered, national and class terms. Despite the emphasis on the Welsh origins of the prince and future King Henry V, Howard and Rackin pointed out that *1 Henry IV* is the only history play in which Shakespeare actually takes his audience to this 'wild country just beyond the English border' and suggested that Shakespeare's Wales is 'inscribed in the same register that defined the dangerous power of women'.[129] Thus, Howard and Rackin proposed that in the second tetralogy women 'threaten to disable their husbands for the public achievements required by the performative conception of male authority by drawing them to sensual pleasures'.[130] In addition, Mistress Quickly, located in the alternative and class-inflected feminine space of the tavern and not easily assimilated into the institution of marriage, 'fractures the hermetically sealed world of aristocratic, masculine history'.[131] In both the spaces of the court and the city, the centre of London and the 'borderless state' of the nation, the play explores, according to this reading, the role of the feminine and its disruption of masculine authority. *Engendering a Nation*, therefore, significantly advanced the scholarly tradition of examinations of the political challenges presented by *1 Henry IV*.

The principal aspects of the long-standing critical tradition on *1 Henry IV*, including the topics of character, genre, the relationship between the play and Shakespeare's other history plays and the depiction of history and the political ideologies of the Elizabethan period continued to be relevant to evaluations of the play in the 1990s. Yet scholarship in the late twentieth century evinced significant changes in approaches to the play and in understandings of it. The fresh interpretations of character, history and ideology, combined with renewed attention to topics such as carnival, nation, and the hitherto-neglected concept of gender, demonstrate the extent to which this play continued to figure prominently in the critical consciousness. They have established the foundations for the new directions of scholarship in the twenty-first century, discussed in Chapter Six and demonstrated by the original research essays in this volume.

Notes

1. Francis Meres, *Palladis Tamia, Wits Treasury Being the Second Part of Wits Common-wealth* (London: Cuthbert Barbie, 1598), p. 282.
2. Samuel Johnson, 'The Plays of William Shakespeare' (1765), in *Henry the Fourth Parts I and II: Critical Essays*, ed. David Bevington (London: Garland Publishing Inc., 1986), pp. 7–8 (p. 7).
3. For example, Mark Van Doren, 'Shakespeare' (1939), in *Henry the Fourth Parts I and II: Critical Essays*, ed. David Bevington (New York and London: Garland Publishing Inc., 1986), pp. 99–116 (p. 99).
4. For an excellent analysis of early responses to the play see Charles Whitney, *Early Responses to Renaissance Drama* (Cambridge: Cambridge University Press, 2006), pp. 70–112.
5. Meres, *Palladis Tamia*, p. 282.
6. Cited in Whitney, *Early Responses*, pp. 94–101.
7. See George Thorn-Drury, *Some Seventeenth-Century Allusions to Shakespeare and his Works* (London: P. J. and A. E. Dobell, 1920), p. 11; Whitney, *Early Responses*, p. 79.
8. Quoted in Rudolph Fiehler, 'How Oldcastle became Falstaff', *Modern Language Quarterly*, 16: 1 (1955), 16–28 (p. 16).
9. For example, Fiehler, 'How Oldcastle became Falstaff'; Gary Taylor, 'The Fortunes of Oldcastle', *Shakespeare Survey* 38 (1985), 85–100.
10. See Gary Taylor et al., eds, *William Shakespeare: The Complete Works* (Oxford: Clarendon 1986), p. 509. See also Taylor, 'The Fortunes of Oldcastle' for justification of this decision. Critics who outline their position against this decision include: Jonathan Goldberg, 'The Commodity of Names: "Falstaff" and "Oldcastle" ' in *1 Henry IV*, in *Reconfiguring the Renaissance: Essays in Cultural Materialism*, ed. Jonathan Crewe (London: Associated University Presses, 1992), pp. 76–88; Kristen Poole, 'Saints Alive! Falstaff, Martin Marprelate, and the Staging of Puritanism', *Shakespeare Quarterly*, 46.1 (1995), 47–75.
11. William Shakespeare, *Poems* (London: Tho. Cotes, 1640), sig. A4r.
12. Francis Beaumont and John Fletcher, *Comedies and Tragedies* (London: Humphrey Robinson and Humphrey Moseley, 1647), sig. F2v.
13. Margaret Cavendish, 'Letter CXIII' (1664), in *Women Reading Shakespeare 1660–1900: An Anthology of Criticism*, ed. Ann Thompson and Sasha Roberts (Manchester: Manchester University Press, 1997), pp. 12–13. See also Marianne Novy, 'Women's Re-visions of Shakespeare 664–1988', in *Women's Re-visions of Shakespeare: On the Responses of Dickinson, Woolf, Rich, H. D., George Eliot, and Others*, ed. Marianne Novy (Chicago: University of Illinois Press, 1990), pp. 1–15.
14. William Winstanley, 'The Lives of the Most Famous English Poets' (1687), in *More Seventeenth-Century Allusions to Shakespeare and his Works*, ed. George Thorn-Drury (London: P. J. and A. E. Dobell, 1924), p. 25.
15. John Dryden, *Of Dramatick Poesy, an Essay* (1668) (London: Jacob Tonson, 1735), p. lxxvi.
16. Aphra Behn, 'An Epistle to the Reader' (1673), in *More Seventeenth-Century Allusions to Shakespeare and his Works*, ed. George Thorn-Drury (London: P. J. and A. E. Dobell, 1924), p. 10.

17. Samuel Pepys, 'Diary' (1667), in *William Shakespeare: The Critical Heritage, 1623–1692 (Volume 1)*, ed. Brian Vickers (London: Routledge, 1974), p. 31. For example, Paul Jorgensen, *Redeeming Shakespeare's Words* (Berkeley, CA: University of California Press, 1962).
18. George Daniel, *Trinarchordia* (1647), cited in Whitney, *Early Responses* (2006) p. 80.
19. Whitney, *Early Responses* (2006) p. 70.
20. Richard Cumberland, 'Remarks Upon the Characters of Falstaff and his Group' (1786), in *Henry the Fourth Parts I and II: Critical Essays*, ed. David Bevington (New York and London: Garland Publishing Inc., 1986), pp. 49–52 (p. 50); Samuel Taylor Coleridge, '*Henry IV*: The Character of Falstaff' (1811), reproduced in *Henry the Fourth Parts I and II: Critical Essays*, ed. David Bevington (New York and London: Garland Publishing Inc., 1986), p. 53.
21. Charles Gildon, 'Remarks on the Plays of Shakespeare' (1710), in *William Shakespeare: The Critical Heritage, 1693–1733 (Volume 2)*, ed. Brian Vickers (London: Routledge, 1996), p. 183; Johnson, 'The Plays', p. 8.
22. Johnson, 'The Plays', p. 8.
23. William Richardson, *Essay on Shakespeare's Dramatic Character of Sir John Falstaff* (London: J. Murray, 1788), p. 1.
24. Richardson, *Shakespeare's Dramatic Character*, pp. 11, 56.
25. Elizabeth Griffith, *The Morality of Shakespeare's Drama Illustrated* (1775) (London: Frank Cass & Co. Ltd., 1971), pp. 227, 228.
26. Cumberland, 'Remarks', p. 50.
27. Corbyn Morris, 'An Essay Towards Fixing the True Standards of Wit, Humour, Raillery, Satire and Ridicule' (1744), in *Henry the Fourth Parts I and II: Critical Essays*, ed. David Bevington (New York and London: Garland Publishing Inc., 1986), pp. 1–5 (p. 3).
28. Richard Stack, 'An Examination of an Essay on the Dramatick Character of Sir John Falstaff' (1788), in *William Shakespeare: The Critical Heritage, 1693–1733, (Volume 2)*, ed. Brian Vickers (London: Routledge, 1974), pp. 469–79.
29. Morris, 'Essay', p. 5.
30. Elizabeth Montagu, 'An Essay on the Writings and Genius of Shakespeare, Compared with the Greek and French Dramatic Poets' (1769), in *Henry the Fourth Parts I and II: Critical Essays*, ed. David Bevington (New York and London: Garland Publishing Inc., 1986), pp. 9–14 (p. 11).
31. Montagu, 'Essay', p. 11.
32. Henry Mackenzie, 'The Lounger' (1786), in *William Shakespeare: The Critical Heritage, 1774–1801 (Volume 6)*, ed. Brian Vickers (London: Routledge, 1981), pp. 440–46 (p. 441).
33. Charlotte Lennox, *Shakespear Illustrated: Or, the Novels and Histories, on which the Plays of Shakespear are Founded, Collected and Translated from the Original Authors* (London: A. Millar, 1754), Volume 3, p. 125.
34. Thomas Davies, *Dramatic Micellanies: Consisting of Critical Observations on Several Plays of Shakespeare* (London: Thomas Davies, 1783), Volume 1, pp. 202–03.
35. Davies, *Dramatic Micellanies*, pp. 202, vi.
36. Elizabeth Inchbald, *King Henry IV, The First Part . . . With Remarks* (1806–1809) (New York: Scholars's Facsimilies and Reprints, 1990), p. 3.
37. Inchbald, *King Henry IV*, p. 4.
38. Inchbald, *King Henry IV*, p. 4.
39. Maurice Morgann, *An Essay on the Dramatic Character of Sir John Falstaff* (1777), in *Henry the Fourth Parts I and II: Critical Essays*, pp. 15–40 (p. 15).

40. Morgann, *Dramatic Character of Sir John Falstaff*, p. 39. Christy Desmet, *Reading Shakespeare's Characters: Rhetorics, Ethics and Identity* (Amherst, MA: University of Massachusetts Press, 1992), p. 52.
41. See Mackenzie 'The Lounger'; Stack, 'Examination of an Essay' (1788); Elmer Edgar Stoll, 'Falstaff', *Modern Philology*, 12.4 (1914), 197–240; John Dover Wilson, *The Fortunes of Falstaff* (Cambridge: Cambridge University Press, 1943).
42. William Hazlitt, from *Characters of Shakespeare's Plays* (1817), in *Henry the Fourth Parts I and II: Critical Essays*, ed. David Bevington (New York and London: Garland Publishing Inc., 1986), pp. 55–64 (p. 64).
43. Hazlitt, 'Characters', p. 55.
44. Hazlitt, Characters', p. 64.
45. A. C. Bradley, 'The Rejection of Falstaff' (1902), in *Henry the Fourth Parts I and II: Critical Essays*, ed. David Bevington (New York and London: Garland Publishing Inc., 1986), pp. 77–98 (p. 78).
46. Bradley, 'Rejection', p. 87.
47. Robert Langbaum, *The Poetry of Experience* (New York: Random House, 1957), in *Henry the Fourth Parts I and II: Critical Essays*, ed. David Bevington (New York and London: Garland Publishing Inc., 1986), pp. 207–22.
48. Wilson, J. D., *Fortunes*, p. 17.
49. Stoll, 'Falstaff', pp. 197–240.
50. Wilson, J. D., *Fortunes*, p. 22.
51. Wilson, J. D., *Fortunes*, p. 36.
52. W. H. Auden, 'The Prince's Dog' (1948), in *Henry the Fourth Parts I and II: Critical Essays*, ed. David Bevington (New York and London: Garland Publishing Inc., 1986), pp. 157–80 (p. 163).
53. Northrop Frye, 'The Argument of Comedy' (1949), in *Henry the Fourth Parts I and II: Critical Essays*, ed. David Bevington (New York and London: Garland Publishing Inc., 1986), pp. 181–86; William Empson, 'Falstaff and Mr Dover Wilson' (1953), in *Shakespeare: Henry IV Parts I and II: A Casebook*, ed. G. K. Hunter (London: Macmillan, 1970), pp. 135–54; Bernard Spivack, 'Shakespeare and the Allegory of Evil' (1958), in *Henry the Fourth Parts I and II: Critical Essays*, ed. David Bevington (New York and London: Garland Publishing Inc., 1986), pp. 221–22.
54. C. L. Barber, *Shakespeare's Festive Comedy: A Study of Dramatic Form and Its Relation to Social Custom* (Princeton, NJ: Princeton University Press, 1959), p. 192.
55. Lewis Theobald, 'The Works of Shakespeare' (1733), in *William Shakespeare: The Critical Heritage, 1693–1733, (Volume 2)*, ed. Brian Vickers (London: Routledge, 1974), pp. 475–528.
56. Edward Dowden, *Shakespeare: A Critical Study of his Mind and Art* (1875), in *Henry the Fourth Parts I and II: Critical Essays*, ed. David Bevington (New York and London: Garland Publishing Inc., 1986), pp. 65–71.
57. Franz Alexander, 'A Note on Falstaff', *Psychoanalytic Quarterly*, 3 (1933), 592–606.
58. Ernst Kris, 'Prince Hal's Conflict', *Psychoanalytic Quarterly*, 17 (1948), 487–506; J. I. M. Stewart, 'Character and Motive in Shakespeare' (1949), in *Shakespeare: Henry IV Parts I and II: A Casebook*, pp. 127–33. ed. by David Bevington (New York and London: Garland Publishing Inc., 1986).
59. Robert Watson, *Shakespeare and the Hazards of Ambition* (Cambridge: Harvard University Press, 1984).
60. Sigurd Burckhardt, 'Shakespearean Meanings' (1968), in *Henry the Fourth Parts I and II: Critical Essays*, ed. David Bevington (New York and London: Garland Publishing Inc., 1986), pp. 289–314.

61. Derek Cohen, 'The Rites of Violence in *1 Henry IV*', *Shakespeare Survey*, 38 (1985), 77–84.

62. For example, Valerie Traub, 'Prince Hal's Falstaff: Positioning Psychoanalysis and the Female Reproductive Body', *Shakespeare Quarterly*, 40 (1989), 456–74.

63. H. B. Charlton, *Shakespearian Comedy* (London: Methuen & Co., 1938), pp. 161–207.

64. Van Doren, 'Shakespeare', pp. 109, 102.

65. Cleanth Brooks and Robert Heilman, *Understanding Drama* (London: George G. Harrap & Co Ltd., 1946), p. 318.

66. R. J. Dorius, 'A Little More than a Little', *Shakespeare Quarterly*, 11 (1960), 13–26.

67. A. P. Rossiter, 'Angel with Horns: The Unity of *Richard III*' (1961), in *Shakespeare's Histories: An Anthology of Modern Criticism*, ed. William Armstrong (London: Penguin, 1972), pp. 123–44.

68. Robert Weimann, *Shakespeare and the Popular Tradition in the Theatre: Studies in the Social Dimension of Dramatic Form and Function*, ed. Robert Schwartz (Baltimore, MD: John Hopkins University Press, 1978).

69. Derek Traversi, *Shakespeare: From Richard II to Henry V* (Stanford, CA: Stanford University Press, 1957), p. 70.

70. Robert G. Hunter, 'Shakespeare, Pattern of Excelling Nature' (1978), in *Henry the Fourth Parts I and II: Critical Essays*, ed. David Bevington (New York and London: Garland Publishing Inc., 1986), pp. 349–58.

71. Graham Holderness, *Shakespeare Recycled: The Making of Historical Drama* (Hemel Hempstead: Harvester Wheatsheaf, 1992), p. 144.

72. Graham Holderness, *Shakespeare's History* (Dublin: Gill and Macmillan, 1985), p. 131.

73. François Laroque, 'Shakespeare's "Battle of Carnival and Lent": The Falstaff Scenes Reconsidered (*1 and 2 Henry IV*)', in *Shakespeare and Carnival: After Bakhtin*, ed. Ronald Knowles (New York: St Martin's, 1998), pp. 83–96.

74. Alice-Lyle Scoufos, *Shakespeare's Typological Satire: A Study of the Falstaff-Oldcastle Problem* (Ohio: Ohio University Press, 1979), esp. pp. 4, 70–133.

75. For example, Robert Fehrenbach, 'When Lord Cobham and Edmund Tilney were at odds': Oldcastle, Falstaff and the date of *1 Henry IV*', *Shakespeare Studies*, 18 (1986), 87–101; Goldberg, 'The Commodity of Names'; Thomas Pendleton, ' "This is not the man" : On Calling Falstaff Falstaff', *Analytical and Enumerative Bibliography*, 4 (1990), 59–71; Poole, 'Saints Alive!' .

76. Harold Bloom, *Ruin the Sacred Truths: Poetry and Belief from the Bible to the Present* (Cambridge: Harvard University Press, 1989), p. 84; Holderness, *Shakespeare Recycled*, pp. 130–77.

77. John Upton, *Critical Observations on Shakespeare* (London: G. Hawkins, 1748), p. 58.

78. See David Scott Kastan, 'Introduction', in *King Henry IV, Part One*, ed. David Scott Kastan (London: Arden Shakespeare, Thomson Learning, 2002), pp. 1–132 (p. 19).

79. See Kastan, 'Introduction', p. 19; Harold Jenkins 'The Structural Problem in Shakespeare's *Henry IV*', in *Shakespeare: Henry IV Parts I and II: A Casebook*, ed. G. K. Hunter (London: Macmillan, 1970), pp. 155–73.

80. Matthias Shaaber, 'The Unity of *Henry IV*', in *Joseph Quincy Adams Memorial Studies*, ed. J. G. McManaway (Washington: Folger Library, 1948), pp. 217–27; Sherman Hawkins, '*Henry IV*: The Structural Problem Revisited', *Shakespeare Quarterly*, 33 (1982), 278–301.

81. G. K. Hunter, '*Henry IV* and the Elizabethan Two part Play', *RES*, 5 (1954), 236–48 (p. 237).

82. E. M. W. Tillyard, *Shakespeare's History Plays* (1944) (London: Penguin Books, 1991), pp. 242, 269.

83. Gerard Langbaine, 'An Account of the English Dramatick Poets (1691)', in *William Shakespeare: The Critical Heritage, 1623–1692, (Volume 1)*, ed. Brian Vickers (London: Routledge, 1974), p. 419.
84. See Tom McAlindon, *Shakespeare's Tudor History: A Study of Henry IV, Parts 1 and 2* (Aldershot: Ashgate, 2001), p. 3.
85. Montagu, 'Essay', p. 9.
86. H. B. Charlton, 'Shakespeare, Politics and Politicians' (1929), in *Shakespeare: Henry IV Parts I and II: A Casebook*, ed. G. K. Hunter (London: Macmillan, 1970), pp. 81–91 (p. 85).
87. Felix E. Schelling, *The English Chronicle Play: A Study in the Popular Historical Literature Environing Shakespeare* (London: Macmillan, 1902).
88. Ronald R. MacDonald, 'Uneasy Lies: Language and History in Shakespeare's Lancastrian Tetralogy', *Shakespeare Quarterly*, 35 (1984), 22–39.
89. Paul Dean, 'Forms of Time: Some Elizabethan Two-Part History Plays', *Renaissance Studies*, 4.4 (1990), 410–30 (p. 426).
90. Bradley, 'Rejection', p. 96; Harold Toliver, 'Falstaff, the Prince and the History Play', *Shakespeare Quarterly*, 16.1 (1965), 63–80.
91. Thomas Courtenay, *Commentaries on the Historical Plays of Shakespeare* (London: Henry Colbourn, 1840), Volume 1, pp. 75–118.
92. Harold Jenkins, 'Shakespeare's History Plays: 1900–1951', *Shakespeare Survey*, 6 (1953), 1–15.
93. A. W. Schlegel, *A Course of Lectures on Dramatic Art and Literature*, translated by John Black (London: Bohn, 1846).
94. Hermann Ulrici, *Shakespeare's Dramatic Art*, translated by L. Dora Schmitz (London: George Bell and Sons, 1876); vol. 2, p. 232.
95. Ulrici, *Shakespeare's Dramatic Art*, p. 238.
96. Ulrici, *Shakespeare's Dramatic Art*, pp. 238, 244.
97. McAlindon, *Shakespeare's Tudor History*, p. 10.
98. Tillyard, *Shakespeare's History Plays*, p. 275.
99. Tillyard, *Shakespeare's History Plays*, p. 282.
100. Tillyard, *Shakespeare's History Plays*, pp. 293–95.
101. Irving Ribner, 'The English History Play in the Age of Shakespeare' (1957), in *Shakespeare's Histories: An Anthology of Modern Criticism*, ed. William Armstrong (London: Penguin, 1972), pp. 29–59 (p. 48).
102. Lily B. Campbell, *Shakespeare's 'Histories': Mirrors of Elizabethan Policy* (1947) (San Marino: The Huntington Library, 1963), p. 15.
103. Richard Simpson, 'The Politics of Shakespeare's Historical Plays', *The New Shakespeare Society Transactions*, 1 (1874), 396–441.
104. Campbell, *Shakespeare's 'Histories'*, p. 5.
105. Alfred Hart, *Shakespeare and the Homilies* (London: Oxford University Press, 1934). Robert Ornstein, *A Kingdom for a Stage: The Achievement of Shakespeare's History Plays* (Cambridge: Harvard University Press, 1972) also cites Elizabethan homilies as an important source of information about contemporary political attitudes.
106. Tillyard, *Shakespeare's History Plays*, p. 244.
107. Sigurd Burckhardt, 'Shakespearean Meanings' , pp. 289–314.
108. Stephen Greenblatt, 'Invisible Bullets: Renaissance Authority and its Subversion, Henry IV and Henry V', in *Political Shakespeare: New Essays in Cultural Materialism*, ed. Jonathan Dollimore and Alan Sinfield (Ithaca, NY: Cornell University Press, 1985), pp. 18–47.
109. Greenblatt, 'Invisible Bullets', p. 29.
110. Greenblatt, 'Invisible Bullets', p. 29.

111. Greenblatt, 'Invisible Bullets', p. 30.
112. Greenblatt, 'Invisible Bullets', p. 38.
113. Michael Taylor, *Shakespeare and Criticism in the Twentieth Century* (Oxford: Oxford University Press, 2001), p. 189.
114. Greenblatt, 'Invisible Bullets', p. 32.
115. David Scott Kastan, *Shakespeare After Theory* (London: Routledge, 1999), p. 129. The essay was first published as ' "The King Hath Many Marching in his Coats", or, What did you do in the War, Daddy?', in *Shakespeare Left and Right*, ed. Ivo Kamps (London: Routledge, 1991), pp. 241–58.
116. Kastan, *Shakespeare After Theory*, p. 134.
117. Kastan, *Shakespeare After Theory*, p. 132.
118. Kastan, *Shakespeare After Theory*, p. 141.
119. Barbara Hodgdon, *The End Crowns All: Closure and Contradiction in Shakespeare's History* (Princeton, NJ: Princeton University Press, 1991), pp. 153, 158–59.
120. Kastan, *Shakespeare After Theory*, p. 131.
121. Richard Helgerson, *Forms of Nationhood: The Elizabethan Writing of England* (Chicago: University of Chicago Press, 1992), p. 227.
122. Helgerson, *Forms of Nationhood*, p. 227.
123. Christopher Highley, *Shakespeare, Spenser, and the Crisis in Ireland* (Cambridge: Cambridge University Press, 1997), p. 87.
124. Montagu, 'Essay', p. 13.
125. Henrietta Lee Palmer, *The Stratford Gallery; or, the Shakespeare Sisterhood: Comprising Forty-Five Ideal Portraits* (New York: Appletin and Co., 1859), p. 283.
126. Palmer, *The Stratford Gallery*, p. 283.
127. Jean E. Howard and Phyllis Rackin, *Engendering a Nation: A Feminist Account of Shakespeare's English Histories* (London: Routledge, 1997), p. 21.
128. Howard and Rackin, *Engendering a Nation*, p. 166. See Valerie Traub, *Desire and Anxiety: Circulations of Sexuality in Shakespearean Drama* (London: Routledge, 1992), pp. 50–70. See also Traub, 'Prince Hal's Falstaff'; Phyllis Rackin, *Stages of History: Shakespeare's English Chronicles* (Ithaca, NY: Cornell University Press, 1990), pp. 203–04.
129. Howard and Rackin, *Engendering a Nation*, p. 168.
130. Howard and Rackin, *Engendering a Nation*, p. 173.
131. Howard and Rackin, *Engendering a Nation*, p. 176.

CHAPTER TWO

Performance History

Graham Atkin

Writing in April 1952, Antony Quayle, in his foreword to an account of *Shakespeare's Histories at Stratford 1951*, welcomed the 'publication of this book in that it rightly binds together the functions of three professions – those of actor, scholar and critic – all of them essential to vital work in the theatre'. Quayle writes regretfully on behalf of all actors that 'when the curtain falls their performance can live only a human span in the failing memories of their audience, and for immortality they must depend on the temper, taste and talent of the dramatic critic'.[1] This chapter aims to do what it can to bind together the functions of actor, scholar and critic and I begin my account with the person of Samuel Pepys – a writer to whom we owe so much – someone we can warm to – someone we might know – someone with at least a little Falstaff in him – and a great theatre-goer, though not perhaps a great dramatic critic. Pepys records seeing the play three times in the 1660s, but it is his entry for 2nd November 1667 that most activates this reader's imagination:

> 2nd. Up, and to the office, where busy all the morning; at noon home, and after dinner my wife and Willett and I to the King's playhouse, and there saw 'Henry the Fourth:' and contrary to expectation, was pleased in nothing more than in Cartwright's speaking of Falstaffe's speech about 'What is Honour?' The house full of Parliament-men, it being holyday with them: and it was observable how a gentleman of good habit, sitting just before us, eating of some fruit in the midst of the play, did drop down as dead, being choked; but with much ado Orange Moll did thrust her finger down his throat and brought him to life again. After

the play, we home, and I busy at the office late, and then home to supper and to bed.[2]

It is fitting that Pepys remembers a nearly dying man saved from the semblance of death, the counterfeit of death, choked perhaps by his own Falstaffian gluttony – saved by the Doll Tearsheet of her days, Moll Orange, who thrusts her finger down his throat and brings him to life again. The Falstaffian figure is found here, revealed to us by Pepys's attentive eye, gorging himself on stage and off, taking the discreet and honourable action of feigning his death, on stage and in the audience. So Cartwright is our first Falstaff to be reviewed, though he is in danger of being upstaged by this 'gentleman of good habit', and Pepys says nothing of any other character in the play. Pepys' low expectations – happily surpassed – may have been due to his earlier attendance, on 8th November 1660, at a production having just read the text, something he felt spoilt the experience somewhat.

Though we know a little about the stages and the actors involved in the earliest performances, and have many references to Falstaff indicating its popularity (see Lamb, Chapter One), we have little information predating Pepys about the play in performance. We do know that during the Civil War the play was produced in a 'droll' under the title *The Bouncing Knight, or the Robbers Robbed*. This was a short version of the play adapted from certain scenes of the play, with Falstaff as the main focus.[3] Kastan highlights that Thomas Betterton produced the best Falstaff yet when he performed the role in 1700, having, in 1682, performed the role of Hotspur with 'fierce and flashing fire'.[4] Betterton's Falstaff appeared in a performance in which the historical action was trimmed while Falstaff's lines were, on the whole, retained. This is suggested also by the title used when this version was published in 1700: *K. Henry IV with the Humours of Sir John Falstaff. A Tragi-comedy*. It is generally thought that Betterton's success enabled the play to avoid the Nahum Tate treatment, or 'Newmodelling', of the period (as was the notorious fate of *King Lear* in 1681). Tate's revised version of *King Lear* held the stage until the mid-nineteenth century, but throughout that period *1 Henry IV* continued to be popular. Following Betterton, James Quin appeared first as Hotspur in 1718–19 and then as Falstaff in 1721–22. He continued in the role until his retirement in 1751, with David Garrick playing Hotspur alongside him at Drury Lane in 1746. Kastan emphasizes that Garrick's Hotspur was criticized as 'not formed to give a just idea of the gallant and noble Hotspur', but Quin's Falstaff was judged 'the most intelligent and judicious Falstaff since the days of Betterton'.[5] Lord Lyttleton praised Quin for 'such perfection . . . he was not an actor . . . he was Falstaff himself'.[6] Therefore it is with incredulity that we learn that Quin cut what is for many one of the most effective and enjoyable scenes of the play, the 'play extempore' from Act II Scene iv. Quin's cut pleased some (Francis Gentleman felt the scene 'rather choaked and loaded the main business' and that it was 'dreadfully tedious in representation') but agitated others, perhaps the most famous of whom was Abraham Lincoln, who demanded 'to know why one of the best scenes in the play, that where Falstaff and Prince Hal alternately assume the character of the king, is omitted in the representation'. James Hackett, the American actor who was asked this by Lincoln at the White House in 1863, reportedly replied that 'it is admirable to read but ineffective on stage, that there is generally nothing sufficiently distinctive about the actor who plays Henry to make an imitation striking'.[7] Indeed, as Scott McMillin confirms, both the play extempore and the Welsh scene were commonly cut or severely reduced during the eighteenth and nineteenth centuries.[8]

Notwithstanding the early Oldcastle/Falstaff controversy, even the earliest references to the play confirm what Pepys' account suggests: that the overwhelming fact about this play is that it is Falstaff's play unless it is placed in the midst of its historical sequence, the 'first tetralogy' spanning the reigns of Richard II, Henry IV and Henry V. Placing it this way does a great disservice to the play, and to Falstaff, and even more especially to Hotspur, who, from the first printed versions of the play, was singled out for a special mention. In the 1623 Folio version, the title of the play is given as 'The First Part of Henry the Fourth, with the Life and Death of Henry sirnamed Hotspurre'. The play is as much Harry Hotspur's (with 18% of the lines) as it is Falstaff's (with 20% of the lines). It is as much Hotspur's as it is Hal's (also with 18% of the lines). The king, who gives his name to this play and its sequel, has a mere 11 per cent of the lines.[9] Yet for Harold Bloom, as for many others, Falstaff is the character who dominates the play, if not the entire work of Shakespeare. Bloom's enthusiasm for Falstaff stems from a performance of the play he saw as a teenager:

> When I was fifteen, I saw Ralph Richardson play Falstaff (with Laurence Olivier as Hotspur), and I have carried the image of Richardson's exuberant and inventive Falstaff in my head for forty-five years now, and find the image informing the text every time I reread or teach the *Henry IV* plays. Richardson's Falstaff was neither an adorable roisterer nor a kind of counter-courtier, eager for possibilities of power. Rather, he was a veteran warrior who had seen through warfare, discarded its honor and glory as pernicious

illusions, and had decided that true life was play, both as we play on stage or in games, and as we play when we are children.[10]

And this view of Falstaff extends right up to his death, recounted by Mistress Quickly in *Henry V*.

> Playing with flowers, and smiling upon his fingers' end, Sir John dies as a child, reminding us again of his total lack of hypocrisy, of what after all makes us love him, of what doubtless drew the Machiavellian Hal to him. Freedom from the superego, authentic freedom, is the liberty to play, even as a child plays, in the very act of dying. (Bloom, p. 5)

However, just as criticism has moved away from the celebration of Falstaff to the story of Hal's education and progression to the throne (see Lamb, Chapter One), so have modern productions. From Richard Burton's 1951 performance of a Hal who knows what he is doing right from the start, up to John Warner's 2007 performance of a depressed and rather gaunt Falstaff, 'a lean-looking Falstaff with a rather sad, sagging beer-belly' as Kate Wilkinson remarks, we can chart the switching emphasis away from the lovable life-affirming rogue towards the calculating rationality of the politician.[11] By the end of *1 Henry IV*, the standard-bearer of the truth-telling, plain-speaking, incapable of seeming anything but what it is, bare-faced honour, Hotspur, is dead. Hal seems to promise rewards to the still tolerated Falstaff, but we know that this will end, and have Hal's 'I do, I will' echoing in our ears. And it is in the foreshadowing harshness of the rejection in the play extempore scene that the shift has occurred. Politics/history will eclipse even Falstaff.

Theatrically, Henry, Hal, Hotspur and the strongest character of them all, Falstaff, dominate the play. When it comes to the history of the play in performance we perhaps cannot avoid a similar domination of character over other considerations (such as setting and costume design, or music and properties). How much more vivid are the characters of a piece like this play in performance as opposed to reading? This is a difficult point to discuss, but the point must be conceded that, in performance, there is a concrete realization of the role which even the most ardent and imaginative reader cannot come close to. In reading, the character remains an idea, but in performance becomes a reality. This is even more true of film. In the close-ups of individual faces the characters of King Henry, Hotspur, Hal and Falstaff, and even Mistress Quickly, in film portrayals by John Gielgud, Norman Rodway, Ken Baxter and Orson Welles, and Margaret Rutherford, capture and preserve some essence of character and the soul of the play more than any ephemeral stage production (even if filmed) ever can.

Outside the shining moments of a few Falstaffs and other characters caught and preserved for us all to see, there is only one wholly fulfilling encounter with the play on film, and that is in Orson Welles's masterpiece, the magnificent *Chimes at Midnight* or *Falstaff* (1965). Welles's film, now happily available to the wide audience it deserves since its release in February 2011 on Region 2 DVD, is one of the great products of that ongoing encounter between the filmic imagination and the Shakespearean mind.

I offer a few notes on these characters and some of the issues that performance raises, agreeing with Bevington that

> any director must take into account . . . the rhythm of the alternation between serious and comic scenes, and the establishment of antithetical, or foil, relationships among the characters: Hotspur and Falstaff, the King and Falstaff, Hal in relation to all three.[12]

A few brief examples from performances of these roles will, I trust, assist in setting the scene. I will concentrate on productions since the end of World War II.

Falstaff

Criticizing Stephen Kemble's Falstaff, famously played in 1818 without padding such was his obesity, J. R. Planche commented that 'he evidently suffered under the exertion; and though his reading of the part was irreproachable, he lacked the natural humour, and was too ill at ease to portray the mere animal spirits of the jovial knight'. Planche goes on to ask a question which strikes to the heart of the difficulty of performing such a mammoth role, 'but did any one ever see Sir John Falstaff except in his mind's eye?'[13] Macready evidently felt, only 8 years later, that Robert Elliston might come close. Having watched Elliston in rehearsal he wrote that 'he made the nearest approach to the joyous humour and unctuous roguery of the character that I had ever witnessed' and felt that this promised success in performing the role of Falstaff sufficiently, 'but, alas! Whether from failure of voice or general deficiency of power, the attempt fell ineffectively upon the audience, and the character was left, as it has been since the days of Quin and Henderson, without an adequate representative' (Salgado, p. 182).

Compare with this 1945, which saw the 'total accomplishment' of Ralph Richardson's Falstaff. Though he was 'the least thirsty Falstaff in remembrance', he was praised for capturing 'the man's wise, agile mind'.[14]

The Stratford-upon-Avon 1951 production, 6 years later presented Antony Quayle in the role. Quayle was hugely made up with big eyebrows and tufts of white hair on top and sides of his head, and a beard and moustache (which from photographs one can clearly see stuck on to gauze) He looked to commentators like a carnival clown, a grotesque scarecrow. But the true fruits of this performance are seen in the 1979 BBC Falstaff for which Quayle, by now in his 60s, drew on his own apprenticeship in the role 28 years earlier. He offers a performance full of lovable ghastliness, such as when he urinates in the bushes before the battle of Shrewsbury while talking to us over his shoulder about the 'gibbets' and 'dead bodies' that he has corruptly recruited as soldiers. Another example, from the end of this scene, shows us Quayle, on hearing that the king is 'encamped', pretending to be busy with preparations by noisily banging a drum and shouting as if for battle-readiness before collapsing, coughing, tossing down the ladle which he used to pound the drum, and delivering, exhausted with his mock aggression, the lines 'Well, to the latter end of a fray and the beginning of a feast| Fits a dull fighter and a keen guest' (IV.ii.77–78). As he says this Quayle eyes the boiled capon that he has skewered on a huge meat fork. He raises the bird, steaming, to his rosy face, blowing the steam away to cool his coming feast. This moment is one of many that could be cited to join with Russell Davies in his praise for Quayle's impressive 'switching on the twinkle at will' which characterized the performance.[15] Richard Last called Quayle's 'underplayed interpretation, full of verbal and visual throw-aways' 'a masterpiece of calculation' (O'Connor and Goodland, p. 342).

This scenic and tonal complexity is characteristic of many of the best-received modern Falstaffs. Commenting on Welles's cutting and rearranging of Shakespeare's text, Bevington argues that 'inevitably some parts of the plays suffer, but in return we are given a remarkably sensitive reading of a fat comic who is at heart insecure and in need of affection'. Welles's Falstaff is to be praised, we are told, because 'beneath his joviality we sense the hurt in Falstaff's frightened eye, the predominant sadness that expresses itself in a series of farewells. To Welles, the film is a story "all in dark colours," a "lament" for Falstaff' (Bevington, p. 85). To be sure, the film from the first frames is possessed of a powerful capacity to capture humanity, such as the opening sequence with Falstaff and Shallow each half-filling the screen, Falstaff more in the foreground with a magical glint in his eyes, the very image of warmth and life. The richness of Welles's voice is felt fully in Falstaff's line 'banish all the world' in which the voice of the actor seems about to fail before it comes through with a depth and sonority that suggest the world.

In contrast, though Bob Pigeon's Falstaff-figure in Van Sant's *My Own Private Idaho*, is described by Scott, the Hal figure, as 'my real father', as 'Father Christmas' and as the 'great psychedelic Papa', there is little in Bob's performance that could be called charismatic. He greets Scott as 'my true son', and on enquiring what time it is, Scott tells him 'what do you care? Why you wouldn't even look at a clock unless hours were lines of coke, dials looked like the signs of gay bars or time itself was a fair hustler in black leather – isn't that right Bob?' The updating of Falstaff jars and jangles, but it certainly makes the medieval knight a modern. Other highly praised modern Falstaffs showing mastery of the character's range include John Woodvine's of 1987 for the English Shakespeare Company. Michael Radcliffe, writing in *The Observer*, called it a 'classic interpretation of breadth, confidence, fastidiousness and humanity' and remarked that Woodvine's 'splintery, dark-etched and saturnine voice relishes every line, reference and joke as though being handed them for the first time' (O'Connor and Goodland, p. 346). Benedict Nightingale writing in *The Times* in April 2000 was very appreciative of Desmond Barrit's seriocomic Falstaff for the Royal Shakespeare Company. For Nightingale, Barrit was a 'troll king who introduces himself by peering out of the same earth like an old mole or the head of a dilapidated John the Baptist'. His particular praise was saved for Barrit's enunciation, in the 'what is honour' speech, of 'the survivor's code with more care and gravity than any Falstaff I can recall' (O'Connor and Goodland, p. 355).

Hotspur

Norman Council has it that Hotspur 'enters battle the picture of an honourable man, secure in conscience and indifferent to death if it provide honour to an otherwise valueless life' and argues that 'his death is displayed as the logical consequence of this attitude'. He goes further: 'his death, immediately juxtaposed with Falstaff's feigning death, is as precisely the true and perfect image of honour as Falstaff's action is the image of life'.[16] These are stark claims, and suggest a great weight of interpretation and meaning of the play resides in the character of Hotspur; his life, his death.

Harry Hotspur's macho energy as 'mad fellow of the north' (II.iv.326) is memorably captured by Welles as he has the fiery Norman Rodway drying his lower body vigorously below the camera frame as he speaks his lines: 'By the Lord, our plot is a good plot as ever was laid, our friends true and constant; a good plot, good friends, and full of expectation; an excellent plot, very good friends'. Marina Vlady's Lady Percy's amused and loving laughter adds to the warmth of this rendering. The ease and comfort between them is evident in every moment, as she pursues her agitated husband and seizes his finger in a touching attempt to assert her love. Similarly, there is something appealing about Tim Pigott-Smith's bombastic rendition of Hotspur in the BBC film version, and his death, with blood glugging out of his mouth, is certainly memorable. Pigott-Smith's Hotspur is a red-headed firebrand, pulsing with energetic animosity. But he does have some sense. Having railed and ranted at Henry's transgressions, he pauses in response to Blount's question 'Shall I return this answer to the King?' and says 'Not so, Sir Walter'.

Hotspur is vital in deed and word, and his manner of speech has been addressed in a variety of ways. In his first scene he rails against the 'popinjay', a performance marking him as the foil to such courtly mannered speech, such exaggerated affectedness. Laurence Olivier, prompted it seems by Lady Percy's reference to him 'speaking thick', played the rebel Hotspur with a slight stammer, particularly with the 'w' sound. This afforded Hal the opportunity of mocking him with a cruel impersonation: 'Fie upon this quiet life, I w-w-want w-w-work' and allowed Olivier to produce 'an effect of heartrending pathos as he struggled to get out his final words – "No, Percy, thou art dust,| A and food for w-w-"'.[17] Michael Redgrave refused such affectation. His pursuit of a memorable characterization of the role in 1951 led him to visit the

> pubs and manor houses of Northumberland in search of a burred 'R' two months before opening ("Hotspur Looks for a Burr in the Bar", *Newcastle Evening Chronicle*, 12 February 1951), and found an accent that could be ignored no more easily than it could be placed. (McMillin, p. 45)

The quest for a genuine taste of the North East in the character is further reflected in the English Shakespeare Company film version of 1990. Here Andrew Jarvis, a 'fierce shaven-headed actor', presented a manic and very Geordie Hotspur, a figure who might have stepped off the Newcastle United football terraces (Loehlin, p. 185).

How does Hotspur die? It tells an audience as much about Hal as about Hotspur. Michael Redgrave as Hotspur ends with blood splattered on the left of his face as Hal kills him. Burton is pictured in one (publicity?) photograph holding his sword as a cross below the hilt. Rodway's Hotspur in *Chimes at Midnight* is a sanguine warrior, with a clarity in his voice and his bright looks that cuts through the gloom of the court and the dirt of the tavern, filling the screen with his thoughts of noble life or death. His death is presented honourably and touchingly by Welles, whereas just 2 years before this film, in 1964, Roy Dotrice's

Hotspur was ignobly stabbed with a dagger and tipped into a pig trough by Ian Holm's ruthless Prince Hal.

In Trevor Nunn's 1982 version, when Hotspur took the stage at Act I, Scene iii he dominated with his charismatic performance of the part of the 'popinjay'. But, as with many productions, comparisons with Hal were subtly made. At the end of this speech, on 'I beseech you', he moved into Worcester's seat and put his arm on the back of the king's chair. There was no pause after Hotspur's speech, and Henry reached for his goblet and coughed slightly, clearly moved (no doubt thinking of the inadequacies of his own son). After the king had left Northumberland, Worcester and Hotspur on stage, Hotspur moved more to the centre of the stage and his activity contrasted notably with the stillness of other figures (e.g., during his long speech from line 158 'Nay, then I cannot blame his cousin King' Hotspur moved between sitting next to Northumberland to the front of the table, to behind them, and then sat at the other end of the table to Worcester's right). On 'pluck bright honour' he was back at front centre-stage. Hotspur's conciliatory line to his uncle, 'good uncle, tell your tale, I have done' was notably drawn out, for comic effect, and his final lines 'O, let the hours be short' were shouted and accompanied by a gesture of a raised, clenched right fist which echoed Hal from the previous scene.

Prince Hal

The early soliloquy is one of the key scenes when deciding how to play the character. Is the Prince of Wales a jovial young scamp who genuinely loves Falstaff but knows that he must reject him, or is he a Machiavellian manipulator planning to use his life of vice to set off his later virtue? Another key moment comes at the aftermath of the battle of Shrewsbury when the prince is confronted by Falstaff lugging the body of Hotspur and claiming the heroic victory over this honourable traitor. A third key moment is the death of Hotspur and what John Dover Wilson calls Hal's 'tender, almost brotherly, speech which he utters over his slain foe'.[18] This offers actors an opportunity to present us with a compassionate prince who respects his adversary – though even now, with a man he has killed lying before him, Hal thinks of the gratitude he is due 'For doing these fair rites of tenderness'. Actors and directors faced with these lines have choices to make, and the choices made at this crucial moment, and the following moment when Hal sees the fallen Falstaff close by, can either work with or against the Hal earlier presented. Do we see a shift towards rejection of Falstaff or a renewal in Hal's tolerance of this 'tun of man'? Does Hal feel anything when he thinks 'poor Jack' dead, or does he know him to be alive and tease him with the prospect of embowelment? Welles answers the question emphatically, with the use of the visible steam of hot breath ascending through the visor of the preposterous knight, noticed by the prince and prompting his words over the counterfeit corpse. Other directors and actors leave us in more doubt as to the prince's feelings and knowledge. In Gus Van Sant's *My Own Private Idaho*, a parallel moment is not possible (there is no 'battlefield scene' as such), leaving those who know the play feeling denied the pleasure of seeing Bob Pigeon cheating death. In the 1979 BBC version, David Gwillim's Hal speaks over the apparently dead Falstaff with tears in his eyes, and the camera catches Anthony Quayle's somewhat surprised reaction.

Hal begins the play not at the court of his father, but in the tavern of his other father. Nunn handled the move from court to tavern by having the platform stage slide away and lights rising on another part of the stage. Falstaff was above, in bed, and comes down to join Hal. He caused laughter from the audience when he swigged some rotten sack, and then there was a hug between Hal and Falstaff, with Falstaff ending up cradling Hal like a mother cradles her baby. He was rewarded with huge laughs for his belch. Hal recited his soliloquy at the end of this scene while moving furniture, slowing down as he went along, clenching his right fist from time to time, facing the audience, and on 'skill' pointing to his own head. Van Sant changes Hal's lines, so that Keanu Reeves, instead of 'I know you all', says

> When I turn twenty-one I don't want any more of this life. My mother and father will be surprised at the incredible change. It will impress them more when such a fuck up like me turns good than if I had been a good son all along. All my bad behaviour I will throw away to pay a debt. I will change when everybody expects it the least.[19]

Bob Pigeon strains to hear in the background, as does Welles's Falstaff, both puzzled, the leafy framing of this moment in the Welles' film replaced by the rubbish strewn alleyway of Van Sant's. And we, as audience, though we wholly hear the speech, are also presented with a character to puzzle over. Michael Coveney felt that Sam West's Hal of 1996, who switched accents depending on whether he was at court or at the tavern created 'an edge and nastiness about Hal that suits the role' while Kate Bassett described West's Hal as 'a snobby public school boy' who was 'slumming it' (O'Connor and Goodland, p. 353).

Some have detected an increasing sense of lofty, almost inhuman, detachment in Prince Harry before the battle of Shrewsbury. In Nunn's 1982 production, in the interview between father and son (III.ii), Hal's language of accountancy was reinforced by David Rintoul's cold performance, but following this, Hal seemed positively affectionate to

Falstaff and the audience's ambivalence towards Hal being further
fuelled. Other performances have found different trajectories. In 1974
Timothy Dalton as Hal was, according to B. A. Young in *The Financial
Times*, 'a skinny, shifty, grubby young man in Eastcheap' who 'smartly
blossoms into nascent royalty on the field at Shrewsbury'. Jonathan
Hammond claimed that Dalton embraced 'effectively the prince's
shrewd calculating nature underlying his carousings with Falstaff and
company' (O'Connor and Goodland, p. 338). Michael Pennington's Hal
for Michael Bogdanov's English Shakespeare Company production in
1987 was described by Andrew Rissik in *The Independent* as particularly wanting. According to Rissik he was 'desperate and graceless' at
Shrewsbury and with the king 'he whines and emotes, a frustrated adolescent' (O'Connor and Goodland, p. 346). But there is plenty more to
say about Hal. The 'play extempore' scene with Falstaff will be discussed
later as a key moment both in establishing the tone of the performance
and the character, and in making him more complex.

King Henry

The traditional portrayal of Henry IV has been in terms of anguished
guilt, highlighting the character's reduced stature compared with the
powerful Bolingbroke of the preceding play, *Richard II*. John Gielgud's
performance as the king in the Welles' *Chimes at Midnight* might be
called the classic example. Here, Henry IV seems at once ennobled and
soured by his burden of conscience. The voice is majestic, but the face
betrays the dyspeptic sufferings of a man for whom life has turned bit-
ter.[20] Welles's casting of Gielgud consciously presents his audience with
an artificial and stylized man of courtly virtuous-seeming operatic rhetoric, against which to set Rodway's passionate Hotspur, against which to
set Baxter's friendly, laughing Hal, against which to play his own oh-so-
human Falstaff. One alternative is indicated by Emrys James's performance as Henry in 1975, praised by Michael Billington for rediscovering
'a character too long overlooked: the king himself' and transforming
him from a 'cold, thin-lipped figure' into 'a passionate paternalist desperate for his son's redemption'. Such a performance served to 'make the
play less a study of the aftermath of usurpation and more an account of
a growing father-son relationship' (O'Connor and Goodland, p. 339).

Another alternative is that offered by Jon Finch in the 1979 BBC
version. This performance has been widely criticized, but Finch is
entirely in keeping with the text in bringing to the fore the question of
the king's anguish and sickness. His Henry is a kind of ghost, haunting
the play, completely upstaged by his son's surrogate father Falstaff.
Nancy Banks-Smith commented on Finch's 'most powerful portrait of

the smoky and incinerated king' (O'Connor and Goodland, p. 342). Even King Henry's most peculiar recent incarnation, as Scott Favor's father, the Mayor of Portland in *My Own Private Idaho*, is less than kingly, claiming that he is being punished for offending God in some way. Perhaps in reaction to this consensus, in 1996 in the English Touring Theatre production directed by Stephen Unwin, Gary Waldhorn played 'a magnificent King Henry' according to John Peter in the *Sunday Times*. Waldhorn's Henry was 'a masterful operator with hooded eyes and an iron will, both remorseful and ruthless' (O'Connor and Goodland, p. 353).

Significant Minor Characters

Some significant minor characters who can make a profound impression in performance should perhaps be mentioned. Glendower is an important foil to Hotspur in the play, and indeed, a foil to Falstaff and to Hal also. Though the text seems to present a figure to be mocked by the truth-speaking Harry Hotspur, there have been performances of the role that have achieved some majesty. In the 1951 Stratford production the Welshman, Hugh Griffith, gave a rendering of 'such a glowering, forceful Glendower that one was prepared to believe him about raising spirits from the vasty deep' (McMillin, p. 49). Though the part of Worcester is a small one, the compelling performance of Fernando Rey in *Chimes at Midnight* is a good example of how, with a certain subtle understatement in the delivery of certain lines and a particularly skilful timing of a wry smile, the character can be made to emblematize manipulative scheming. In Nunn's 1982 version the figure of Worcester was employed in another way, 'made visible during the tavern revels, as a reminder of a reckoning not yet made' (Bevington, p. 84). One of the celebrated features of the play in production is Bardolph's nose. Just how monstrous, carbuncular, big and red can Bardolph's nose be made? Judging from photographs of the 1951 Bardolph, played by Michael Bates, extremely. Mistress Quickly, played by Margaret Rutherford in Welles's film, provides a memorable and lasting mixture of exasperation and affection towards her impossible customer. And Marina Vlady in *Chimes at Midnight* makes a charming Lady Percy, and the evident love between her and Norman Rodway's Hotspur brings a rare breath of domestic bliss into the heart of Welles's film.

The 'Play Extempore' Scene (2.iv)

One of the great scenes in the play, and indeed in all of Shakespeare, is the 'play extempore' scene in which Falstaff and Hal each play King Henry and the prince (II.iv). Though omitted from nineteenth-century performances, in the modern era it is firmly established as an expected high point. The 1951 Stratford Memorial Theatre production starring Richard Burton as Hal and Antony Quayle as Falstaff made the scene the centrepiece of the play. The set designer Tanya Moiseiwitch had conceived a stage with huge timbers and drapes above. There was a balcony at the rear of centre-stage, behind the main playing area, with steps on both sides, and a cheese-wedge shaped platform in mid-stage right, referred to in the prompt-book as 'the cheese' to enable players some extra prominence. Tables and chairs provided the movable furniture. The set allowed crowds to gather all round the players.

The play scene in 1951, interpreted from a black and white photograph, shows Falstaff sitting on a chair on the table, with Hal standing across the stage by the 'cheese' and others gathered around. There are many, many tankards in the scene, and a barrel in the foreground. This contrasts nicely with the stage images produced in the court scenes in which one photograph shows the king standing above at stage right and many scribes sit below him in file. Lady Percy and Hotspur, played by Barbara Jefford and Michael Redgrave, are a handsome young couple with the look of Hollywood film stars (again, in promotional photographs for the production).

Though there is no film record of this stage version of the play there is, as well as still photography, the marvellous prompt book from the production kept in the Shakespeare Archive in Stratford-upon-Avon. The notes accompanying this particular scene make evident the amount of on-stage levity that was conjured. The blocking of the scene placed 'Falstaff on top of table pushed by others' and 'Prince above cheese'. Mistress Quickly's interjections are greeted by 'Applause' and the prompt book has plentiful directions for 'laughter and Oh's!' punctuating Falstaff's playful speeches of self-justification and self-defence. The crowd 'cheers as Falstaff hands cushion and sceptre to Hal', and, having laughed and oh'd and cheered through the rest of the quoted lines there are 'loud cheers' after Falstaff's finale 'banish all the world'. Falstaff retires behind an arras in this production, a sketch illustration in the prompt book showing clearly how the prince sits at the table and Poins sits on the table before the arras, playing cards to distract the Sheriff and his men. After the Sheriff's 'I think it be two o'clock' the prompt book simply states 'Snore'.

McMillin argues that Burton's 'growing seriousness of tone' in the performance of this scene meant that 'the rejection was virtually occurring already' and that this performance set a new standard in the theatre

to use the final lines of the exchange – Hal's "I do, I will" in answer to Falstaff's "Banish plump Jack and banish all the world" – as a profound moment of realization, on everyone's part, that Falstaff will suffer rejection when the moment is ripe for Hal's royal personality to be declared. (McMillin, p. 7)

This aspect of the 1951 production seems to be agreed upon by scholars, that the directors Anthony Quayle and John Kidd 'envisaged the break between Hal and his companion as inevitable from the start' (Bevington, p. 81). Following this precedent, Gwillim's Hal in the BBC version becomes increasingly steely-eyed in this scene, and his 'I do, I will' leaves Quayle's Falstaff spluttering and shocked.

Nunn's 1982 production of the play took a very different tack, focusing on Falstaff's inner knowledge, for example, utilizing a long, long pause before Falstaff's 'I knew ye as well as he that made thee'. For the play extempore Falstaff was hoisted up on a table on which his chair was placed, and Hal stood on the table next to him. Mistress Quickly's laugh was strange and croaky, and elicited as much laughter from the audience as anything Falstaff said or did. As Falstaff delivered the line 'His name is . . . Falstaff' it was the whole on-stage audience who provided the 'Falstaff'. (In Welles's *Chimes at Midnight* it is his page, played by Welles's own daughter, who provides the name.) Following this speech there were cheers and applause from the on-stage audience, and cheers following 'my noble lord from Eastcheap' and 'who means your Grace?' The light-hearted delivery of 'I do, I will' from Prince Hal (while pointing at Falstaff with 'sceptre'), coincided with Hal taking the cushion|crown off his head, as if he spoke for himself – though with an untroubled and rising voice. The scene was not haunted with a sense of the later rejection present in so many performances, and when Hal gave Falstaff two hugs before he hid behind the arras the audience were unlikely to feel that this is a Hal who will banish plump Jack. The arras here was erected on the stage (as it was not part of the architecture of this stage, similar to the 1954 version). When the sheriff and his man came to find Falstaff, the delivery of the line 'as fat as butter' contained a pause of 6 or 7 seconds before 'butter', a pause usually rewarded by a great laugh from the audience. At the end of this scene Prince Hal dismissed Poins (not Peto) rather bad-temperedly with a 'good morrow' and, occupying a position at front of stage centre crossed himself as if beginning a penitent pilgrimage from tavern to throne.

In 2007, at the Courtyard Theatre in Stratford-upon-Avon, the scene was presented so forcefully as a repudiation of Falstaff (David Warner) by an unfriendly Hal (Geoffrey Streatfield) that one critic, Kate Wilkinson, called it 'nasty, a far stronger rejection than that at the end of *Part 2* and uncomfortable to watch'. For Wilkinson Streatfield's Hal 'was not an

engaging Machiavel but rather a bit of a two-dimensional damp squib'
and the production overall offered 'little insight into the play' and provided 'little humour to make up for that loss' (Wilkinson, p.183).

It is Orson Welles, in *Chimes at Midnight*, who seems to get the balance of ingredients from his troupe (himself, his daughter playing the
page, Keith Baxter as Hal, and the wonderful Margaret Rutherford as
Mistress Quickly, occupying a front row seat to enjoy the theatrics of
one of her favourite performers) just right. The play extempore is a joy
for the audience in the tavern and the audience in the cinema or on the
sofa, and Falstaff holds sway as the Lord of Misrule, whether he plays
the king or the prince. McMillin describes how the Boar's Head Tavern
which Welles created was

> a panoply of entrances, passageways, windows, bedrooms, and
> balconies through, around, and under which people dart, run
> twist, duck. No one just walks anywhere. Keith Baxter, who played
> Hal, said that the camera track at the tavern was laid on an S, 'and
> the actors as well as the camera were made to move in very intri-
> cate ways'.[21]

Through full use of the resources of the film-maker in the 1960s Welles,
in his rendering of Shakespeare's play extempore scene, achieves a profound comic climax that captures Falstaff in his tavern world.

Speaking Better Welsh (III.i)

One scene in particular allows, indeed requires, actors and directors to
supply not only their own interpretation, but their own text. In the
scene dramatizing the meeting of the rebel leaders, a meeting which
took place, according to Holinshed, at the Archdeacon's house in Bangor
(III.i), Shakespeare's text indicates that Welsh should be both spoken
and sung, but supplies no words itself. Wales and the Welsh language
are set centre stage. In his description of the division of the kingdom
Mortimer identifies one portion: 'All westward, Wales beyond the
Severn shore | And all the fertile land within that bound | To Owen
Glendower' (III.i.74–76). Glendower's account of his prodigious birth
challenges Hotspur with these words: 'Where is he living, clipped in
with the sea, | That chides the banks of England, Scotland, Wales, |
Which calls me pupil or hath read to me?' (III.i.43–45). Hotspur undermines Glendower's pomposity with the dismissive 'I think there's no
man speaks better Welsh' (III.i.49). Kastan comments that 'it isn't clear
whether the phrase means "utter more nonsense" or "brags more outrageously"'.[22] It is not clear who is the more preposterous here, Glendower

or Hotspur. In the ensuing argument, over whether Hotspur will change the course of the river Trent, Glendower replies to Hotspur's 'Who shall say me nay?' with 'Why, that will I', to which Hotspur responds 'Let me not understand you, then: speak it in Welsh' (III.i.114–16). In Quayle's 1951 version Hugh Griffiths provided a certain Welsh authenticity not only in his performance as Glendower, but through writing the added Welsh text. Griffiths' Welsh text, introduced for this production, was preserved and used again in the next Stratford performance of the play in 1964 (when Griffiths played Falstaff himself). The scene seems to have been a great success in 1951, as is attested to by this witness:

> With admirable restraint the producer allowed this scene to take its own time and – as never before in my experience – it was given in full, with long and passionate speeches in Welsh for Glendower's daughter. For one listener, at least, there was no sense of flagging, but it might have been otherwise without Hugh Griffith's Glendower; no ranting pomposo, this, for all his occasional flamboyances, but the dangerous, enigmatical and compelling personality that alone can cast the spell the scene demands.[23]

The 1951 production also gave Glendower's daughter, Lady Mortimer, played by Sybil Williams, a significant Welsh-speaking part. The stage direction '*Glendower speaks to her in Welsh, and she answers him in the same*' (III.i.193) became, in performance, an exchange between father and daughter that ended with the following lines:

> *Glendower*   Na, na. Nid lle i wragedd yw rhyfeloedd, fy
> ngeneth
> Rhaid i ti aros a chanlyn gyda mi.
> *Lady M.*   (furious) Nis gallaf aros hebbdo. Mae'n rhaid i mi
> gael mynd;
> a chaiff neb fy arbed chwaith.

The translation offered in the same 1951 prompt book is:

> *Glendower*   Impossible; you must remain here.
> *Lady Mortimer* That I will not do. I go with him. Nothing
> shall stop me.

The translation for the Welsh is inadequate (which could give rise to a critical discussion in itself). Mortimer, her own husband, cannot properly understand her passionate words, though he does claim a capacity to interpret her emotion and her language: 'I understand thy looks. That pretty Welsh, | Which thou pourest down from these swelling heavens, | I am too perfect in, and but for shame | In such a parley should I answer thee' (III.i.196–99). Following her next speech, which in this 1951 performance ends with the Welsh 'Iaith cariad yw, cariad sy'n llosgi'm bron' (in the prompt book this is translated as 'I must always be with thee, to comfort and arm thee for battle', but a more accurate and very different translation reads: 'it is like the language of love, love is burning within my breast'), Lady Mortimer kisses Mortimer and he replies:

> I understand thy kisses, and thou mine,
> And that's a feeling disputation;
> But I will never be a truant, love,
> Till I have learnt thy language, for thy tongue
> Makes Welsh as sweet as ditties highly penned,
> Sung by a fair queen in a summer's bower
> With ravishing division to her lute. (III.i.200–06)

Shakespeare's text suggests Hotspur seems somewhat charmed by the Prospero-like powers of Glendower to summon up music from musicians who 'hang in the air a thousand leagues hence' when he grudgingly comments 'Now I perceive the devil understands Welsh'. Yet his giddy humour makes him a presence that jars with the atmosphere of enchantment, and even Lady Percy's plea that he should 'Lie still, ye thief, and hear the lady sing in Welsh' elicits the coarse response from Hotspur 'I had rather hear Lady, my brach, howl in Irish' (III.i.231–32).

Nunn's 1982 staging of the scene between the rebels featured Hotspur with a map so small that one might easily forget it. Glendower was a genial host, giving out wine. Following the benchmark established in earlier performances Nunn engaged with the need for spoken Welsh, making full use of its comic potential for an audience who, largely, would not understand it, thus putting the audience in the position of the monoglot Mortimer, who kisses his lady to stop her talking. Glendower was presented as a druidic conjuror, and Hotspur showed no respect for him or his daughter in his mocking the solemnity of the moment. The Welsh song was handled sympathetically; as a harp was played Lady Mortimer sang for almost 3 minutes in Welsh, with Mortimer lying in her lap. Hotspur and Kate were sitting to one side. The audience was granted a peaceful interlude, away from the boisterous tavern and the formal court, though Hotspur's unimpressed presence provided a discordant counterpoint to the sweet sense of harmony. The music of Lady Mortimer's song is echoed as the scene ends, and one feels a keynote of the production has been struck – the mournful

division of the kingdom. The tragic aspects of the play are brought to
the fore.

The 2007 Stratford production prompt book contains the Welsh
poetry of Mererid Hopwood, Sianed Jones and Mary Lloyd Jones (set to
the music of Sianed Jones) for the song of the Welsh lady. The seriousness with which the production presented the Welsh scene, the respect
accorded the Welsh language and song, is noteworthy. Let us hope that
future productions rise to the challenge of this most potent and enchant-
ing scene.

The Battle of Shrewsbury, the Death of Honour and the Death of Falstaff

1Henry IV does not end with Falstaff's death, but on the battlefield at
Shrewsbury. The whole of the fifth act takes place on or near to the
Shrewsbury battlefield, and directors and actors have addressed its performance challenges in different ways. The 1964 RSC production, part
of a cycle of the histories, was influenced by Jan Kott's critical work
Shakespeare Our Contemporary, which director Peter Hall read in type-
script, which arguably 'governed the productions' view of politics as a
cycle of totalitarian violence and corruption'. Prince Hal, played by Ian
Holm, was, 'another Machiavellian climber, who retained a degree of
detachment while learning to manipulate those around him'. Hal's
'moments of triumph were tempered by an insistence on the brutality of
the political arena he inhabited' as, for example, when he achieved his
victory at Shrewsbury 'by knifing Hotspur in the gut and tipping him
into a pig trough' (Loehlin, p. 162). Few productions of the play have
moved as far away from heroism as this one. For McMillin, 'anti-
heroism can do no more with the Battle of Shrewsbury than dump
Hotspur into a pig trough'. Holm and Dotrice engaged in a 'tremen-
dously menacing and disturbing fight, a demonstration of the battlefield brutality that ran through the entire cycle', and those who witnessed
the fight 'took no pleasure in knowing that a hero-King of England was
emerging out of such violence' (McMillin, p. 65). The direction of Peter
Hall, John Barton and Clifford Williams

> showed the influence of Bertolt Brecht in the squalid tavern
> scenes and frightening renditions of battle, emphasizing through-
> out the contrast between a gargantuan capacity for life (embodied
> most of all in Hugh Griffith's ebullient Falstaff) and the emotion-
> ally sterile world of political struggle. Hal (Ian Holm) was cold-
> blooded, self-contained. (Bevington, pp. 82–83)

Just 1 year after the grim 1964 stage production came the release of *Chimes at Midnight*, surely the most Falstaffian of all Shakespearean productions. As McMillin notes, 'if Falstaff had made films, he would have made something like this one'. McMillin cites

> the subterfuges and improvisations Welles had to employ in order to do the film at all: not just getting the money to build his own Boar's Head Tavern in Spain by telling his producer it would be the Admiral Benbow Inn in the *Treasure Island* he was promising to make, but also dressing Prince Hal in a leather tunic first worn by Jayne Mansfield in *The Sheriff of Fractured Jaw*, also shot in Spain, or dealing with the departure of Gielgud after the first four weeks of shooting by using a double for Henry IV's striking entrance in the battle scene, where only the bottom of his robe is visible. (McMillin, p. 95)

Before the Battle of Shrewsbury we catch a glimpse of Sir John's preparations. As the men ride by, flames lick the cauldron in the front and just for a few seconds we glimpse Falstaff turning his head in the dust of war to look to his right as the soldiers ride by and he carries in his left arm a huge ladle, a great big cauldron cooking pot in the foreground under which is going a healthy fire. And there he is, our friend Falstaff, preparing for battle. Even as the bloodbath approaches, and later in the very heat and chaos of the battle itself, Falstaff – who Hal calls 'chewet' (chatterer) – is able to prattle and natter. Falstaff remains Falstaff. And Falstaff remains alive. Is it his high point or his low point when he jests with Hal by lending him a bottle of sack rather than his pistol and makes the awful joke 'There's that will sack a city'? The joke is wearing thin on Hal who asks 'what, is it a time to jest and dally now?' as he throws the bottle at him. The answer is, for Hal, no, but for Falstaff the answer is always yes. And it is Falstaff's presence on the Shrewsbury battlefield which undermines any sense of heroic deeds through jests and dalliances.

Perhaps the greatest achievement of Welles's magnificent film is the long nearly 10 minute sequence representing the battle of Shrewsbury, a clattering startling succession of shots of figures in combat. There is no speech, from Falstaff or anyone else. There is no Shakespeare. This is unlike any battle of Shrewsbury before or since. Welles begins by showing us the absurd preparations of fully-armoured knights being hoisted up and lowered on to their warhorses in a 'parody of the steed-mounting in Olivier's *Henry V*' (McMillin, p. 97). Most absurd of all is Falstaff, whose rope breaks as he is being hoisted onto his horse, and who must survive the day on foot. McMillin provides some extensive examples of sequences of shots in the film, but a brief example of four consecutive shots will, I hope, give a sufficient flavour here:

> 759 . . . a rider in armor moves to the right. He suddenly throws up his arms and plunges off his horse toward the camera, which follows the beginning of his fall.
> 760 . . . footsoldiers, silhouetted in combat. The foreground is dominated by a horse, lying on its side, twisting and writhing with an arrow in its side.
> 761 . . . A series of horses, moving very close to the camera, initially block out any image. After the pass, two men in Long Shot are seen struggling, with a body lying on the ground next to them.
> 762 . . . a horseman with lance moves to the right and away from the camera. He unseats another horseman riding toward him, striking him with the lance. As he then moves further into the background at the right, a foot soldier crosses the foreground to the left, only his head visible.[24]

We are a long way from Shakespeare's theatre, where the chorus in *Henry V* has to implore us to 'make imaginary puissance' so that we might 'into a thousand parts divide one man' or 'think, when we talk of horses, that you see them | Printing their proud hoofs i'th'receiving earth'.[25] Welles shows us the thousand men and the horses, and the muddy earth in which they writhe, stuck with arrows. No other battle of Shrewsbury sequence, filmed or staged, has ever come close to Welles's brilliance here. 'What we see is Falstaffian' argues McMillin 'for this amazing camera work does externalize Falstaff's cynicism about honour'.[26] It is a cynicism which extends to the dramatic critic, as, for example, in Richard Last's description of the great heroic Harry-to-Harry final combat of the BBC version of 1979. Last dismissed the rendition as 'a Western-style roll in the dust which sounded like a crate of sardine-tins being shaken up'.[27]

As a counterpoint to the impressive rhetoric and heroic appearances of King Henry, Prince Hal and Harry Hotspur in the build up to the battle, Welles brings forward the figure of Falstaff in his huge suit of armour, uttering a thought that, given the horrendous carnage about to be unleashed upon the screen, provides a sense of everyday comforts: 'I would 'twere bedtime Hal, and all well' (V.i.125). Whereas stage Falstaffs generally are able to dominate the battlefield with their interjections, in Welles's film Falstaff is reduced to an absurd figure moving about to avoid combat while thousands of men and horses are slaughtered to an incredibly mixed soundtrack of clashing metal, yells, cries, groans, neighs, ominous music, the blast of trumpets and an angelic choir. To survive in the midst of such mayhem is an achievement in itself.

Of Shrewsbury, Ian Mortimer writes that 'all the chroniclers agree that it is one of the bloodiest battles ever fought on English soil'. Mortimer quotes from Jean de Waurin's account of the battle as follows:

> after the arrows were exhausted, they put their hands to swords and axes with which they began to slay each other. And the men and horses were slain in such wise that it was pitiable to see. None spared his fellow, mercy had no place.[28]

Falstaff understands the carnage to come only too well when he defends his choice of recruits to Hal earlier with 'They'll fill a pit as well as better. Tush, man, mortal men, mortal men' (IV.ii.65–66). This was the lesson that the gentry learned at Shrewsbury, that 'loyal service' 'necessitated facing the risk of an indiscriminate and ignoble death, whichever side they were on'.[29] Though Falstaff survives and the forces of the king are victorious, the mood is sombre and uncomfortable as Falstaff brings the dead body of Hotspur before Hal and Henry. Falstaff's dishonourable actions in Quayle's BBC TV version involve us all as he frequently looks directly through the camera to us, the intimacy of the relationship difficult to deny. Gwillim's Hal placed the blue sash of his colours over Hotspur's face in a tender and honourable moment – immediately undone by Quayle's prodding of the body and his decision to 'swear I killed 'im'. Here he pauses, looks directly at us with a look of surprise on his face, as though we, the audience, or even I, the individual viewer, might object to his dishonour. He persuades us that his action is sensible, the sort of thing we might ourselves do if we were in his particular situation. The truth, if we turn to the historians, is that 'no one knows who wielded the blow which stopped Hotspur',[30] and that it is 'thanks largely to an unknown archer' that King Henry IV 'won his only full-scale battle'.[31] For Shakespeare to have Prince Hal kill Hotspur on the Shrewsbury battlefield seems no less a corruption of historical truth than for Falstaff to claim that he killed Hotspur. When Antony Quayle explains his combat with Hotspur to Hal and others, 'we fought a long hour by Shrewsbury clock', they all look to the left of the frame as if to see the clock. It is a moment worthy of Monty Python.

Earlier in the play, in an attempt to defend his tall tale of the Gad's Hill robbery, Falstaff asks Hal 'is not the truth the truth?' (II.iv.222). In their argument Hal claims to present the 'plain tale' of truth, but the truth of Hal's story is itself many-layered. Falstaff's truth is ever-shifting and 'in performance, we have to add "staged truth", which is inevitably interpretive, and another truth as received or interpreted by a particular

audience'. In Act II, Scene iv Shakespeare has shown how the history of
a recent event, the Gad's Hill robbery, 'is as coloured, twisted, added
upon, and generally misread as events that happened ages ago'.[32] Like
the combatants on Welles's Shrewsbury battlefield, history is mired in
the mud and it is impossible to see the truth clearly. Larsen suggests that
'perhaps Shakespeare was New Historicist before the moniker had been
coined, acknowledging at least the possibility of multiple histories as he
created a dramatic history his characters – historical and fictional –
could populate with at least the appearance of historical veracity'.[33] Falstaff's presence at the battle provides a counter-narrative to the chronicle
accounts. Among the shouts, of 'St George' from the Royalists and
'Esperance' for the rebels, we hear the plainly-stated battle-cry of
Shakespeare's Falstaff, 'give me life'. Barry Stanton's Falstaff in the English
Shakespeare Company film version of the stage production steals the
entire show by rising from his counterfeited death and pulling a No
Entry traffic sign breast-plate, battered from the combat he has survived, out from under his shirt. The audience laugh, the audience
applaud, for the life and soul of this world is still with us, the irrepress-
ible Falstaff lives to run away another day.

At the end of Welles's film a narrator reads from Holinshed's *Chronicles*. Peter Conrad comments:

> 'For conclusion' this unseen historian commends Henry V's ref-
> ormation, and guarantees that he will remain 'famous to the world
> alway'. Ralph Richardson, whose voice constructs this version of
> the past and anticipates the verdict of the future, was renowned
> for his Falstaff – he played the part at the Old Vic in 1945, with
> Olivier as both Hotspur and Shallow – though he is here enlisted
> to pass judgement on the antique reprobate. Welles knew this flat-
> tering preview of the new regime to be untrue, and advised Bax-
> ter against playing Henry V who was, he said, a shit. But history
> is written by the winners, whether or not they owe their victory to
> money or industrial might or slick public relations.[34]

Richardson's Holinshed speaks over the image of the huge trundling
up-slope struggle of Falstaff's coffin-wagon. For though Falstaff does
not die in either part of *Henry IV*, his reported death from *Henry V* is
used by Welles to complete the story with Falstaff's huge presence centre
screen. Mistress Quickly, here played, and surely never better played, by
the marvellous Margaret Rutherford, provides a fitting epitaph:

> Nay, sure, he's not in hell; he's in Arthur's bosom, if ever man went
> to Arthur's bosom. 'A made a finer end, and went away an it had

been any christom child. 'A parted even just between twelve and one, even at the turning o'th'tide. For after I saw him fumble with the sheets and play wi'th' flowers, and smile upon his fingers' ends, I knew there was but one way; for his nose was as sharp as a pen, and 'a babbled of green fields. 'How now, Sir John?' quoth I, 'what, man! Be o' good cheer.' So 'a cried out 'God, God, God!' three or four times. Now I, to comfort him, bid him 'a should not think of God; I hoped there was no need to trouble himself with any such thoughts yet. So 'a bade me lay more clothes on his feet. I put my hand into the bed and felt them, and they were as cold as any stone. Then I felt to his knees, and so up'ard, and all was as cold as any stone. (*Henry V*, II.iii.9–25)

And yet Falstaff, that great counterfeiter of death, was to live again in *The Merry Wives of Windsor*. Apparently Elizabeth shared a desire with many of her subjects who wished to see Falstaff's performance go on, and at the queen's command the bouncing knight was resurrected and given a new lease of lusty life. And on Falstaff's performance goes.

Notes

1. John Dover Wilson and T. C. Worsley, *Shakespeare's Histories at Stratford 1951* (London: Max Reinhardt Stellar Press, 1952), foreword, no page number.
2. *The Diary of Samuel Pepys Volume VII*, ed. Henry B. Wheatley (London: G Bell, 1926), pp. 183–84.
3. *King Henry IV Part 1*, ed. David Scott Kastan (London: Arden Shakespeare, Thomson Learning, 2002), pp. 80–81.
4. Kastan, *King Henry IV*, p. 83.
5. Kastan, *King Henry IV*, p. 85.
6. Ronald Knowles, *The Critics Debate: Henry IV Parts I and II* (Basingstoke: Macmillan, 1992), p. 23.
7. Kastan, *King Henry IV*, p. 85.
8. Scott McMillin, *Shakespeare in Performance: Henry IV Part One* (Manchester: Manchester University Press, 1991), p. 8.
9. *Complete Works of William Shakespeare*, ed. Jonathan Bate and Eric Rasmussen (Basingstoke: Macmillan, 2007), p. 899.
10. *Sir John Falstaff*, ed. Harold Bloom (Broomall, PA: Chelsea House, 2004), p. 2.
11. Kate Wilkinson, 'Review of Shakespeare's *Richard II, Henry IV Part 1, Henry IV Part 2*, and *Henry V* (directed by Michael Boyd and Richard Twyman for the Royal Shakespeare Company) at the Courtyard Theatre, Stratford-upon-Avon 2007' in *Shakespeare*, 4, Nos. 1–4, March – December 2008, 181–87 (p. 183).
12. *Henry IV, Part One*, ed. David Bevington (Oxford: Oxford University Press, 1987–1994), p. 67.
13. Gamini Salgado, *Eyewitnesses of Shakespeare* (London: Sussex University Press, 1975), pp. 180–81.
14. J. C. Trewin, *Shakespeare on the English Stage 1900–1964* (London: Barrie and Rockliff, 1964), p. 194.

15. *A Directory of Shakespeare in Performance, 1970–2005*, ed. John O'Connor and Katherine Goodland (Basingstoke: Macmillan, 2006), p. 341.
16. Norman Council, *When Honour's at the Stake: Ideas of honour in Shakespeare's Plays* (London: George Allen and Unwin Ltd, 1973), p. 49.
17. James N. Loehlin, *The Shakespeare Handbooks. Henry IV: Parts I and II* (Basingstoke: Palgrave Macmillan, 2008), p. 153.
18. John Dover Wilson, *The Fortunes of Falstaff* (Cambridge: Cambridge University Press, 1964), p. 66.
19. *My Own Private Idaho*, dir. Gus Van Sant (New Line Cinema, 1991), 32:16- 32:37.
20. T. F. Wharton, *Text and Performance: Henry the Fourth Parts 1 and 2* (London: Macmillan, 1983), p. 45.
21. McMillin, *Shakespeare in Performance*, p. 96.
22. Kastan, *King Henry IV*, p. 242.
23. Richard David, 'Shakespeare's History Plays: Epic or Drama?', *Shakespeare Survey*, 6 (1953), 129–39 (135).
24. McMillin, *Shakespeare in Performance*, p. 98.
25. *Henry V* (Prologue, lines 24 and 26–27) in *King Henry V*, T. ed. W. Craik (London: Arden Shakespeare, Routledge, 1995).
26. McMillin, *Shakespeare in Performance*, p. 98.
27. O'Connor and Goodland, *Directory of Shakespeare*, p. 342.
28. Ian Mortimer, *The Fears of Henry IV: The Life of England's Self-Made King* (London: Vintage, 2008), pp. 373, 270.
29. Mortimer, *Fears*, p. 376.
30. Mortimer, *Fears*, p. 272.
31. J. L. Kirby, *Henry IV of England* (London: Constable, 1970), p. 158.
32. Darl Larsen, *Monty Python, Shakespeare and English Renaissance Drama* (London: McFarland, 2003), p. 82.
33. Larsen, *Monty Python*, p. 75.
34. Peter Conrad, *Orson Welles: The Stories of His Life* (London: Faber and Faber, 2003), p. 343.

CHAPTER THREE

Current Critical Research:
The State of the Art

Jonathan Hart

1 Henry IV is a splendid play that achieves so much in history and comedy and encompasses a great deal more.[1] This comic history has many important attributes. There are different worlds in the play – Wales, court, rebel camp and tavern – that find their representation in the main plot and alternative or sub-plot. Prince Hal has a rival in Hotspur, whom Henry IV finds more promising than his own son, and a surrogate father-figure, Falstaff, a kind of Lord of Misrule, who is a counterbalance to the king. *1 Henry IV* is full of theatricality, sometimes conscious and other times not. Hotspur seems to be histrionic without knowing it, but Falstaff and Hal alternate roles in the tavern and play at king and prince and much else. The play celebrates and explores language in many forms – the battle of wits between Hotspur and Kate, Glendower and Hotspur, Hal and Falstaff; the lamentations of Henry IV, the politic or even Machiavellian schemes and plans of Hal; the bawdy exchange of the tavern, and much else. Language, structure and character create a play of rule and misrule, politics and 'impolitics', debauchery and war, corruption and reform. The audience is drawn into the relation between Hal and Falstaff and torn by it as well. Just as the tragic figure of Hamlet threatens to burst the seams of his eponymous play and of tragedy more generally, the comic character of Falstaff pushes at the boundaries of *1 Henry IV* and of the history play in general.

The constructions of masculinity and femininity in the various worlds of *1 Henry IV* are part of the comic, political and historical representation. Gender and genre live in creative tension. Legal and economic questions arise and the relationship between Wales and England raises issues about English and British identities and alternative histories to the official or traditional history of England. Shakespeare re-imagines the work of the chronicles by Hall, Holinshed and others and makes this history vital through the power of language, character and story. The power of drama and the drama of power is part of Shakespeare's on-going legacy.

The approach I am taking is one of a multilingual and multicultural overview, a survey of the state of criticism and not a privileging of a few well-known critics. This method may make some uncomfortable because they desire me to make more value judgements, to use my authorial voice more or to concentrate on a few works in greater detail, but I have resisted this temptation because there is too much emphasis on criticism in English and often only that of a few critics I have chosen the chronological approach within each topic because a historical way to discuss a history play seems appropriate. I am not interested in reinscribing centres and peripheries. My linguistic shortcomings limited my view, and thus, reluctantly I had to concentrate on some Western European languages, whereas in a more perfect world with a less imperfect author, the reader would have been exposed to important works in Asian, eastern European and other languages. From this overview, I hope the reader will be able to go to the critical works that interest him or her. The task at hand was vast, so while I tried to make myself aware of everything that had been written on *1 Henry IV* in this period, I could not include it all, and had to focus on what seemed to be the most debated areas of that criticism. Many of the characters of *1 Henry IV* reappear in Shakespeare's sequels, *2 Henry IV* and *Henry V*, and Falstaff and other comic characters also turn up in *The Merry Wives of Windsor*. Unless noted otherwise, references to characters are to their presence in *1 Henry IV* rather than in these later plays.

Genre, Theatricality and History

Despite deconstruction's questioning of genre, it is a subject that does not seem to go away in the criticism of this play, and in *1 Henry IV* genre calls attention to history and to the performing of the past in the theatre. The question of genre persists, and E. M. W. Tillyard's notion of the epic nature of Shakespeare's history finds different expression in Ann Lecercle's argument that in *1 Henry IV*, Shakespeare presents a kind of Homeric epic with a Christian ethics.[2] The work in genre, theatricality and history is wide-ranging and there is no one method that seems to have taken hold. Some concentrate on texts and others on contexts; some tend towards form and others towards content. For instance, Kiernan Ryan discusses the role of Marxism in the relation of past, present and future, how history and the utopian future relate through the present.[3]

Moreover, Judith Mossman finds the influence of Plutarch in both parts of *Henry IV*, something that is usually reserved for the Roman plays.[4] Tom McAlindon examines the affinities between historical works in sixteenth-century England and in the nation at the time of Henry IV and, in another work, discusses the contemporary intellectual and historical context and the critical reception of both parts of *Henry IV*.[5]

For Lisa Hopkins, New Historicism can veer towards the ahistorical in discussions of the Elizabethan history play, including *1 Henry IV*.[6] Paul Dean sees the *Henry IV* plays and *Henry V* as representing ideology across the spectrum while showing partisan views.[7] Others continue to examine the history play in more formal terms. For Giuseppe Martella, the mixing of tragic and comic elements is an interesting aspect of the frame of history in the *Henry IV* plays.[8] Content and themes are also persistent focus of criticism. Time and power in the first three plays of the second tetralogy, including *1 Henry IV*, are central concerns of Jutta Schamp's work.[9] Critics can remind others that Shakespeare is making the past dramatic, that he is staging history. Content also affects form. For Heather Dubrow, domestic loss, such as burglary in *1* and *2 Henry IV*, is a key theme in Shakespeare across the genres.[10] Representations of brotherhood are the main reason, according to Lisa Hopkins, that the *Henriad* cannot be considered a full epic like Homer's *Iliad*.[11] Jonathan Shaw sees history plays like *1* and *2 Henry IV* as emphasizing the importance of time and in particular the relation between the temporal and the eternal.[12]

Shakespeare's histories draw on his past and present and we use him in our time and culture. Richard Simon explores parallels between Oliver Stone's *Platoon* and *1 Henry IV*.[13] Through common sources in the visual arts, Cathleen McLoughlin sees a connection between the *Henry IV* plays and Rabelais's *Gargantua and Pantagruel*.[14] Michele Stanco sees *1 Henry IV* as a mixture of history and comedy that involves education.[15] For Philippe Chardin, *1 Henry IV* effectively combines comedy and theatricality.[16] In a collection that discusses the staging of *1 Henry IV* in a comparative context ranging from ancient Greek theatre to that of modern France, the editor, François Lecercle, contributes an essay that examines Henry IV's description of his desired crusade that he has to abandon before he has begun.[17]

Critical concerns with the making of the nation through the history play and the nature of historical representation recur in various contexts. There is a theatricality to Shakespeare's history and politics. According to Derek Cohen, the *Henry IV* plays represent the ambivalence of uncertainty and authority in the history of the nation.[18] For Ronald Knowles, argument of speech and action of the characters is an important part of Shakespeare working out his representation of history in both *Henry IV* plays.[19] Pascale Drouet likens Hal in the tavern scene in Act II to the Master of the Revels, both protecting the actors even as they are supposed to censor them.[20] For Nathalie Rivère de Carles, the arras, in the *Henry IV* plays, serves a theatrical purpose in the visual prop and the verbal description.[21] In Michael Flachmann's view, Shakespeare uses language to produce a representation of history that relies on parody.[22] Self-conscious theatricality, a play-within-a-play or metatheatre in works like *1 Henry IV*, in Jesús Maestro's view, calls attention to the nature of representation, a dramatic technique that Shakespeare shares with Cervantes.[23]

Thematic, historical and artistic unity and disunity continue to interest critics. Shakespeare represents many elements in *1 Henry IV*, so critics look for keys in the smallest details inside and outside the play to 'unlock' the secrets of its form and content, seeing the world in a grain of sand. For Alessandro Vescovi, the idea of the voyage unifies the *Henry IV* plays and *Henry V*.[24] Charles Edelman argues that in *1* and *2 Henry IV* Shakespeare's use of past or present gestures towards Brecht's epic theatre.[25] For Alan Stewart, the robbing of the carriers in Act II, Scene ii of *1 Henry IV* shows the exposure to corruption, embodied by Falstaff and Hal.[26] According to Anthony Davies, a strong representation of the king and of the Percies counterbalances Hal and Falstaff.[27] The rejection of Falstaff by Hal – as opposed to the relation between the prince and king, which is the focus of the *Henriad* according to Robert Shaughnessy – can be seen in theatrical terms but also in a post-war theatricality that draws on psychological realism.[28]

Hal as a Character, and as a Machiavel or Christian Prince

Although the study of character is supposed to be moribund, something A. C. Bradley did to counter Aristotle at the turn of the twentieth century, it is still very much alive, with Hal and Falstaff receiving the most attention. Character is relational, and Hal lives in contrast with Falstaff, Henry IV, Hotspur and others in the various worlds of the play. Prince Hal is controversial figure in criticism, on stage and film.[29] Is he a Machiavel or a Christian prince, or perhaps a mixture of both? For Michèle Vignaux, morality and individual responsibility is a chief concern of *1 Henry IV* and the other plays of the second tetralogy.[30] Richard Hardin sees Hal as learning that a king is not above the law and implies that while the authority of kingship comes from God, it is being desacralized in Shakespeare's second tetralogy.[31]

Hal's relation to others is part of his definition as a character and this continues to feed the debate on his religious and political attributes.

Robert Reid frames Hal and Falstaff in terms of the four humours, Hal being sanguine and Falstaff being phlegmatic.[32] In discussing Hal, Tim Spiekerman says that in his youth he learns from his relation to Falstaff that the prince must go even further than Henry IV in Machiavellism; Spiekerman later generalizes his discussion of Machiavelli and Shakespeare and the politics of pessimism and the limitations of the political.[33] For Dennis Quinn, Hal represents proper wit whereas Falstaff is excessive and Hotspur deficient in wit.[34] Jane Kingsley-Smith balances Hal's pastoral of exile against the banishment of Falstaff.[35] Hal, according to Michael Davies, rejects Falstaff as part of a Reformation drama, a Calvinist conversion that makes the prince a hero in the context of Elizabethan Protestantism.[36] Examining Act V, Scene iii of *1 Henry IV*, Derek Peat sees in Hal's throwing of a bottle of sack at Falstaff a gesture of rejection and maintains that how this is performed affects the audience's view of Falstaff.[37] According to Harry Berger, Jr., Falstaff collaborates with Hal in the story of the prodigal son leading up to his rejection of Falstaff.[38] Hal is *like* a son to Falstaff but *is* a son to Henry IV.

The relation between father and son in Shakespeare, including in the *Henry IV* plays, is, in Lawrence Danson's view, in part connected to the anxiety and aggression of the son.[39] Leah Scragg discusses Hal and *1 Henry IV* in terms of the tale of the prodigal son.[40] Beatrice Groves sees Hal in Christian terms, as he moves from Lent to reconciliation with his father.[41] Moreover, Marvin Krims examines the relation of Hal to his father and to Falstaff, and sees an increasing identification with Henry IV allowing for an identity that accepts violence and war.[42] In another article he argues that Hal's wild and aggressive side in the *Henry IV* plays is acted out in *Henry V*, so that Oedipal aggression becomes military violence.[43] Wayne Rebhorn contrasts Hal's rhetoric with Henry IV's, the one being given to manipulation and the other to eloquence.[44] In these plays, according to David George, Shakespeare represents Hal as searching for a father as he comes of age.[45] Élisabeth Rallo discusses the relation between Henry IV and Hal and how the king shifts from fear of, to admiration for, his son.[46]

Laura Di Michele explores the eventual suppression of the popular voice with Hal's rejection of Falstaff.[47] David Ruiter discusses Hal as a means of controlling Falstaff's festivity.[48] For Ellen Summers, Hal's speech in Act II, Scene i suggests that the audience exercises judgement, which is a counterbalance to those who thought playgoing to be immoral.[49]

Other connections inside and outside the play round out the critical reception of Hal in recent years. For Jean-Louis Claret, Hal's plans in Act I, Scene ii of *1 Henry IV* to dissimulate connects him with Richard III, Iago and Edmund.[50] Avery Plaw sees Prince Hal, who later becomes

Henry V, as a figure who embodies Machiavelli's politics, which the *Henry IV* plays and *Henry V* criticize.[51] Daniel Colvin discusses Hal's use of clothing and disguise in terms of identity and role-playing.[52] Hal's containment of petty criminals in *1 Henry IV* represents, for Nick Cox, an allaying of the fear of criminals and vagrants in Elizabethan England.[53] Charles Forker examines the political aspects of reconciliation in the context of the relation between Hal and Falstaff in *1* and *2 Henry IV*.[54] Aysha Pollnitz places the education of Prince Hal in the context of the political anxieties in the late years of the reign of Elizabeth I.[55] The study of Hal is relational, characterological and historical. Like Falstaff, he is unlikely to fade from the interests of those studying Shakespeare.

Falstaff and Oldcastle

Just when critics think they have Falstaff figured out, he slips out of their grasp. Critics have to focus on one element or a few aspects to create a coherent interpretation, but they then come to realize that theirs is but one view of a multi-dimensional character. What's in a name? The old controversy about the name of Shakespeare's fat knight gathered new momentum with the decision to replace 'Falstaff' with 'Oldcastle' in the Oxford *Complete Works* of 1986. In 1985, Gary Taylor argued that censorship had changed Oldcastle for Falstaff so that the name should revert to the original. In 1992, Jonathan Goldberg argued that the name change was the result of revision, and the traces of the name Oldcastle in the text reflect this rather than indicate censorship.[56] David Kastan sees Stanley Wells's and Gary Taylor's decision to use the name Oldcastle in the Oxford Shakespeare as problematically ignoring the intricacy of the text.[57]

The modern 'Oldcastle controversy' has many sides – religious, political and dramatic. Text and context are once more involved in the debate. Silvestro Severgnini discusses how Shakespeare made Falstaff out of Oldcastle.[58] For Janet Spenser, Shakespeare creates Falstaff from the religious violence, from the remains of the martyr.[59] Douglas Brooks sees parallels between the construction of Oldcastle as martyr and of Shakespeare as author.[60] For Benjamin Griffin, a treacherous likeness of opposites links Oldcastle and Falstaff .[61] In two instances, Paul White weighs into the debate: in the first, he shows the tension between political factions (Essex versus Cobham and Cecil) and topical interpretation in relation to Shakespeare's Oldcastle controversy and the acting company; in the second, White re-examines the religious and political controversy over Lord Cobham and Oldcastle in the context of a shift from patronage to the commercial theatre.[62] For Ellen Caldwell, Falstaff has a proto-Protestant voice that mocks the Catholic trappings of the monarchy, one reason that Hal (Henry V) has to banish him, thus becoming an iconoclast.[63] Shakespeare, according to Arthur Marotti, represented Falstaff–Oldcastle in a mixed fashion, so that Catholic and Protestant become intertwined in their representation.[64] According to Kristen Poole, the *Henry IV* plays, especially in the role of Falstaff, show that Puritans are represented as licentious and transgressive.[65] Gary Hamilton examines the mockery and rejection of Falstaff in terms of John Foxe's narrative, which represents him as a Calvinist martyr.[66] In Hugh Grady's view, Falstaff combines the carnivalesque with city comedy and questions the power of the state.[67] For Peter Milward, the Falstaff of *1 Henry IV* is like a sacred fool who parodies religious doctrine.[68] Susan Penberthy discusses Falstaff's promise of reform in religious terms and, more specifically, in the context of idleness.[69]

A parodic aspect of the debate also exists. James Bednarz thinks that Cobham's family forced Shakespeare to change Oldcastle's name to Falstaff and that Shakespeare and Jonson came to parody this family in *Merry Wives of Windsor* and *Every Man in His Humour* respectively.[70] For David Crosby, the tavern scene at Act II, Scene iv allows Hal and Falstaff to mock Oldcastle as martyr and suggests something about the debate over martyrdom in Shakespeare's time.[71] Christopher Kendrick considers Shakespeare's use of parody in *1 Henry IV* as a means of questioning royal and aristocratic power.[72]

Falstaff, Festivity, and Carnival

Festivity and carnival are persistent concerns in criticism relating to this play. Festivity and religion are not mutually exclusive as there is a Catholic as well as Puritan element to the religious controversy of Shakespeare's England. Analyzing *1* and *2 Henry IV* among other plays, Phebe Jensen sees Shakespeare's representation of the festive as being connected with tradition and Catholicism.[73] There are religious and political aspects to this misrule. Robert Bell argues that the representation of Falstaff shows the power of folly.[74] With a twist on C. L. Barber's festive comedy, Charles Whitney examines festivity in Act IV, Scene ii in terms of topical political and economic allusions.[75] Pierre Iselin discuss the comic political aspects of the grotesque and tragic bodies in *1 Henry IV*.[76] Ann Lecercle examines the relation between subversion and order, the carnivalesque and the monarchy.[77] Jonathan Hall also examines carnival in the play in the context of the relation between comedy and nation.[78] Elsewhere, Hall considers the *Henry IV* plays as representing Falstaff as representing chaos and dissension and *Merry Wives of Windsor* as making this character serve more bourgeois ends.[79] Bente Videbaek examines Falstaff's major clowning role in the context of Shakespeare's other clowns.[80] Nathalie Vienne-Guerrin relates the rhetoric of insults between Hal and Falstaff to the uses of the carnival and later looks at their flyting to show the ambivalence and change in their relationship (she also examines this aspect in film versions).[81] François Laroque draws on Mikhail Bakhtin's idea of the grotesque and the carnivalesque in relating the Falstaff scenes to Brueghel's painting *The Battle of Carnival and Lent* and also, in another piece, sees Falstaff in the *Henry IV* plays as a mock king whose carnival destabilizes the meaning of the crown.[82]

Falstaff's irreverence, satire and comic spirit can also be interpreted in terms of philosophy, as R. V. Young does, when arguing that Falstaff's questioning of honour, as understood in relation to William of Occam's nominalism and universals, represents a questioning of universals.[83] Harold Bloom sees Falstaff and Hamlet as the fullest expression of the human among Shakespeare's characters and argues that Shakespeare is central in the exploration of humanity.[84] From the philosophical to the grotesque, Falstaff has always welcomed a copia of commentary. In an analysis of Falstaff, Alan Lutkus includes a discussion of the critical reception of the *Henry IV* plays.[85] Falstaff is, for Michael Shurgot, part of the staging of subversion in *1 Henry IV*.[86] Another example of this focus is Madalina Nicolaescu's view that Falstaff questions honour in a way that is carnivalesque and deconstructs the ideal of honour at court.[87] Michele Stanco, discusses the ideas of guilt and punishment and the rejection of Falstaff.[88]

Falstaff is also a figure of nation, politics and geography. Michael Dobson discusses the role of Falstaff in making Shakespeare the national poet of Britain.[89] Jonathan Bate sees Falstaff as embodying the English nation.[90] For Steven Earnshaw, Falstaff and the Boar's Head Tavern pose a threat to order and come to be contained by king and government.[91] Giorgio Melchiori sees the Falstaff of the *Henry IV* plays as a Mediterranean character; he also discusses the transformation of the characters in the *Famous Victories of Henry the Fifth* into their counterparts in Shakespeare's plays, finding more emphasis on language in the later plays.[92] Herbert Weil compares Falstaff and Montaigne as tellers of truth.[93] Drawing on Nietzsche's idea of the good European, Michael Szczekalla discusses Falstaff as a self-critical European.[94]

Military aspects also supplement the elements of Falstaff, the clown, fool and 'professor' of religion. William Leahy analyzes Falstaff in the context of the situation of Elizabethan soldiers.[95] For David Kastan, Falstaff questions with his clowning unity and closure, kingship and history, class and authority in both *Henry IV* plays.[96] In Guillaume Winter's view, the tavern is a place of festivity, inversion and change in the *Henry IV* plays, whereas it is an infernal place of temptation in the works of Puritans.[97]

Falstaff welcomes variations on a range of critical themes from religious through social to psychological concerns introduced much earlier than the 1990s but developed in the past decade or two. For Douglas Hayes, in *1 Henry IV*, Shakespeare presents Falstaff as a Vice given to a rhetoric that subverts.[98] David Ellis examines Falstaff as a character and concentrates on his psychology and his considerable ability to evoke laughter.[99] According to Joachim Frenk, in all the plays in which he appears, Falstaff is the spirit of carnival who is sacrificial victim as well as critic of social class.[100] Norman Holland calls attention to the use of enthymemes, or rhetorical syllogisms that are truncated: they are founded on a tacit assumption that is assumed to be true, by Falstaff and Hotspur, which indicates their propensity to imagination and wishful thinking, thus implying that language can say something about the psychology of characters.[101] For Bert Cardullo, Shakespeare's representation of Falstaff in all the plays in which he appears constitutes part of the shifting perspectives and sympathies that the audience is asked to consider.[102] Michael Steppat uses Bakhtin's theory of the carnivalesque to argue that Shakespeare's representation of Falstaff show the power of theatre to transform new political and social energy.[103] David Ellis discusses the jokes played on Falstaff in the *Henry IV* plays.[104]

Language and memory are also keys to Falstaff's role. There is copia in his copiousness. In Isabel Karremann's view, the *Henry IV* plays are about memory, and Falstaff represents forgetfulness.[105] Christopher Ivic discusses fratricide in the context of the English civil wars and terms of remembering and forgetting.[106] Wolfgang Klooss places Falstaff's drinking and eating in *1* and *2 Henry IV* in context of a wider discourse on these topics in the period.[107] Elena Levy-Navarro argues, in the context of Elizabethan discourse on obesity as signifying excess, that Hal's thinness and Falstaff's fullness in the *Henry IV* plays have an intricate relation, including a representation of political ambitions, expansion and morality that asserts and questions their status.[108] Christopher McDonough draws on sources among the ancients to gloss Falstaff's comparison of honour to a 'mere scutcheon' as in the classical literary tradition of the *rhipsaspis* (shield-tosser), a coward who abandons his shield on the battlefield.[109] Karen Marsalek relates the resurrection of Falstaff to plays with that theme like the Chester *Antichrist*.[110] There is, then, a looking outward and backward, inward and ahead in the contexts for Falstaff and *1 Henry IV*. An example of a recurrent theme is gender, and the thin prince and the fat knight are in the thick of that preoccupation with masculinity and femininity.

Gender, Masculinity and Femininity

In the past couple of decades or so, there has been increasing interest in gender in *1 Henry IV*, building on the feminism of the 1960s and 1970s. The concern with the feminine also developed a study of the masculine. In the comedies cross-dressing has also been widely discussed, and this has also been translated into discussions of the history plays. Valerie Traub examines representations of female reproduction in *1 Henry IV*.[111] Phyllis Rackin thinks that the erotic in heterosexual relations can be negative in *1 Henry IV*.[112] J. L. Simmons sees a submerging of the feminine in the play as in Shakespeare's sources.[113] Marvin Krims sees Hotspur as embodying unconscious conflicts that entail an anti-feminine prejudice.[114] In *1 Henry IV*, Mistress Quickly, according to John Crawford, mentors male characters, one of several characters across the canon playing such a role.[115]

Work on gender can go beyond these characters. The work of Phyllis Rackin and Jean Howard, discussed in Edel Lamb's chapter (Chapter One), relates gender to the transformation of England from kingdom to nation.[116] Anne Larue discusses Falstaff in terms of mother earth as well as a father-figure and harlequin.[117] Cheang Wai-fong considers Mistress Quickly to be a comic voice that presents alternatives and disrupts history.[118] Madalina Nicolaescu discusses the relation between violence and representations of females across the genres, including *1 Henry IV*.[119]

Masculinity is not far from the surface of a play in a time of war. For Donald Hedrick, Hotspur represents a masculinity that contains within it its own crisis.[120] Barbara Cobb considers Shakespeare's representation of strong male monarchs in the second tetralogy a reminder of the problem of succession and the insecurities surrounding an old and childless queen.[121] According to Roberta Barker, Hotspur's masculinity and sense of honour in this play has created contradictions in criticism and theatre that range from the tragic to through the comic to the historical.[122] Michael Mangan examines representations of lovers and soldiers in this and other Shakespeare plays, as well as the role of violence in representations of masculinity.[123] Richard Grennell considers that charges of witchcraft feminize Glendower in *1 Henry IV*.[124] Harry Berger, Jr. examines the horse as a marker of gender, sexuality and class.[125] For Karen Love, Falstaff embodies the grotesque and the carnivalesque and uses language to subvert the boundary between male and female.[126]

The nature of clowning is also tied up with questions of gender and sexuality. Augustin Redondo compares Falstaff and Sancho Panza and sees them as festive characters whose buffonery allows to call social conventions into question.[127] For Frances Barasch, Mistress Quickly's conflation of 'harlequin' and 'harlot' at Act II, Scene iv suggests a metatheatrical comparison of Falstaff and the harlequin of the Italian theatre.[128] Christian Billing examines the representation of Falstaff's body and character in terms of politics and gender, especially masculinity.[129] Vin Nardizzi discusses the images of grafting in relation to Hal and in connection with sex and queer sexuality.[130] Gender has social and political implications, and the critics discuss economics, politics and law more generally in relation to *1 Henry IV*.

Economic, Political and Legal Criticism (Value and Exchange)

Politics and the relation of the public and private have long been part of the criticism of this play. E. A. Rauchut considers the political, legal and economic aspects of King Henry asking for Hotspur's prisoners, something that suggests the division between the Crown and the aristocratic code of chivalry.[131] The Realpolitik and militarism of the 1590s, as embodied by Robert Cecil, are central to Curtis Breight's analysis of the *Henry IV* plays and *Henry V*.[132] Harry Berger, Jr. discusses the relation between ethics and complicity in *1 Henry IV*.[133] Andreas Höfele explores the notion of the queen's two bodies and its relation to monarchy and the image of royal power and relates that to the tension between the elevation and reduction of kingship in the second tetralogy.[134] Expediency and violence, war and politics, particularly in terms of sovereignty, concern Jean-Christophe Mayer in regard to the *Henriad*.[135] Avraham Oz sees Jerusalem as a national preoccupation in Shakespeare's English histories, an ideological force behind the building of England.[136] In terms of dearth, James Berg discusses the monarchy in the first three plays of the second tetralogy.[137] Sometimes there are legal aspects to this political world. Victoria Time, for instance, examines *1 Henry IV* in terms of law, justice and criminology and sees parallels between modes of thinking then and now.[138] Using *1* and *2 Henry IV* as illustrations, Ian Ward argues for the connection between constitutions and literature.[139]

Although poetics and rhetoric were once centres of studies of this and other Shakespearean plays, this area is sometimes neglected and its neglect takes on a politics of its own. A detailed study of the rhetoric of the colour red in *1 Henry IV* by Raphaëlle Costa de Beauregard is an alternative to analyses that focus mainly on politics and ideology.[140] Bikang Huang discusses the ideology of politics and argues that Hal uses images of political and legal violence to contain Falstaff's subversion.[141] Nina Levine connects the rise of Hal and the rise of credit in her analysis of economic metaphors of exchange.[142] The rhetoric of copia and cornucopia in the *Henry IV* plays is, according to Laetitia Coussement-Boillot, a way of representing a nostalgia for, and a rejection of, abundance.[143] For Glen Mynott, *1* and *2 Henry IV* represent tensions between monarchy and aristocracy and the notion of chivalry is part of that friction.[144] The king's two bodies continue to inform debate on politics in Shakespeare's histories: Albert Rolls discusses this theory in relation to subjectivity in the *Henry IV* plays.[145]

This analysis of language continues in the realm of law, politics and economics. Lorna Hutson examines legal and political limits to royal power and humanist ideas of the civic in Shakespeare's *Henry IV* plays.[146] She also discusses Falstaff's defiance of law and justice in the context of the legal and political theory (including that of the body politic) in Edmund Plowden and Ernst Kantorowicz.[147] Jesse Lander examines coins and coinage to discuss political and economic value and the counterfeiting of kingship.[148] Walt Turner discusses political legitimacy in terms of the language of legal and counterfeit coins.[149] According to Barbara Kreps, Shakespeare uses rhetoric, mainly through puns and economic metaphors, to represent a questioning of the legitimacy of the rule of Henry IV.[150] James Knowles examines the contemporary context for the play's division between royal and aristocratic powers.[151] François Lecercle discusses political discourse in terms of manipulation in the language of Henry IV and Hal.[152] Jennifer Low examines the relation between the judicial duel and the monarch as source of law and justice and how the duel can subvert the authority of the monarchy.[153]

The language of religion is never too far from other discourses in *1 Henry IV*. Timothy Rosendale discusses the importance of signs in the wake of the Reformation and, in particular, in the attempt to represent a unified image of the monarch.[154] Clifford Davidson argues that Shakespeare saw the Coventry mystery plays, whose representation of rebellion influenced his own in the *Henry IV* plays.[155] For Uwe Klawitter, these plays are important for the relation between ideology and the people.[156] Jesús López-Peláez Casellas discusses honour in *1 Henry IV* in terms of contradiction partly because the ends of power are not always honourable.[157] Otherness and the relation between I and others, as discussed in Martin Buber and Emmanuel Levinas, is the focus of David Ruiter's analysis of Hal's relationship with Francis and Henry V's relations with others.[158] Jean-Louis Claret argues that interest in the Crusades was waning in the sixteenth century, and that *1 Henry IV* translates the focus on the Crusades in *Richard II* into a religious war against France.[159]

The debates over the personal and social aspect of characters and events in this play show the interdisciplinary and interlocking critical discourses, developing not in a linear fashion but as a web or weave of various concerns in economics, law and politics. Critical analysis often examines particular threads or details, exploring their larger implications. For instance, Mark Taylor examines the world of the tavern in terms of privacy.[160] Another aspect of the private and the public, of the personal and the political is honour, which can be expressed through language and gesture in *1 Henry IV* and the other plays of the second tetralogy as Joan Hartwig argues.[161] David Quint discusses *1 Henry IV* and other plays in terms of the tension between aristocracy and monarchy.[162] Stephen Dickey examines the ceremonial functions of cushions and crowns in *1 and 2 Henry IV*.[163] For Patricia Cahill, the *Henry IV* plays represent the ambivalence over the militarization of the state under Elizabeth I.[164] Alicia Marchant examines *1 Henry IV* in terms of space, mainly centre and periphery, as a means of discussing a kingship in the context of dislocated nature and laws.[165] For Benedict Robinson, religion and politics mix in representations of Islam, particularly in Shakespeare's references to Turks and to Amurath in the *Henry IV* plays and *Henry V*.[166] Alexander Welsh sees Shakespeare's discussion of honour in the second tetralogy leading him to a consideration of honour in the Roman plays.[167]

'New British History' or Rewriting the History of the 'Atlantic archipelago'

In this area the relationships between England, Wales, Ireland and Scotland are foregrounded. England is defined according to the places that surround it and they in turn find definition in their relation with England. There is also an attempt at decentring English hegemony of the British Isles. Critics try to examine Shakespeare and *1 Henry IV* from other perspectives, ranging from internal colonization to alternative worlds beyond England itself.

The reader can find critics concerned at once with Ireland, Wales and Scotland, so I have made no attempt to divide them neatly. For instance, Shawn Holliday sees the theme of usurpation in the plays of the second tetralogy, including *1 Henry IV*, as a warning against Elizabeth I's misguided policy in Ireland.[168] Bradley Greenburg views Wales as a counterbalance to England in *1 Henry IV*.[169] Mapping, boundaries and displacement as well as location and dislocation (exile) are important to *1 Henry IV*, and David Read examines Act III, Scene i to explore how characters are concerned with these matters.[170] Combining notions of gender and the meeting of cultures and languages at the borders, Terence Hawkes discusses how Welshness make Falstaff and Mortimer effeminate and how Anglicization affects Glendower and Fluellen even in their names.[171]

The connections among the 'British' peoples or nations form a critical web. A complex of relations among Ireland, Scotland, Wales and England occur in Christopher Highley's reading of Shakespeare's English history plays, and his interpretation of *1 Henry IV* involves a displacement and a screening of Scotland to represent the crisis in Ireland.[172] Claire Lamont notes the connection between the plays and wider British culture in the form of ballads about Douglas and Percy.[173]

Theatre is concerned with space and time in the history play. This representation can have political and cultural implications. Mapping is one such example. Maps do not, according to Bruce Avery, work toward building a community in *1 Henry IV*.[174] More work on mapping as ideology and as questioning what is known occurs in Garrett A. Sullivan, Jr.'s study, which examines *1 Henry IV* and other plays about England and Britain. Analysis of characters, stereotyping, language and self-conscious theatricality also help the reinterpretation of the British Isles in this and other plays. For Reese Davies, Glendower is Shakespeare's representation of a Welsh hero.[175] Matthew Greenfield sees the staging of past and present British identity being played out through metatheatricality.[176] Megan Lloyd examines the negative stereotyping of Welsh and Wales in *1 Henry IV*.[177] For Kate Chedgzoy, the English use representations of the feminine to construct an idea of Welshness from the language to the nation.[178]

In addition to culture, religion plays a role in this new interpretation of the cultures of this Atlantic archipelago. Joan Fitzpatrick connects the play's complex representation of an unruly Britain with the hypothesis that Shakespeare was Catholic: this religious identity allowed the playwright to understand power and marginalization from different points of view.[179] Lisa Hopkins suggests that the ambiguity of Wales and Welshness complicates gender (especially the feminine) and genre (especially comedy).[180] For Andrew Murphy, for example, the foreign/familiar Ireland in the play should be seen in the context of Hugh O'Neill and the Nine Years War (1594–1603), and is a key to understanding identity in the British Isles in these years.[181]

Staging, theatrical and linguistic performance and representation are all issues in this new mapping of the cultures of the British Isles. In the context of performance, Peter Holland discusses the maps in *1 Henry IV* and *King Lear* as the mapping of the division of England that has historical as well as geographical implications.[182] In the context of identity and authority, Lloyd Kermode examines Welshness, Britishness and strangers in the second tetralogy and *Cymbeline*.[183] Huw Griffiths analyzes the representation of the Welsh and their use of language in *1 Henry IV* in terms of performance and comedy.[184] Megan Lloyd argues that in *1 Henry IV* Shakespeare represents Lady Mortimer as a figure of the power of Wales and its language.[185]

This overview of recent criticism shows that there is continuity even in those who would break with the critical past. Text, context and performance are inescapable. Even as the criticism seems to depart the scene, it returns to it. The worlds of *1 Henry IV* of court, tavern, Wales and rebel camp keep actors, directors, critics, readers and audiences coming back to many of the same concerns even when they would like to discard received opinion.

Directions that Future Criticism May Take

Language is at the heart of Shakespeare's achievement, and his accomplishment in helping to transform the chronicle play into the history play, which is one of his most original contributions as an artist in terms of genre, depends on how memorable and accomplished his poetry and prose are. On Shakespeare's stage, the hero is all too often, if not nearly always, the language.

Although Shakespeare's dramatic poetics has been a topic for the ages, it is inexhaustible and is at the heart of Shakespeare's achievement as a dramatic historian. For many, the history of the reign of Henry IV will be experienced through Shakespeare's history plays. Their compression, variety and virtuosity separates Shakespeare from all but the greatest historians and perhaps all historians. As a dramatic poet he can play with the sequence of time and with facts more than a historian can. Shakespeare's language makes him more memorable than the historical narratives or chronicles from which he worked. Though historical contexts have been at the centre of much research over the past few decades, it might be time to concentrate a little more on discourse, rhetoric and poetics. More specifically, this study could be informed by historical milieu. How is the language of manipulation and persuasion and how are the aesthetics of speech and writing used to promulgate religious, social and political positions? There is a range of language within each character and among characters who are parts of the worlds of the play – Wales, rebel camp, court and tavern. These are possible or fictional worlds within the large imaginative and historical world of the play. Leibnitz's theory of possible worlds, and refractions of it in fictional worlds as set out by Thomas Pavel, might be a suggestive way to consider *1 Henry IV*.

Another related way of thinking about language in a play that is fictional and historical, comic and serious, is to frame it in terms of otherness or alterity. That might create a field theory of gender, class and race as well as religion, internal and external politics and colonization. For instance, Lady Mortimer's and Glendower's Welshness is a form of otherness without which the audience would have a hard time understanding the aspirations of English language, culture and polity. Hotspur's poetics is one in which masculinity attempts to come to terms with but also efface the feminine, as represented by his wife, Kate. Henry IV's language of pilgimage and Falstaff's puritanical cant give different dimensions to religion and make the audience distinguish between aspiration and hypocrisy. Each character is other to the next, and Hal speaks in various registers and uses language to negotiate the alterity of the tavern, the rivalry of the rebel camp, the legitimacy of Mortimer in Wales, and the alienation he experiences from king and court. There are private and public aspects of this otherness: Hal must negotiate the estrangement from his father, who is also king. The family and the state are superimposed on each other while being estranged from each other. Each aspect has its own otherness and is multi-layered. The women of the tavern have a language from a different class and culture to that of Lady Mortimer and Kate.

In *1 Henry IV*, Shakespeare draws on rhetoric and poetics to create a powerful use of language that makes the fictional history of the play memorable and enduring both as instruction and delight. How does Shakespeare take this body of theory and practice and transform it into his powerful art? This question can also be explored specifically in relation to the history play. The very language that makes the history plays memorable might be much more the language of the poet than of the historian and actually distract the reader and audience from the historical record. Alternatively, as I have suggested, the memorability of Shakespeare's language invites reader and audience to consider the past. Poetics and rhetoric, as well as the language of history, are part of a European context, ancient and modern. Shakespeare's formal education was in Greek and Latin and involved the classics and the Bible, as well as influences from Europe and beyond, so that his language already had a broad cultural and linguistic framework. Text and context have an interplay and are other to each other. The elements that make up Shakespeare's language and the varied and sometimes contradictory elements of his characters' speech create a complex understanding of fiction and history. The history play is oxymoronic because it yokes the fiction of drama with the fact of history. The crusades, the Reformation, the expansion of Europe are all in the details of the language of *1 Henry IV* not to mention discourses of sexuality, politic and economics. Here, Shakespeare's language is both familiar and strange in its public and private utterance, and what was familiar in his time might be strange to us now. The otherness of language even within the culture of English combines with historical estrangement to make the study of

Shakespeare's poetics, rhetoric and discourse in *1 Henry IV* a renewable resource. Whether or not students of the play take this course, it is a field that has an ever-shifting configuration with great potential for fruitful labours.

Notes

1. For discussion of and excerpts from work from the 1970s and 80s, see *Shakespeare's History Plays: Richard II to Henry V*, ed. Graham Holderness (New York: St. Martin's Press, 1992). Pre-1990s criticism of the play is discussed in Ronald Knowles, *The Critics Debate: Henry IV Parts I and II* (Basingstoke: Macmillan, 1992) and Jonathan Hart, *Theater and World: The Problematics of Shakespeare's History* (Boston: Northeastern University Press, 1992). The latter includes an extensive bibliography to about 1990 or so, including work on Shakespeare's histories and *1 Henry IV*. For my most recent discussion of *1 Henry IV* and the history plays at length, see *Shakespeare: Poetry, History, and Culture* (New York: Palgrave Macmillan, 2009). I have not included references to my own work in the body of this essay.

2. Ann Lecercle, 'Epics and Ethics in *1 Henry IV*', in *French Essays on Shakespeare and His Contemporaries: 'What Would France with Us?'* ed. Jean-Marie Maguin and Michèle Willems (Newark, DE: University of Delaware Press, 1995), pp. 175–88.

3. Kiernan Ryan, 'The Future of History in *Henry IV*', in *Henry IV Parts 1 and 2*, ed. Nigel Wood (Buckingham: Open University Press, 1995), pp. 92–125.

4. Judith Mossman, 'Plutarch and Shakespeare's *Henry IV Parts 1 and 2*', *Poetica: An International Journal of Linguistic-Literary Studies*, 48 (1997), 99–117.

5. Tom McAlindon, 'Pilgrims of Grace: *Henry IV* Historicized', *Shakespeare Survey* 48 (1996), 69–84 and his *Shakespeare's Tudor History: A Study of Henry IV, Parts 1 and 2* (Aldershot: Ashgate, 2001).

6. Lisa Hopkins, 'New Historicism and History Plays', *Shakespeare Yearbook*, 6 (1996), 53–73.

7. Paul Dean, 'Shakespeare's Historical Imagination', *Renaissance Studies* 11 (1997), 27–40.

8. Giuseppe Martella, '*Henry IV*: The Frame of History', in *Mnema per Lino Falzon Santucci*, ed. Paola Pugliatti (Messina: Siciliano, 1997), pp. 55–85.

9. Jutta Schamp, *Repräsentation von Zeit bei Shakespeare: Richard II, Henry IV, Macbeth* (Tübingen: Niemeyer, 1997).

10. Heather Dubrow, *Shakespeare and Domestic Loss: Forms of Deprivation, Mourning, and Recuperation* (Cambridge: Cambridge University Press, 1999).

11. Lisa Hopkins, 'The Iliad and the Henriad: Epics and Brothers', *Classical and Modern Literature*, 19 (1999–2000), 149–71.

12. Jonathan Samuel Shaw, *History Plays of Shakespeare: A Revaluation* (Allahabad: Kitab Mahal, 1999).

13. Richard Keller Simon, *Trash Culture: Popular Culture and the Great Tradition* (Berkeley, CA: University of California Press, 1999).

14. Cathleen T. McLoughlin, *Shakespeare, Rabelais, and the Comical-Historical* (New York: Lang, 2000).

15. Michele Stanco, 'Historico-Tragico-Comical Kings: Genre Conventions and/as Emblems of Power in Shakespeare's Histories', in *The Iconography of Power: Ideas and Images of Rulership on the English Renaissance Stage*, ed. György Endre Szonyi and Rowland Wymer (Szeged: IATE Press, 2000), pp. 117–45.

16. Philippe Chardin, 'De la grandeur du désastre à l'héroï-comique du désastreux', *Littératures*, 45 (2001), 267–77.

17. François Lecercle, 'La croisade avortée: Shakespeare, Henry IV, première partie, acte I, scène 1', in *Théâtres de la guerre: La mise en scène de la guerre dans Les Perses d'Eschyle, la première partie de Henry IV de Shakespeare, Les Paravents de Genet*, ed. François Lecercle (Paris: Klincksieck, 2001), pp. 211–19. On the representation of war in the same volume, see David Lescot, 'La mise en drame de la guerre', pp. 67–77. On the battle of Shewsbury in *1 Henry IV*, also see , Daniel Mortier, 'Le théâtre de la guerre', pp. 47–65.

18. Derek Cohen, *Searching Shakespeare: Studies in Culture and Authority* (Toronto: University of Toronto Press, 2003).

19. Ronald Knowles, *Shakespeare's Arguments with History* (Basingstoke: Palgrave, 2002).

20. Pascale Drouet, 'Répétitions et différenciations à Eastcheap dans *1 Henry IV* de Shakespeare', *Imaginaires: Revue du Centre de recherche sur l'imaginaire dans les littératures de langue anglaise* 9 (2003), 9–20.

21. Nathalie Rivère de Carles, 'Tenture et théâtre, de Minerve à Thespis', *Anglophonia*, 13 (2003), 83–96.

22. Michael Flachmann, 'Parrot, Parody, and Paronomasia: Damnable Iteration in *Henry IV, Part I*', *Journal of the Wooden O Symposium*, 4 (2004), 45–52.

23. Jesús G. Maestro, 'Cervantes y Shakespeare: El nacimiento de la literatura metateatral', *Bulletin of Spanish Studies* 81 (2004), 599–611.

24. Alessandro Vescovi, 'A journeyman to grief: L'idea di viaggio in *Enrico IV* ed *Enrico V*', in *Shakespeare Days – I edizione Milano, 16-23-30 maggio 2002: Atti del convegno* ed. Luisa Camaiora (Milan: Università Cattolica, 2004), pp. 245–55.

25. Charles Edelman, 'Shakespeare and the Invention of the Epic Theatre: Working with Brecht', *Shakespeare Survey*, 58 (2005), 130–36.

26. Alan Stewart, *Shakespeare's Letters* (Oxford: Oxford University Press, 2008).

27. Anthony Davies, 'Falstaff's Shadow', in *Shakespeare on Screen: The Henriad*, ed. Sarah Hatchuel and Nathalie Vienne-Guerrin, (Mont-Saint-Aignan: Publications des Universités de Rouen and du Havre, 2008), pp. 99–117.

28. Robert Shaughnessy, ' "I do, I will": Hal, Falstaff, and the Performative', in *Alternative Shakespeares 3*, ed. Diana E. Henderson (London: Routledge, 2008), pp. 14–33.

29. In addition to the stagings and film productions of *1* and *2 Henry IV*, there is also a movie about Hal, *Young Prince Hal*, directed by Philip R. Frey and produced by Ray Salah for television, 1997.

30. Michèle Vignaux, *L'invention de la responsabilité. La deuxième tétralogie de Shakespeare* (Paris: Presses de l'École Normale Supérieure, 1995).

31. Richard F. Hardin, *Civil Idolatry: Desacralizing and Monarchy in Spenser, Shakespeare, and Milton* (Newark, DE: University of Delaware Press, 1992).

32. Robert L. Reid, 'Humoral Psychology in Shakespeare's Henriad', *Comparative Drama*, 30 (1996–97), 471 502.

33. Tim J. Spiekerman, 'The Education of Hal: *Henry IV, Parts One and Two*', in *Shakespeare's Political Pageant: Essays in Literature and Politics,* ed. Joseph Alulis and Vickie Sullivan (Lanham, MD: Rowman and Littlefield, 1996), pp. 103–24. See Tim J. Spiekerman, *Shakespeare's Political Realism: The English History Plays* (Albany, NY: State University of New York Press, 2001).

34. Dennis Quinn, 'Pastimes and the Prince: Hal and *Eutrapelia*', *Ben Jonson Journal*, 4 (1997), 103–14.

35. Jane Kingsley-Smith, *Shakespeare's Drama of Exile* (Basingstoke: Palgrave Macmillan, 2003).

36. Michael Davies, 'Falstaff's Lateness: Calvinism and the Protestant Hero in *Henry IV*', *Review of English Studies*, 56 (2005), 351–78.
37. Derek Peat, 'Falstaff Gets the Sack', *Shakespeare Quarterly* 53 (2002), 379–85.
38. Harry Berger, Jr., 'The Prince's Dog: Falstaff and the Perils of Speech-Prefixity', *Shakespeare Quarterly*, 49 (1998), 40–73.
39. Lawrence Danson, 'Shakespeare and the Misrecognition of Fathers and Sons', in *Paternity and Fatherhood: Myths and Realities*, ed. Lieve Spaas, (Basingstoke: Macmillan, 1998), pp. 236–45.
40. Leah Scragg, *Shakespeare's Alternative Tales* (London: Longman, 1996).
41. Beatrice Groves, 'Hal as Self-Styled Redeemer: The Harrowing of Hell and *Henry IV Part 1*', *Shakespeare Survey*, 57 (2004), 236–48.
42. Marvin B. Krims, 'Prince Hal's Play as Prelude to His Invasion of France', *Psychoanalytic Review*, 88 (2001), 495–510.
43. Marvin B. Krims, 'Prince Hal's Aggression', *PsyArt: A Hyperlink Journal for Psychological Study of the Arts*, (2002), 1–21; see Krims, *The Mind According to Shakespeare: Psychoanalysis in the Bard's Writing* (Westport, CT: Praeger, 2006).
44. Wayne A. Rebhorn, *The Emperor of Men's Minds: Literature and the Discourse of Rhetoric* (Ithaca, NY and London: Cornell University Press, 1995), 56–62.
45. David George, 'Sons without Fathers: Shakespeare's Second tetralogy', in *Shakespeare's Second Historical Tetralogy: Some Christian Feature*, ed. Beatrice Batson (West Cornwall, CT: Locust Hill Press, 2004), pp. 27–55.
46. Élisabeth Rallo, 'Tel père, tel fils? Paternité et filiation dans *Henry IV* de Shakespeare', in *Femmes, familles, filiations: Société et histoire*, ed. Marcel Bernos and Bitton, Michèle Bitton, (Aix-en-Provence: Publications de l'Université de Provence, 2004), 205–14.
47. Laura Di Michele, 'Shakespeare's History Plays as a "Scene" of the Disappearance of Popular Discourse', in *Italian Studies in Shakespeare and His Contemporaries*, ed. Michele Marrapodi and Giorgio Melchiori (Newark, DE: University of Delaware Press, 1999), pp. 128–51.
48. David Ruiter, *Shakespeare's Festive History: Feasting, Festivity, Fasting, and Lent in the Second Henriad* (Aldershot: Ashgate, 2003).
49. Ellen Summers, '"Judge, my masters": Playing Hal's Audience', in *Shakespeare's Second Historical Tetralogy: Some Christian Features*, ed. Beatrice Batson (West Cornwall, CT: Locust Hill Press, 2004), pp. 165–78.
50. Jean-Louis Claret, 'Aveu et redemption dans le théâtre de Shakespeare', in *Cultures de la confession: Formes de l'aveu dans le monde anglophone*, ed. Sylvie Mathé and Gilles Teulié (Aix-en-Provence: Publications de l'Université de Provence, 2006), pp. 27–38.
51. Avery Plaw, 'Prince Harry: Shakespeare's Critique of Machiavelli', *Interpretation: A Journal of Political Philosophy*, 33 (2005), 19–43.
52. Daniel L. Colvin, '(Re)covering the Self: Hal and the Psychology of Disguise', in *Staging Shakespeare: Essays in Honor of Alan C. Dessen*, ed. Lena Cowen Orlin and Miranda Johnson-Haddad (Newark, DE: University of Delaware Press, 2007), pp. 45–59.
53. Nick Cox, 'The Great Enlargement: The Uses of Delinquency in *Henry IV Part One*', *Literature and History*, 8 (1999), 1–19.
54. Charles R. Forker, 'The State of the Soul and the Soul of the State: Reconciliation in the Two Parts of Shakespeare's *Henry IV*', *Studies in Medieval and Renaissance History*, 4 (2007), 289–313.
55. Aysha Pollnitz, 'Educating Hamlet and Prince Hal', in *Shakespeare and Early Modern Political Thought*, ed. David Armitage et al. (Cambridge: Cambridge University Press, 2009), pp. 119–38.

56. Gary Taylor, 'The Fortunes of Oldcastle', *Shakespeare Survey*, 38 (1985), 85–100 and Jonathan Goldberg, 'The Commodity of Names: "Falstaff" and "Oldcastle" in *1 Henry IV*, in *Reconfiguring the Renaissance: Essays in Critical Materialism*, ed. Jonathan Crewe (Lewisburg, WV: Bucknell University Press, 1992), pp. 76–88.
57. David Scott Kastan, *Shakespeare After Theory* (London: Routledge, 1999).
58. Silvestro Severgnini, 'Shakespeare da Oldcastle a Falstaff, per predenza', *La rivista illustrata del Museo teatrale alla Scala*, 7 (Autumn 1994), 31, 34–35.
59. Janet M. Spencer, 'Violence and the Sacred: Holy Fragments, Shakespeare, and the Postmodern', *Christianity and Literature*, 50 (2000–01), 613–29.
60. Douglas A. Brooks, *From Playhouse to Printing House: Drama and Authorship in Early Modern England* (Cambridge: Cambridge University Press, 2000).
61. Benjamin Griffin, 'Marring and Mending: Treacherous Likeness in Two Renaissance Controversies', *Huntington Library Quarterly*, 60 (1998), 363–80.
62. Paul Whitfield White, 'Shakespeare, the Cobhams, and the Dynamics of Theatrical Patronage', in *Shakespeare and Theatrical Patronage in Early Modern England*, ed. Paul Whitfield White and Suzanne R. Westfall, (Cambridge: Cambridge University Press, 2002), pp. 64–89; White, 'Shakespeare and Religious Polemic: Revisiting *1 Henry IV* and the Oldcastle Controversy', in *Shakespeare's Second Historical Tetralogy: Some Christian Features*, ed. Beatrice Batson (West Cornwall, CT: Locust Hill Press, 2004), pp. 147–64.
63. Ellen M. Caldwell, '"Banish all the wor(l)d": Falstaff's Iconoclastic Threat to Kingship in *1 Henry IV*, *Renascence*, 59 (2006–07), 219–45.
64. Arthur F. Marotti, 'Shakespeare and Catholicism', in *Theatre and Religion: Lancastrian Shakespeare*, ed. Richard Dutton et al. (Manchester: Manchester University Press, 2003), pp. 218–41.
65. Kristen Poole, *Radical Religion from Shakespeare to Milton: Figures of Nonconformity in Early Modern England* (Cambridge: Cambridge University Press, 2000).
66. Gary D. Hamilton, 'Mocking Oldcastle: Notes toward Exploring a Possible Catholic Presence in Shakespeare's Henriad', in *Shakespeare and the Culture of Christianity in Early Modern England*, ed. Dennis Taylor and David N. Beauregard (New York: Fordham University Press, 2003), pp. 141–58.
67. Hugh Grady, 'Falstaff: Subjectivity between the Carnival and the Aesthetic', *Modern Language Review*, 96 (2001), 609–23.
68. Peter Milward, 'Shakespeare's Sacred Fools', *Renaissance Bulletin*, 29 (2002), 19–28.
69. Susan Penberthy, 'Falstaff's Reformation: Virtue in Idleness', in *The Touch of the Real: Essays in Early Modern Culture in Honour of Stephen Greenblatt*, ed. Philippa Kelly (Crawley: University of Western Australia, 2002), pp. 143–58.
70. James P. Bednarz, 'Biographical Politics: Shakespeare, Jonson, and the Oldcastle Controversy', *Ben Jonson Journal*, 11 (2004), 1–20.
71. David Crosby, 'Examination and Mockery in *Henry IV, Part One*', *Journal of the Wooden O Symposium*, 4 (2004), 24–34.
72. Christopher Kendrick, *Utopia, Carnival, and Commonwealth in Renaissance England* (Toronto: University of Toronto Press, 2004).
73. Phebe Jensen, *Religion and Revelry in Shakespeare's Festive World* (Cambridge: Cambridge University Press, 2008).
74. Robert H. Bell, 'The Anatomy of Folly in Shakespeare's Henriad', *Humor*, 14 (2001), 181–201.
75. Charles Whitney, 'Festivity and Topicality in the Coventry Scene of *1 Henry IV*', *English Literary Renaissance*, 24 (1994), 410–48.
76. Pierre Iselin, '"Thou hast damnable iteration!": Anatomie de la citation dans *Henry IV, Part 1*', in *Le grotesque au theatre* (special issue of *Cercles*, October 1992), ed.

Jean-Pierre Maquerlot (Mont-Saint-Aignan: Centre d'Etudes en Littérature, Linguistique et Civilisation de Langue Anglaise and Centre d'Etudes du Théâtre Anglo-Saxon, 1992), pp. 25–36.

77. Ann Lecercle, 'Of Benches and Wenches: Subversion de l'espace et topologie de la tyrannie dans *I Henry IV*', in *L'espace littéraire dans la littérature et la culture anglo-saxonnes*, ed. Bernard Brugière (Paris: Presses de la Sorbonne Nouvelle, 1995), pp. 33–40.

78. Jonathan Hall, *Anxious Pleasures: Shakespearean Comedy and the Nation-State* (Madison, NJ: Fairleigh Dickinson University Press, 1995).

79. Jonathan Hall, 'The Evacuations of Falstaff', in *Shakespeare and Carnival: After Bakhtin*, ed. Ronald Knowles (New York: St Martin's Press, 1998), pp. 123–51.

80. Bente A. Videbaek, *The Stage Clown in Shakespeare's Theatre* (Westport, CT: Greenwood, 1996).

81. Nathalie Vienne-Guerrin, 'L'anatomie de l'insulte dans *1 Henry IV*', *Bulletin de la Société de stylistique anglaise*, 17 (1996), 21–35; her 'Les jeux de l'injure dans *Henry IV*', in *Shakespeare et le jeu*, ed. Pierre Kapitaniak and Yves Peyré (Paris: Société Française Shakespeare, 2005), pp. 185–99; and her 'Flyting on Screen: Insults in Film Versions of *Henry IV*', in *Shakespeare on Screen: The Henriad*, ed. Sarah Hatchuel and Nathalie Vienne-Guerrin (Mont-Saint-Aignan: Publications des Universités de Rouen and du Havre, 2008), pp. 119–45.

82. François Laroque, 'Shakespeare's *Battle of Carnival and Lent*: The Falstaff Scenes Reconsidered (*1* and *2 Henry IV*)', *Shakespeare and Carnival: After Bakhtin*, ed. Richard Knowles (New York: St Martin's Press, 1998), pp. 83–96 and François Laroque, 'Les rois de carnaval dans le théâtre de Shakespeare: Le cas de *Jules César* et d'*Hamlet*', in *Figures de la royauté en Angleterre de Shakespeare à la Glorieuse Révolution*, ed. François Laroque, and Franck Lessay (Paris: Presses de la Sorbonne Nouvelle, 1999), pp. 49–60.

83. R. V. Young, 'Juliet and Shakespeare's Other Nominalists: Variations on a Theme by Richard Weaver', *Intercollegiate Review*, 33 (1997), 18–29.

84. Harold Bloom, *Shakespeare: The Invention of the Human* (New York: Riverhead Books, 1998).

85. Alan Lutkus, 'Sir John Falstaff', *Fools and Jesters in Literature, Art, and History: A Bio-Bibliographical Sourcebook*, ed. Vicki K. Janik (Westport, CT: Greenwood, 1998), pp. 176–84.

86. Michael W. Shurgot, *Stages of Play: Shakespeare's Theatrical Energies in Elizabethan Performance* (Newark, DE: University of Delaware Press, 1998).

87. Madalina Nicolaescu, '"What is honour?": Falstaff's Deconstruction of Chivalric Values in *1 Henry IV*', *Studii de limbi si literaturi moderne* (2000), 287–96.

88. Michele Stanco, 'Le sette vite di Falstaff: Giustizia penale e giustizia poetica in *Henry IV (1 e 2)* e *Henry V*', in *Shakespeare e Verdi*, ed. Giovanna Silvani and Claudio Gallico, (Parma: Facoltà di Lettere e Filosofia, Università degli Studi de Parma, 2000), pp. 99–117.

89. Michael Dobson, 'Falstaff after John Bull: Shakespearean History, Britishness, and the Former United Kingdom', *Shakespeare Jahrbuch*, 136 (2000), 40–55.

90. Jonathan Bate, 'Shakespeare Nationalised, Shakespeare Privatised', *English*, 42 (1993), 1–18.

91. Steven Earnshaw, *The Pub in Literature: England's Altered State* (Manchester: Manchester University Press, 2000).

92. Giorgio Melchiori, 'Falstaff mediterráneo', *Contrastes: Revista cultural* 12 (2000), 24–29 and his 'Hal's Unrestrained Loose Companions', *Memoria di Shakespeare*, 1 (2000), 19–32.

93. Herbert Weil, 'Montaigne and Falstaff', *Shakespeare Newsletter*, 58 (2008), 49, 54, 60, 70.

94. Michael Szczekalla, 'Shakespeare als gutter Europäer', *Anglistik*, 16 (2005), 25–34.

95. William Leahy '"Thy hunger-starved men": Shakespeare's *Henry* Plays and the contemporary Lot of the Common Soldier', *Parergon*, 20 (2003), 119–34.

96. David Scott Kastan, *Understanding Falstaff* (San Diego: San Diego State University, 2003).

97. Guillaume Winter, '"In the suburbs of your good pleasure": Les lieux de plaisir à Londres à la fin du XVIe et au début du XVIIe siècles', in *Enfers et délices à la Renaissance*, ed. François Laroque and Franck Lessay (Paris: Presses Sorbonne Nouvelle, 2003), pp. 31–41.

98. Douglas W. Hayes, *Rhetorical Subversion in Early English Drama* (New York: Peter Lang, 2004).

99. David Ellis, 'Falstaff and the Problems of Comedy', *Cambridge Quarterly*, 34 (2005), 95–108.

100. Joachim Frenk, 'Falstaff erzählen und zeigen', *Wissenschaftliches Seminar Online* 3 (2005), 16–23 (www.shakespeare-gesellschaft.de/publikationen/seminar/ausgabe2005. html, accessed 24 March 2011).

101. Norman N. Holland, '"The barge she sat in": Psychoanalysis and Diction', *PsyArt: An Online Journal for the Psychological Study of the Arts* (2005) (www.clas.ufl.edu/ipsa/journal/2005_holland09.shtml#holland09, accessed 24 March 2011).

102. Bert Cardullo, 'One Dramatic Character, Two Artistic Media: Shakespeare's Falstaff in Drama and Film', *Lamar Journal of the Humanities*, 31:2 (2006), 43–68.

103. Michael Steppat, 'Globe of Sinful Continents: Desires in the Henriad', in *Anglistentag: 2005 Bamberg Proceedings*, ed. Christoph Houswitschka, Gabriele Knappe and Anja Müller (Trier: Wissenschaftlicher Verlag Trier, 2006), pp. 145–58.

104. David Ellis, *Shakespeare's Practical Jokes: An Introduction to the Comic in His Work* (Lewisburg, PA: Bucknell University Press, 2007).

105. Isabel Karremann, '"Drinking of the wyne of forgetfulnesse": The Ambivalent Blessings of Oblivion and the Early Modern Stage', *Wissenschaftliches Seminar Online* 6 (2008), (www.shakespeare-gesellschaft.de/publikationen/seminar/ausgabe2008/karremann.html, accessed 24 March 2011).

106. Christopher Ivic, 'Reassuring Fratricide in *1 Henry IV*', in *Forgetting in Early Modern English Literature and Culture: Lethe's Legacies,* ed. Christopher Ivic and Grant Williams (London: Routledge, 2004), 99–109.

107. Wolfgang Klooss, 'Feasting with Falstaff: Luxus und Verschwendung im kulinarischen Diskurs von Shakespeares England', in *Texting Culture – Culturing Texts: Essays in Honor of Horst Breuer*, ed. Anja Müller-Wood (Trier: Wissenschaftlicher Verlag, 2008), pp. 71–91.

108. Elena Levy-Navarro, *The Culture of Obesity in Early and Late Modernity: Body Image in Shakespeare, Jonson, Middleton, and Skelton* (New York: Palgrave Macmillan, 2008).

109. Christopher M. McDonough, '"A mere scutcheon": Falstaff as *Rhipsaspis*', *Notes and Queries*, 55 (2008), 181–83.

110. Karen Marsalek, 'Marvels and Counterfeits: False Resurrection in the Chester *Antichrist* and *1 Henry IV*', in *Shakespeare and the Middle Ages,* ed. Curtis Perry and John Watkins (Oxford: Oxford University Press, 2009), pp. 217–40.

111. Valerie Traub, *Desire and Anxiety: Circulations of Sexuality in Shakespearean Drama* (London: Routledge, 1992).

112. Phyllis Rackin, 'Historical Difference/Sexual Difference', in *Privileging Gender in Early Modern England*, ed. Jean R. Brink (Kirksville, MO: Sixteenth Century Journal Publishers, 1993), pp. 37–63.

113. J. L. Simmons, 'Masculine Negotiations in Shakespeare's History Plays: Hal, Hotspur, and "the foolish Mortimer"', *Shakespeare Quarterly*, 44 (1993), 440–63.

114. Marvin B. Krims, 'Hotspur's Antifeminine Prejudice in Shakespeare's *1 Henry IV*', *Literature and Psychology*, 40 (1994), 118–32.

115. John W. Crawford, 'Secondary Wisdom: The Role of Women as Mentors in Shakespeare's Plays', *The Learning, Wit, and Wisdom of Shakespeare's Renaissance Women*, ed. John W. Crawford (Lewiston, NY: Mellen, 1997), pp. 63–93.

116. Jean E. Howard and Phyllis Rackin, *Engendering a Nation: A Feminist Account of Shakespeare's English Histories* (London: Routledge, 1997).

117. Anne Larue, 'La fantasme de la terre-mère dans trois pièces de guerre: *Les Perses, 1 Henry IV, Les Paravents*', in *Théâtres de la guerre: La mise en scène de la guerre dans Les Perses d'Eschyle, la première partie de Henry IV de Shakespeare, Les Paravents de Genet* (Paris: Klincksieck, 2001), pp. 79–103 and Anne Larue, *A la guerre comme au théâtre: Les Perses, Henry IV, Les Paravents* (Paris: Editions du Temps, 2000).

118. Cheang Wai-fong, 'Laughter, Play, and Irony: Rereading the Comic Space in Shakespeare's Second tetralogy', *NTU Studies in Language and Literature*, 10 (2001), 51–74.

119. Madalina Nicolaescu, *Meanings of Violence in Shakespeare's Plays* (Bucharest: Editura Universitatii Bucuresti, 2002).

120. Donald K. Hedrick, 'Male Surplus Value', *Renaissance Drama*, 31 (2002), 85–124.

121. Barbara Mather Cobb, ' "Suppose that you have seen the well-appointed king": Imagining Succession in the Henriad', *Cahiers Élisabéthains* 70 (2006), 33–38.

122. Roberta Barker, 'Tragical-Comical-Historical Hotspur', *Shakespeare Quarterly*, 54 (2003), 288–307.

123. Michael Mangan, *Staging Masculinities: History, Gender, Performance* (Basingstoke: Palgrave Macmillan, 2003).

124. Richard W. Grinnell, 'Witchcraft, Race, and the Rhetoric of Barbarism in *Othello* and *1 Henry IV*', *Upstart Crow*, 24 (2004), 72–80.

125. Harry Berger, Jr., 'A Horse Named Cut: *1 Henry IV*, 2.1.', in *Renaissance Historicisms: Essays in Honor of Arthur F. Kinney*, ed. James M. Dutcher and Anne Lake Prescott (Newark, DE: University of Delaware Press, 2008), pp. 193–205.

126. Karen Love, *Lies before Our Eyes: The Denial of Gender from the Bible to Shakespeare and Beyond* (Oxford: Lang, 2005).

127. Augustin Redondo, 'En torno a dos personajes festivos: El shakesperiano Falstaff y el cervantino Sancho Panza', in *Entre Cervantes y Shakespeare: Sendas del Renacimiento/Between Shakespeare and Cervantes: Trails along the Renaissance*, ed. Zenón Luis Martínez and Luis Gómez Canseco (Newark, DE: Juan de la Cuesta, 2006), pp. 161–82.

128. Frances K. Barasch, 'Harlequin/Harlotry in *Henry IV, Part One*', in *Italian Culture in the Drama of Shakespeare and His Contemporaries: Rewriting, Remaking, Refashioning*, ed. Michele Marrapodi (Aldershot: Ashgate, 2007), pp. 27–37.

129. Christian M. Billing, *Masculinity, Corporality, and the English Stage 1580–1635* (Aldershot: Ashgate, 2008).

130. Vin Nardizzi, 'Grafted to Falstaff and Compounded with Catherine: Mingling Hal in the Second tetralogy', in *Queer Renaissance Historiography: Backward Gaze*, ed. Vin Nardizzi, Stephen Guy-Bray and Will Stockton (Farnham: Ashgate, 2009), pp. 149–69.

131. E.A. Rauchut, 'Hotspur's Prisoners and the Laws of War in *1 Henry IV*', *Shakespeare Quarterly*, 45 (1994), 96–97.

132. Curtis C. Breight, *Surveillance, Militarism, and Drama in the Elizabethan Era* (Basingstoke: Macmillan; New York: St. Martin's Press, 1996).

133. Harry Berger, Jr., *Making Trifles of Terrors: Redistributing Complicities in Shakespeare*, ed. Peter Erickson (Stanford, CA: Stanford University Press, 1997).

134. Andreas Höfele, '"The great image of authority": Königsbilder in Shakespeare's Theatre', *Shakespeare Jahrbuch*, 133 (1997), 77–97.

135. Jean-Christophe Mayer, 'Pro Patria Mori: War and Power in the Henriad', *Cahiers élisabéthains*, 51 (1997), 29–46.

136. Avraham Oz, 'Nation and Place in Shakespeare: The Case of Jerusalem as a National Desire in Early Modern English Drama', in *Post-Colonial Shakespeares*, ed. Ania Loomba and Martin Orkin (London: Routledge, 1998), pp. 98–116.

137. James E. Berg, '"This dear, dear Land": "Dearth" and the Fantasy of the Land-Grab in *Richard II* and *Henry IV*', *English Literary Renaissance*, 29 (1999), 225–45.

138. Victoria M. Time, *Shakespeare's Criminals: Criminology, Fiction, and Drama* (Westport, CT: Greenwood, 1999).

139. Ian Ward, 'Shakespeare, the Narrative Community, and the Legal Imagination', in *Law and Literature*, ed. Michael Freeman and Andrew D. E. Lewis (Oxford: Oxford University Press, 1999), pp. 117–48.

140. Raphaëlle Costa de Beauregard, *Silent Elizabethans: The Language of Colour in the Miniatures of Nicholas Hilliard and Isaac Oliver* (Montpellier: Centre d'Etudes et de Recherches sur la Renaissance Anglaise, Université Paul Valéry – Montpellier III, 2000).

141. Bikang Huang, *Politics in Form: Imagery and Ideology in Shakespeare's History Plays* (Beijing: Peking University Press, 2000).

142. Nina S. Levine, 'Extending Credit in the *Henry IV* Plays', *Shakespeare Quarterly*, 51 (2000), 403–31.

143. Laetitia Coussement-Boillot, *Copia et cornucopia: La poétique shakespearienne de l'abondance* (Bern: Lang, 2008).

144. Glen Mynott, 'Chivalry, Monarchy, and Rebellion in Shakespeare's *Henry IV, Parts One and Two*', in *The Iconography of Power: Ideas and Images of Rulership on the English Renaissance Stage*, ed. György Endre Szonyi and Rowland Wymer (Szeged: IATE Press, 2000), pp. 147–60.

145. Albert Rolls, *The Theory of the King's Two Bodies in the Age of Shakespeare* (Lewiston: Mellen, 2000).

146. Lorna Hutson, 'Not the King's Two Bodies: Reading the 'Body Politic' in Shakespeare's *Henry IV*, Parts 1 and 2', in *Rhetoric and Law in Early Modern Europe,* ed. Victoria Kahn, and Lorna Hutson (New Haven, CT: Yale University Press, 2001), pp. 166–98. On the law in the *Henry IV* plays and elsewhere, see also Lorna Hutson, *The Invention of Suspicion: Law and Mimesis in Shakespeare and Renaissance Drama* (Oxford: Oxford University Press, 2007).

147. Lorna Hutson, '"Our old storehouse": Plowden's Commentaries and Political Consciousness in Shakespeare', *Shakespeare Yearbook*, 7 (1996), 249–73.

148. Jesse M. Lander, '"Crack'd crowns" and Counterfeit Sovereigns: The Crisis of Value in *1 Henry IV*', *Shakespeare Studies*, 30 (2002), 137–61

149. Walt Turner, 'Coins, Cons, and the Caduceus: The Making of a Sovereign in Shakespeare's *Henry Plays*', *Shakespeare and Renaissance Association of West Virginia: Selected Papers*, 27 (2004), 1–10.

150. Barbara Kreps, 'Power, Authority, and Rhetoric in Shakespeare's Lancastrians', in *The Complete Consort: Saggi di anglistica in onore di Francesco Gozzi*, ed. Roberta Ferrari and Laura Giovannelli (Pisa: Pisa University Press, 2005), pp. 63–76.

151. James Knowles, '*1 Henry IV*', in *A Companion to Shakespeare's Works*, ed. Richard Dutton and Jean E. Howard, 4 vols. (Oxford: Blackwell, 2003), 2: 412–31.

152. François Lecercle, '"Ne'er seen but wonder'd at": La mise en scène politique dans *Henry IV* de Shakespeare', in *Cité des hommes, cité de Dieu: Travaux sur la littérature de la Renaissance en l'honneur de Daniel Ménager* (Geneva: Droz, 2003), pp. 163–76.

153. Jennifer Low, *Manhood and the Duel: Masculinity in Early Modern Drama and Culture* (New York: Palgrave Macmillan, 2003).
154. Timothy Rosendale, 'Sacral and Sacramental Kingship in the Lancastrian Tetralogy', in *Shakespeare and the Culture of Christianity in Early Modern England*, ed. Dennis Taylor and David N. Beauregard (New York: Fordham University Press, 2003), pp. 121–40.
155. Clifford Davidson, 'The Coventry Mysteries and Shakespeare's Histories', *Shakespeare's Second Historical Tetralogy: Some Christian Features*, ed. Beatrice Batson (West Cornwall, CT: Locust Hill Press, 2004), pp. 3–25.
156. Uwe Klawitter, *Die Darstellung des einfachen Volkes in Shakespeares Dramen: Eine ideologiekritische Studie* (Trier: Wissenschaftlicher Verlag Trier, 2004).
157. Jesús López-Peláez Casellas, ' "And dressed myself in such humility": Honour and Disguising in Shakespeare's *1 Henry IV*', in *Masquerades: Disguise in Literature in English from the Middle Ages to the Present*, ed. Jesús López-Peláez Casellas, David Malcolm, Pilar Sánchez Calle (Gdansk: Wydawnictwo Uniwersytetu Gdanskiego, 2004), pp. 38–54.
158. David Ruiter, 'Harry's (In)Human Face', in *Spiritual Shakespeares*, ed. Ewan Fernie (London: Routledge, 2005), pp. 50–72.
159. Jean-Louis Claret, 'La prise de croix n'aura pas lieu: L'idée de croisade dans *Henry IV* de Shakespeare', in *Religious Writings and War/Les discourse religieux et la guerre*, ed. Gilles Teulié (Montpellier: Université Paul-Valéry, 2006), pp. 103–24.
160. Mark Taylor, 'Falstaff and the Origins of Private Life', *Shakespeare Yearbook*, 3 (1992), 63–85.
161. Joan Hartwig, ' "Mine honor's pawn": Gage-Throwing and Word-Play in Shakespeare's Second tetralogy', *CEA Critic* 68, (2006), 3–11.
162. David Quint, 'The Tragedy of Nobility on the Seventeenth-Century Stage', *Modern Language Quarterly*, 67 (2006), 7–29.
163. Stephen Dickey, 'The Crown and the Pillow: Royal Properties in *Henry IV*', *Shakespeare Survey*, 60 (2007), 102–17.
164. Patricia A. Cahill, *Unto the Breach: Martial Formations, Historical Trauma, and the Early Modern Stage* (Oxford: Oxford University Press, 2008).
165. Alicia Marchant, 'Cosmos and History: Shakespeare's Representation of Nature and Rebellion in *Henry IV Part One*', in *Renaissance Poetry and Drama in Context: Essays for Christopher Wortham*, ed. Andrew Lynch and Anne M. Scott (Newcastle: Cambridge Scholars, 2008), pp. 41–59.
166. Benedict Robinson, 'Harry and Amurath', *Shakespeare Quarterly*, 60:4 (2009), 399–424.
167. Alexander Welsh, *What Is Honor: A Question of Moral Imperatives* (New Haven, CT and London: Yale University Press, 2008).
168. Shawn Holliday, ' "Now for our Irish wars": Shakespeare's Warning against England's Usurpation of Ireland in the Lancastrian Tetralogy', *Pennsylvania English*, 20:2 (1996), 12–23.
169. Bradley Greenburg, 'Romancing the Chronicles: *1 Henry IV* and the Rewriting of Medieval History', *Quidditas*, 26–27 (2005–06), 34–50.
170. David Read, 'Losing the Map: Topographical Understanding in the Henriad', *Modern Philology*, 94 (1996–97), 475–95.
171. Terence Hawkes, 'Bryn Glas', *European Journal of English Studies*, 1 (1997), 269–90.
172. Christopher F. Highley, *Shakespeare, Spenser, and the Crisis in Ireland* (Cambridge: Cambridge University Press, 1997).
173. Claire Lamont, 'Shakespeare's Henry IV and "the old song of Percy and Douglas" ', in *Shakespearean Continuities: Essays in Honour of E. A. J. Honigmann*, ed. John Batchelor, Tom Cain, and Claire Lamont (Basingstoke: Macmillan, 1997), 56–73.

174. Bruce Avery, 'Gelded Continents and Plenteous Rivers: Cartography as Rhetoric in Shakespeare', in *Playing the Globe: Genre and Geography in English Renaissance Drama*, ed. John Gillies and Virginia Mason Vaughan (London: Associated University Presses, 1998), pp. 46–62.

175. Rees Davies, 'Shakespeare's Glendower and Owain Glym Dwr', *Historian*, 66 (2000), 22–25.

176. Matthew Greenfield, '*I Henry IV*: Metatheatrical Britain', in *British Identities and English Renaissance Literature*, ed. David J. Baker and Wily Maley (Cambridge: Cambridge University Press, 2002), 71–80.

177. Megan Lloyd, '*Speak it in Welsh': Wales and the Welsh Language in Shakespeare* (Lanham, MD: Lexington Books-Rowman and Littlefield, 2007).

178. Kate Chedgzoy, 'The Civility of Early Modern Welsh Women', in *Early Modern Civil Discourses*, ed. Jennifer Richards (Basingstoke: Palgrave Macmillan, 2003), pp. 162–82.

179. Joan Fitzpatrick, *Shakespeare, Spenser, and the Contours of Britain: Reshaping the Atlantic Archipelago* (Hatfield: University of Hertfordshire Press, 2004).

180. Lisa Hopkins, 'Welshness in Shakespeare's English Histories', in *Shakespeare's History Plays: Performance, Translation and Adaptation in Britain and Abroad*, ed. A. J. Hoenselaars (Cambridge: Cambridge University Press, 2004), pp. 60–74.

181. Andrew Murphy, 'Ireland as Foreign and Familiar in Shakespeare's Histories', in *Shakespeare's History Plays: Performance, Translation and Adaptation in Britain and Abroad*, ed. A. J. Hoenselaars (Cambridge: Cambridge University Press, 2004), pp. 42–59.

182. Peter Holland, 'Mapping Shakespeare's Britain', in *Spectacle and Public Performance in the Late Middle Ages and the Renaissance*, ed. Robert E. Stillman (Leiden and Boston: Brill, 2006), pp. 157–81.

183. Lloyd Kermode, *Aliens and Englishness in Elizabethan Drama* (Cambridge: Cambridge University Press, 2009).

184. Huw Griffiths, '"O, I am ignorance itself in this!": Listening to Welsh in Shakespeare and Armin', in *Shakespeare and Wales: From the Marches to the Assembly*, ed. Willy Maley and Philip Schwyzer (Farnham: Ashgate, 2010), pp. 111–26.

185. Megan Lloyd, 'Rhymer, Minstrel Lady Mortimer, and the Power of Welsh Words', in *Shakespeare and Wales: From the Marches to the Assembly*, ed. Willy Maley and Philip Schwyzer (Farnham: Ashgate, 2010), pp. 59–73.

CHAPTER FOUR

New Directions: The Madcap and Politic Prince of Wales: Ceremony and Courtly Performance in *Henry IV*

Alison Findlay

At a decisive moment of his career – the night before the Battle of Agincourt – Henry V, erstwhile madcap and politic Prince of Wales, stops to think about the ceremonial existence that now surrounds him at court:

> And what art thou, thou idol Ceremony?
> What kind of god art thou, that suff'rest more
> Of mortal griefs than do thy worshippers?
> What are thy rents? what are thy comings in?
> O Ceremony, show me but thy worth!
> What is thy soul of adoration?
> Art thou aught else but place, degree and form
> Creating awe and fear in other men? (*Henry V*, IV.i.228–35)[1]

Ceremony exists absolutely on the surface and in the immediate moment of enactment. Its full meaning is constituted by the diverse surface elements of which it is made, as Henry's speech goes on to detail: the form of words spoken (the 'titles blown from adulation'); the specific gestures enacted ('flexure and low bending'); the textiles and objects that are used (the 'intertissued robe', balm, sceptre, ball, mace); the positions of those enacting the ceremony and – often equally important – those participating as witnesses or spectators (the 'tide of pomp'); the place in which all these elements congregate and, finally, their precise orchestration according to a set pattern or form, such as in an entry to the royal presence, or an investiture as Prince of Wales.

Even as Henry V empties ceremony of significance, referring to it as an 'idol', whose essence, or 'soul', is no more than its constituent, superficial parts, he appreciates the importance of courtly ceremony as a means to create awe and fear among people. Indeed, this is something the character recognizes from his first soliloquy in *1 Henry IV;* it forms the basis of his strategy to 'imitate the sun', glittering 'like bright metal on a sullen ground' in order to 'show more goodly and attract more eyes' (I. ii.175–193). Chris Fitter points out the slippage between 'goodly' and 'godly' in Elizabethan ears,[2] which suggests that, from the beginning of his dramatic life, Hal/Henry is self- consciously constructing himself according to the post-Reformation model of kingship, where the monarch's sacred body is reconfigured through theatrical or ceremonial display. For Henry, the 'idol' ceremony is not an empty term. In the post-Reformation context in which the character speaks, it is an essential part of kingship. Paul Kleber Monod has argued that at the turn of the sixteenth century, monarchs could no longer simply claim that they embodied holiness as their predecessors had done; they needed to 'imitate it' and 'display it to their subjects' by means of rituals which proclaimed their divinely-sanctioned authority to rule.[3] Ceremony, which has been defined as a superficial or secondary form of ritual in which supernatural powers are not immediately invoked,[4] was thus an essential tool to re-connect the monarch with the divine. Henry recognizes 'the deep value of surfaces', to borrow a term from the philosopher of aesthetics, Richard Shusterman. As this discussion will explore, Shusterman's theories offer a useful set of tools for analysing how the representations of courtly ceremony might have worked in performances of *Henry IV.*

Shusterman argues that a surface – for example an entry to the royal presence – is experienced as a unique event in space and time by the participants but it also reaches beyond the site of enactment to a world elsewhere – a wider community across time and space and, in some cases, to a spiritual entity. The surface is immediate but invokes the presence of depth – emotionally, spiritually and historically via the weight of tradition. By marking off an event or object from its immediate context, the artistic frame of the ceremony intensifies its emotional and sensuous immediacy and simultaneously puts it in a larger socio-historical framework.[5] Ceremonies in the English royal court worked in precisely this way, invoking a tradition of divinely-sanctioned kingship. John Adamson and Fiona Kisby have persuasively demonstrated that the formal routines of the Tudor and Stuart royal households on ordinary days and holy days were still governed by ceremonies that were infused with liturgical symbolism.[6]

A ceremony on stage, however, is not a real ceremony but a fictional representation of an already framed act. It is thus doubly framed. How do we read such surfaces in *1 Henry IV*? They are obviously still spectacular events but do they carry any of the emotional, spiritual and historical charge of their originals when reproduced on stage? Critical studies have explored how theatre 'empties out' rituals and ceremonies of power and it is certainly possible to read *1Henry IV* as a negation or emptying out of the prodigal son paradigm, as Robert Hornback's essay (Chapter 6) does.[7] Nevertheless, it has also been argued that objects re-presented on stage can function as the materials of memory – carrying traces of their former existence that resonate with the actors and audiences who use or view them in their new theatrical context. I propose that courtly ceremonies in Shakespeare's play operate in this way: that the surface forms enacted on the stage retain a power like their originals, to invoke deep political, emotional and spiritual resonances for those present. Actors or audiences engage via their own anticipated, enacted or fantasy experiences of these rituals of royal authority.

The performance site changes the resonance of each courtly ceremony, of course. What would Henry V's lines on the 'idol' ceremony mean when pronounced at court in Whitehall Palace on 7 January 1605? What effect would his questions 'What are thy rents? what are thy comings in?' or his demand 'O Ceremony, show me but thy worth!' have created the night after the hugely extravagant *Masque of Blackness* was presented in the relatively insubstantial banqueting house made of canvas and wood? When the stage King Henry proclaimed 'Art thou aught else but place, degree and form / Creating awe and fear in other men?' in front of the ruling monarch, what did these lines mean?

My investigation of courtly ceremony in *1 Henry IV* will focus on its relation to the Jacobean court, examining the formal interview between King Henry IV and Prince Hal rehearsed in the tavern in Act II and then enacted at court in Act III, Scene ii. Since admission to the royal presence was strictly controlled, via a series of connecting courtyards and public rooms,[8] the play had 'populuxe' appeal, giving spectators in the public theatre the illusion of gaining privileged access to the monarch.[9] In performance at the Curtain and the Globe, the tavern scene's self-conscious play-acting acknowledges the fact that, for the majority of spectators, entry to the palace and to the monarch's presence was just as fantastic – and probably just as terrifying – as the play *King Cambyses* which Falstaff cites as his model. Chris Fitter's essay (Chapter 5) shows how Shakespeare's play dramatizes a difference between the court and the common people. The majority of common spectators in the public theatres are educated by the text. Prince Hal's behaviour teaches them a healthy scepticism about royalist appeals to their emotions, cautioning them against any identification with the 'sham respect of wooing lords' who will always banish plump

Jack and 'all the world' in the pursuit of an exclusive, courtly identity (II.v.438–39).

In public performances of Act III, Scene ii, a throne representing the state served as a focal point to illuminate the theatre's decorations – painted pillars, images on the tiring house wall, and elaborately-starred heavens – which alluded to the decorations of palaces. For spectators from the court, the prince's entrance to the presence amidst these surroundings may have evoked the dangerous excitement of their own hopes or memories of proximity to power. For those better acquainted with the tavern, the material props used by Falstaff and Hal – the chair, dagger, cushion-crown and cup of sack – would probably carry stronger associations with the potential to spill over into Act III, Scene ii and contaminate the appearance of the stage properties used for throne, sceptre and crown. Records of etiquette in the royal household book of Henry VIII show that the scene parodies occasions when the king made semi-public appearances in the chapel royal. Falstaff's selection of his crown, dagger, and cup of sack parodically mimic the crown and chalice of St Edward, still used in Tudor and Stuart royal processions to invest the monarch with the full sacred authority borne by monarchs of a bygone age.[10] Falstaff and Hal's idle ceremony in *1 Henry IV* subverts the early modern fragile illusion of 'idol ceremony' and painted pomp. In Jacobean revivals, Falstaff's debauched performance of monarchy could have been read in the context of the scandals of James's court, and ceremony could be shabby rather than glorious.

1 Henry IV seems to have been produced at court at least four times so it behoves us to speculate on what effects the play might have created there, in addition to registering how it teaches radical lessons to a public theatre audience, as Chris Fitter's chapter (Chapter Five) explores. The first recorded occasion of a court performance, over November and Christmas 1612, is an especially interesting event on which to construct an impression of the effects of a court performance. At Whitehall, its presentation in the Hall or Great Chamber in front of a royal audience offered very different surfaces against which to read the text. Both the Hall and the Great Chamber were rooms of some importance in the Tudor palace (the first place to which visitors on formal business were conducted). Their surfaces would have been lavishly decorated with painted and marbled finishes, tapestries with rich effects of gold and silver thread, and windows of coloured glass. John Astington points out that the plan for the investiture of Henry, as Prince of Wales, gives a likely impression of the arrangement of the auditorium for a court performance in the Hall or Great Chamber.[11] A wooden platform is erected for the state, from which the monarch watches at one end of the room. Raised wooden bench seating runs round the edge of the room, with boxes for other especially important spectators: the queen and her children (on the right of the state) and ambassadors and possibly senior courtiers or favourites (to the left). The rehearsal and presence scenes of *Henry IV* mirror this arrangement. Falstaff, the carnival king, proclaims, 'This chair shall be my state, this dagger my sceptre, and this cushion my crown' opposite the originals (II.v.344). Shortly afterwards, the actors playing the king and prince present more persuasive copies of regal ceremony with no qualifying metatheatrical reference to distinguish them from the royal spectators.

How might the doubling effects have worked in a court performance? William Sanderson's history of the reign of James gives the following description of the court as theatre and theatre at court:

> The splendor of the *King, Queen Prince and Princess* with the rest of the royall yssue, the concourse of strangers hither from forrein Nations, the multitude of our own people from all parts of our three Kingdoms gave a wonderfull glory to the Court, at this time, the only Theatre of Majesty; . . . .And it was prudentiall in state to set it forth, with all moderate additions of *Feasts, Masks, Comedies, Balls* and such like . . . . They are necessary *Mirrors*, wherein mens Actions are reflected to their own view. Indeed some men privy to the uglyness of their own guilt have been violent, not onely to crack but to break in pieces all those *Looking-glasses, least their own deformities recoyle, and become eye-sores to themselves.*[12]

The entertainments are a reflection of royal glory, but they can also, *Mousetrap*-like, turn the court's eyes critically upon itself. When its ceremonies are reproduced within the court walls with different actors, the King's Men offered the king (if he were present) and his courtiers the opportunity to re-view their actions – of formal supplication, welcome, admonishment and banishment – as though from the outside. A strong emotional undercurrent must have coloured the 1612 performance of *1Henry IV*. It was part of the traditional Christmas festivities, but this year the presentation of mirth and good cheer associated with Falstaff must also have been, to some extent, superficial in the wake of Prince Henry's sudden death on 6 November. Did Falstaff's line 'Weep not sweet Queen for trickling tears are vain', and his stage direction 'convey my tristful Queen | For tears do stop the floodgates of her eyes' (II.v.359–60) make reference to grief behind the tears of laughter? Or to a stage exit which mirrored Queen Anne's absence?

John Astington suggests that the Lord Chamberlain and Master of the Revels chose plays for the festive season that 'stayed clear of the sensitive matter of the death of princes', arguing that although an epic battle closes the play, it is dominated by the comic 'wit and exploits of the fat knight Falstaff' (Astington, p. 203). Its comedy would undoubtedly have been appropriate to the festive mood of the season in anticipation of the wedding between Frederick, Elector Palatine to James's daughter, Elizabeth. Nevertheless, in the wake of Prince Henry's death, many of the scripted exchanges between prince and king must have carried other weird resonances as well. In addition to Shakespeare's king, there are of course two more Henries in the play itself: the prince and Percy. Notably, the Chamber account lists the play as 'The Hotspurr' rather than the fat knight. Prince Henry has been just such a Hotspur, an 'infant warrior' or 'Mars in swaddling clothes' (III.ii.112–13), the blazing star of Protestant militarism. Far from lying 'respectfully dormant at court' in the performance of 1612, the politics of princely education in Shakespeare's script engages with a complex pattern of political and emotional negotiations between the king, the dead prince, the new heir apparent (Charles) and Prince Frederick.

From the perspective of courtly spectators, Hotspur's code of honour and Prince Hal's apparently prodigal nature must have evoked memories of the ambivalent nature of Prince Henry's royal identity as honourable hero and potential rebel. Immediately after his death he was celebrated as 'the flower of Knights | Mirrour of man-hood'; in eulogies collected by James Maxwell.[13] The King's Men's 1612 court performance of 'The Hotspurr', who boasts 'it were an easy leap | To pluck bright honour from the pale-faced moon' (I.iii.199–200), would surely have recalled Prince Henry's endless enthusiasm 'To vault and leap, to wrastle, ride and runne' in the 'arte of warre' (Maxwell, C2v.). The Crown prince's royal style appears to have been modelled on that of his namesake, Henry IV of France, whose public image emphasized personal charisma, masculine military prowess and an unflagging sense of energy and movement. It was very different to James I's strategy to recuperate the mystique of divinely-appointed monarchy through learned scriptural allusion, peacemaking and comparisons of himself to David and Solomon.[14] James apparently found the precocious militarism of Prince Henry threatening. The Venetian Ambassador had noted as early as 1607 that James was jealous 'to see his son so beloved and of such promise that his subjects place all their hopes in him'. After Henry's death, Sir John Holles lamented that his detractors told James that 'Absolom-like he might with better facility snatch the sceptre out of his father's fist'.[15] Performed in Whitehall, Henry IV's praise of Hotspur 'this Mars in swaddling clothes, | This infant warrior', and admonishment of his son in Act III, Scene ii, must have engaged with James's erstwhile insecurities about his son, and the French king before their deaths (Henry IV had been assassinated in 1610). The play's critical presentation of Hotspur's chivalric, military ideals collapsing to nothing more than 'food for worms' (V.i.85) may have offered a vindication of James's method of grounding British royal authority on scriptural models of wisdom and peace. Nevertheless, in a court immediately in mourning for the loss of Prince Henry, the player King Henry's fears that his degenerate heir was likely to 'fight against me' under Percy's pay (III.ii.126), were more likely to have had a poignant effect.

As a story of princely reformation, the courtly performance of *1 Henry IV* probably had even stronger associations the new heir apparent, Prince Charles. It seems almost ludicrous to compare the 'madcap' Hal with the reserved, sensitive Prince Charles, but they do share a similarity in being completely overshadowed by flamboyant brother figures. Prince Charles's gallant older brother was, like Hotspur, 'this same child of honour and renown', 'this all-praised knight' and, in the immediate aftermath of Prince Henry's death, Charles looked likely to remain unthought of, just as Hal felt (III.ii.139–41). On the night Henry died, James I sent a message to tell Prince Frederick, rather than Charles, that he would adopt him as a first-born son and presented him with the Order of the Garter previously worn by Henry.[16] In the Christmastide performance of *Henry IV,* Charles watched his fictional counterpart dutifully listen to the player king prefer Hotspur: 'Now by my sceptre and my soul to boot | He hath more worthy interest to the state | Than you, the shadow of succession' (III.ii.98–99). Shakespeare's prince robustly defends himself with the promise

> I will redeem all this on Percy's head
> And in the closing of some glorious day
> Be bold to tell you that I am your son. (III.ii.132)

For Charles and other spectators at the court performance, the story of the politic prince mapped out a route to recreate Charles as the 'illustrious hope of Great Britain'.[17] James Maxwell's 1612 verses argued that, after the death of Henry, any dream of future glory for Britain lay with Charles 'the choice of *Albion* | Whose towardeness doth tell he is another | Great-hearted Henrie' (B3). This 'tender toward Knight' had grace, wit, modesty and skill at running the ring, which would bring honour 'One day by his brave actes to Brittaine' (C2v). Perhaps the fat knight's assurance to Hal 'thou art essentially made without seeming so' (II.iv.449–50) gave the 'unthought of' spectator prince confidence.

Seventeenth-century accounts certainly saw him following Prince Hal's pattern of emerging like the sun from the 'base contagious clouds . . . to be more wondered at' (I.ii.185–87). Sir William Sanderson observed that

> whilst the Elder Brother Henry was hopeful to succeed, this *Prince* may be said to be the less looked upon . . . . directed by such as knew the forwardness of the former, to make himself rather less than he was, then to appear more than he should be . . . And it may be referred to his wisedome (not to his meekness) so far to comply with that Policy; And therefore we find him, the less apparent to open examination, till time and opportunity might present him to the publique.[18]

Similarly, Perrinchief notes that 'Some that at a distance looked upon the prince's actions, ascribed them to a Narrowness of Mind and an Incapacity of Greatness', while those who knew him better recognized his strategic choice 'to wait for a certain, though delayed Grandeur, rather then by the Compendious way of Contrasts get a precocious Power and leave too pregnant Example of ruine'.[19]

On 24 March 1616, the anniversary of James's accession, Charles was formally invested as Prince of Wales amid a wealth of pomp and ceremony in the Hall at Whitehall, possibly the same venue in which he had watched the politic prince promise to 'be bold to tell you that I am your son'. The fact that two subsequent performances of *1 Henry IV* took place at Whitehall on significant occasions (1 January 1625, the year in which Charles was to ascend the throne, and on 29 May 1639, the ninth birthday of his heir, Charles II), could suggest that the play's rituals of maturation held special significance for Charles. Indeed, the first court performance in 1612 may have been close to Charles's twelfth birthday, on 19 November.

A representation of *1 Henry IV* in a third playing space, the country house of Sir Edward Dering, brings another dimension to courtly performance in Shakespeare's play and perhaps makes a further comment on Charles's pathway to the crown. The script conflating Parts 1 and 2 of *Henry IV* was commissioned by Sir Edward Dering in Surrenden, Kent. The scribe, who was paid at the end of February 1623, faithfully copies the ceremonial interviews between Falstaff, Prince Hal and King Henry IV from the printed Quarto of *1 Henry IV*.[20] Since Dering's other printed texts and manuscripts (including a cast list) point to a tradition of domestic performance, it seems likely that the *Henry IV* MS was also prepared with a production in mind. Laetitia Yeandle has persuasively argued that the transcription was produced in January or early February 1623 and pointed out that Dering's account book also includes a payment of 17s 6d (a considerable sum) for 'ffor heads of haire and beardes' on 18 February 1623, perhaps to use in a performance?

Surrenden Dering Manor, which lies between Maidstone and Ashford, was rebuilt in 1631 and damaged by fire in 1952 making it difficult to recover any material traces of the surfaces against which *Henry IV* might have been performed. One change of surface we can be fairly confident about is the actors: how did that ceremonial exchange between father than son, king and heir apparent, fat knight and politic prince change when lines were spoken by members of the aristocracy (Sir Edward Dering and his circle of friends and family)? Such subjects were a lynchpin in the commonwealth, providing government at a local level. If Sir Edward Dering and his brothers took the roles of the royals and the fat knight, while neighbouring gentry, friends and tenants performed the rebels and the tavern, the formal exchanges could have been a reminder of the small ceremonies used every day to structure the little commonwealths of household and region in relation to each other and to the kingdom and the Court.

Sir Edward Dering was ambitious to improve his connections at Court, especially between the death of his first wife in 1622 and his remarriage to Anne Ashburnham, which made him a distant relative of the Duke of Buckingham. Could his preparation of the manuscript be connected to his courtly aspirations? Dering commissioned the manuscript at the same time Prince Charles and Buckingham conducted their incognito trip to Madrid to see the Infanta. As Sir Henry Wotton noted:

> They began their motion on Thursday the 18th of *February*, from the Marquesse his House of late purchase at *New Hall* in *Essex*, setting out with disguised Beards, and with borrowed names of *Thomas* and *John Smith*. And then attended by none but *Sir Richard Gresham*, Master of the Horse to the Marquess, and of inward trust about him.[21]

The party, also including Endymion Porter, made their way to Dover, from where they embarked on 19 February, 1623, the day after Dering had paid for 'ffor heads of haire and beardes'. Is it possible that the Dering prepared the manuscript – and the wigs and beards – for a visit by the prince and Buckingham, or in commemoration of their exploits? Surrenden Dering lay on one of the routes to Dover, though not on the way they finally took, via Canterbury. The date of the voyage was probably agreed in consultation with James whose lucky number was 19 since his children born on that day of the month (including Charles) had survived. If, somehow, Dering knew of the proposed trip, a performance of the conflated Parts 1 and 2 of *Henry IV* on 18 February would have been highly appropriate to mark a critical stage in Charles's path to the crown.

Did Dering envisage Charles and Buckingham as spectators of a gentry performance to celebrate the final Gad's Hill escapade in the politic prince's education? Certainly the events of the Spanish expedition broadly paralleled the path of Shakespeare's heir apparent. Having travelled in lowly disguise (though apparently not so concealed as to avoid detection from those who suspected), Charles blossomed into royal splendour on his arrival in Madrid. He ordered ornate clothing fit for a king, embroidered with gold and silver. He fashioned himself as the flower of chivalry, cropping the honours that had previously graced his elder brother's brows, and proudly displaying the insignia of the Order of the Garter on a bright, blue ribbon. James sent him 'the roabes of the Order, qwich you must not forgette to weare on St George's-daye'.[22] In spite of appearances, Charles's spectacular assumption of 'this new: and gorgeous garment majesty' (Dering MS Act V, Scene 10, line 3) must surely have carried elements of regret: memories of the brother whose place he had filled and the ailing father whom he must prepare to succeed. The Dering manuscript of *Henry IV* catered to the prince's retrospective and prospective viewpoints:

Yett weepe that Harryes dead and so will I:
But Harry Lives that shall convert these teares
By number into howers of happines. (Act V, Scene 10 lines 18–20)

declares Prince Harry, as if confidently fulfilling the hopes of glorious succession that Maxwell's verses of 1612 had identified in Charles: specifically the idea that he should be Henry's phoenix. The last words of the Dering manuscript belong to the prince: 'Vanityes Farewell; we'll now act deeds for Chronicles to tell'. As an elegant compliment to mark Charles's political maturity, the Dering manuscript of *Henry IV* styled the crown prince as a figure likely to make his mark as 'the mirror of all Christian kings' (*Henry V*, Chorus 2, line 6).

Charles's style of kingship did not follow the models suggested by any of his royal or dramatic predecessors. He was certainly not the warrior monarch like Henry IV, King of France, his elder brother Prince Henry, or Shakespeare's character Hotspur. Like his father, he refused to become involved in European religious battles until he was forced into this one. Instead he commissioned expensive paintings of himself in the role of Saint George that were displayed exclusively within the court rather than to his subjects.[23] Prince Hal's identity as a prodigal prince (and his father Bolingbroke's role in *Richard II*) offered a model of

'confessionalized' monarchy in which the king refashioned his authority by aligning himself with religious reformers and his subjects, presenting himself as a paradigm for personal and national moral reform.
Charles (like most monarchs of the time) rejected this, probably because
it would limit his sacral claims and royal authority.[24] Far from identify-
ing with his sinful subjects, or even following his father's style of Calvinist kingship, he aligned himself with Arminian theology (which
promoted the importance of human free will and pious acts as well as
divine grace and was regarded as too closely aligned with Catholicism
to be tolerated by Calvinists). This produced a Caroline model of kingship in which the monarch did indeed 'shine like bright metal on a sullen ground' but whose mirror of Christian kinship was so elitist and
self-referential that it proved brittle in a world where monarchy's sacred
signs could no longer function independently. The court performances
of *1 Henry IV* in 1612, 1625 and 1629 suggest it was a play peculiarly
fitted for a Prince of Wales to watch in a world where the sacred signs of
kingship were being differently refashioned by every monarch in
Europe, to recuperate some of their sacred power to legitimate royal
authority. In *1 Henry IV*, Douglas tells the king 'I fear thou art another
counterfeit | And yet, in faith, thou bear'st thee like a king' (V.i.34–35).
Charles's spectacularly theatrical self-representations, which paid little
attention to his subjects as audience, suggest that he had not heeded the
warnings of the Shrewsbury battlefield.

Notes

1. All Shakespeare references are to the texts in *The Norton Shakespeare,* ed. Stephen
   Greenblatt, et al. (London and New York: W. W. Norton, 1987)
2. See Chris Fitter, ' "The Devil Take Such Cozeners": Radical Shakespeare in *1 Henry
   IV*', Chapter Five.
3. Paul Kleber Monod, *The Power of Kings: Monarchy and Religion in Europe 1589–1715*
   (New Haven, CT: Yale University Press, 1999), p. 83.
4. See, for example, Max Gluckman and Mary Gluckman, 'On Drama, Games and Athletic
   Contests', in *Secular Ritual,* ed. Sally F. Moore and Barbara Meyerhoff (Amsterdam: Van
   Gorcum, 1977), pp. 227–43 (p. 231), and Richard Firth, *Tikopia Ritual and Belief*
   (Boston: Beacon Press, 1967), who writes 'whereas other ritual procedures are believed
   to have a validity of their own, ceremonial procedures, while formal in character, are
   not believed in themselves to sustain the situation or effect a change in it' (p. 13).
5. Richard Shusterman, *Surface and Depth: Dialectics of Criticism and Culture* (Ithaca,
   NY: Cornell University Press, 2002), p. 1.
6. John Adamson, *The Princely Courts of Europe: Rituals, Politics and Culture under the
   Ancien Regime 1500–1750* (London: Weidenfeld and Nicholson, 1999), Fiona Kisby,
   ' "When a King Goeth a Procession": Chapel Ceremonies and Services, the Ritual Year
   and Religious Reforms at the Early Tudor Court', *Journal of British Studies,* 40:1
   (2001), 44–75, and Fiona Kisby, ed., 'Religious Ceremonial at the Tudor Court:
   Extracts from Royal Household Regulations', in *Religion, Politics and Society in*

Sixteenth Century England, ed. Ian W. Archer, et al., Camden Fifth Series, Volume 22 (London: Royal Historical Society Publications, 2003), pp. 1–34.

7. 'Falstaffian "Gross Indecorum," "Contrarietie," and Arrested Prodigality: Anachronism and Colliding Generational Sensibilities in *1 Henry IV*, Chapter Six.

8. Severe punishments operated for disorder in the Presence chamber. For example, it was decreed that that anyone using 'anie worde of reprouche whereby a quarrell may arise' was to be fined and imprisoned for 4 months (or 8 months for Presence Chamber or beyond) and banished from court for a year. See G. P. V. Akrigg, *Jacobean Pageant: The Court of James I* (London: Hamish Hamilton, 1962), p. 250.

9. The theory of populuxe theatre is developed by Paul Yachnin in Anthony B. Dawson and Paul Yachnin, *The Culture of Playgoing in Shakespeare's England* (Cambridge: Cambridge University Press, 2001) and refined in ' "The Perfection of Ten": Populuxe Art and Artisanal Value in *Troilus and Cressida*', *Shakespeare Quarterly*, 56 (2005), 306–27.

10. See Kisby 'When a King Goeth a Procession' and 'Religious Ceremonial', and for more on the coronation ceremony see Alice Hunt, *The Drama of Coronation: Medieval Ceremony in Early Modern England* (Cambridge: Cambridge University Press, 2008), pp. 24–25.

11. John H. Astington, *English Court Theatre 1558–1642* (Cambridge: Cambridge University Press, 1999), pp. 45–46, 48–49 (Plate 4).

12. William Sanderson, *A Compleat History of the Lives and Reigns of Mary, Queen of Scotland, and of Her Son and Successor, James the Sixth, King of Scotland* (London: H. Meseley, R. Tomlins and G. Sawbridge, 1658), pp. 366–67.

13. James Maxwell, *The Laudable Life and Deplorable Death of Our Late Peerless Prince Henry* (London: Thomas Pavier, 1612), B2v.

14. See Monod, *Power of Kings*, p. 95–97 for further information on the relationship between Henry IV of France and King James, and Roy Strong, *Henry Prince of Wales and England's Lost Renaissance* (London: Pimlico, 2000) for Prince Henry's use of the French king as a model.

15. Sir John Holles to Lord Gray, HMC Portland IX , and *Relazione* of 1607 Nicolo Molin *CSP Venetian* 1603–07, pp. 513–14, cited in Roy Strong, *Henry Prince of Wales* , pp. 3 and 9. Maxwell neatly captures and deflects the allusions to Prince Henry as Absolom:

> So far was he inclin'd not to rebell
> With Absalom, who hellishly did aime
> His King and father to expell:
> So far I say was Henry from this straine
> That from his cradle to his mournfull end
> He never did his father once offend. (B2v)

16. Charles Carlton, *Charles I: The Personal Monarch* (London: Ark Paperbacks, 1983), p. 14.

17. Thomas Middleton, *Civitatis Amor* (London: Thomas Archer, 1616).

18. Sir William Sanderson, *A Compleat History* p. 1 (B1v).

19. Richard Perrinchief, *The Royal Martyr, or, The History of the Life and Death of King Charles I* (London: R. Royston, 1676), p. 4.

20. See Laetitia Yeandle, 'The Dating of Sir Edward Dering's Copy of "The History of Henry King the Fourth" ', *Shakespeare Quarterly*, 37 (1986), 224–26. Quotations from the manuscript are from *William Shakespeare, 'The History of King Henry the Fourth' As Revised by Sir Edward Dering*, ed. George Walton Williams and G. B. Evans (Folger Shakespeare Facsimiles: University of Maryland Press, 1974).

21. Sir Henry Wotton, *Reliquiae Wottonianae,* 4th ed. (London, B. Tooke & T. Sawbridge: 1685), pp. 214–16.

22. Lesley Ellis Miller, 'Dress to Impress: Prince Charles Plays Madrid, March–September 1623', in *The Spanish Match: Prince Charles's Journey to Madrid, 1623,* ed. Alexander Samson (Aldershot: Ashgate, 2006), pp. 27–50 (pp. 39–40).

23. Monod, *Power of Kings,* pp. 105–07 describes how Charles's remoteness from the people and rejection of warrior kinship undermined his own position.

24. See Monod, *Power of Kings,* p. 53 for a discussion of confessionalization as a royal style.

CHAPTER FIVE

New Directions: 'The Devil Take Such Cozeners!': Radical Shakespeare in *1 Henry IV*

Chris Fitter

'Suspicion all our lives shall be stuck full of eyes' (V.ii.8)

One minute or less into *1 Henry IV*, there arrives an arresting definition of agency. King Henry's speech deploring civil conflict specifies not subjects, countrymen, or soldiers but 'eyes', that 'of one substance bred | Did lately meet in the intestine shock | And furious close of civil butchery'.[1] These 'opposèd eyes', he hopes, will now 'March all one way, and be no more opposèd | Against acquaintance, kindred and allies' (I.i.9, 11–16). Those traumatizing eyes, close and butchering and still on the march, are a matter of more than an apparently quaint synecdoche: for a warfare of the deadly gaze accurately figures a world of hostile espials, of potentially lethal social penetrations, active at the heart both of the play, and of the political climate of contemporary London.

Remarkably, the crises of that precise juncture – *1 Henry IV* was almost certainly written and first performed somewhere between the later part of 1596 and the autumn of 1597 – have yet to be taken fully into account in mapping the tense political co-ordinates of this drama. For this was a time of an almost unprecedented and semi-hysterical government surveillance of commoners: and it proved, for any mutinous-seeming pauper or labourer, apprentice or servant, a bloody period of immediate whippings on the open street, and even a killing season in the many months when martial law was unleashed. 'Majesty might never yet endure | The moody frontier of a servant brow' (I.iii.18–19) summed up the new authoritarian intolerance. Martial law had been imposed in July 1595; and in early 1596 two Provost-Marshals were created – 'mobile executioners', as Curtis Breight calls them [2] – each with a dozen armed attendants *en suite*, to patrol the London streets, empowered in the words of the proclamation of July 1595 'without delay to execute upon the gallows by order of martial law'.[3] 'If the devil and mischance look big upon [us]' (IV.i.58–59), the poorer commons knew, the gaze of authority could thus mean immediate lynching. 'On my face he turned an eye of death' (I.iii.143) was thus scarcely an alarm confined to Hotspur. Dread of *l'oeil farouche* of vengeful central power – '[We] durst not come near your sight' (V.i.63) –was a state of mind shared by the London masses with the drama's rebels.

For the violent paranoia of the ruling classes, panicked by metropolitan scenes of large-scale popular rebellion, had successfully engineered in the lower orders a symmetrical paranoia. 'Affrighted with their bloody looks' (I.iii.104), both poles of a sharply divided society, each of which had recently tasted blood, now feared the worst. The threatening mutuality of 'opposèd eyes' owed much to a dramatic new escalation of class tensions. Such was the scale of upper-class alarm that, as one London official, the wardmote of Tower ward, expressed it in 1597

> Yt will come to pass yt the people will shortly growe careless of lawes & maiestrates, and in thend fall to flat disobedience & open contempt whereof we do percieve & fynd to our greatte greafes a marvelous inclynacion & beginning already.[4]

Bringing governing-class anxiety to that boiling point was popular reaction to the series of failed harvests from 1594–97 – among the most disastrous harvests in English agrarian history. 'It is difficult to exaggerate the extent to which people in the late sixteenth and early seventeenth century were conscious of the threat of dearth', write John Walter and Keith Wrightson. This was 'the spectre which haunted early modern Europe, one of the principal factors contributing to the profound insecurity of the age'.[5] Even in London, beneficiary of foodstuffs impounded from the provinces, 1597 saw a sharp rise in the number of burials across seven of the poorer intramural parishes.[6] The impact of the failed harvests on a city whose population had doubled between 1580 and 1600

> more than doubled the price of wheat and carried that of barley, oats, peas and beans, the food of the poor, proportionately even higher. Probably for the first time in Tudor England large numbers of people in certain areas died of starvation.[7]

In consequence, notes historian Jim Sharpe, the dearth 'had become central to the poor's consciousness and to their conversation . . . [generating] a continual undercurrent of adverse comment among the lower orders'.[8] In September 1596, for example, Somerset J. P. Edward Hext wrote to Burghley that there were many in his area who 'especyally in this time of dearthe' were encouraging their fellows 'to all contempte bothe of noble men and gentlemen, contynially bussynge into there eares that the ritche men have gotten all into their hands and will starve the poore'.[9] In London, such was the climate of popular vitriol against well-fed authority – rumoured to be exacerbating the dearth for private profit – that a royal proclamation was eventually issued, in September 1597, to defend against slander the lord mayor, the Privy Council, 'and any public person who shall be appointed under her majesty for the good government of her highness' people'. Such 'untrue and slanderous report . . . raised by evil-disposed and malicious persons' would be met, the proclamation threatened, with 'some severe punishment' (Hughes and Larkin, vol. 3, pp. 182–83). Henry IV refers with like anxiety of contempt to 'poor discontents' and 'moody beggars, starving for a be time | Of pell-mell havoc and confusion' (V.i.81–82). Yet, in a Latin tag still current, *venter non habet aures*: the stomach has no ears. As stories reached London of cannibalism in the north of England, and as the cost of the poor's staple diet shot up – 'Poor fellow never joyed since the price of oats rose. It was the death of him' (II.i.11–12) – politically edged complaint was irrepressible.

If the threat of the gallows – or 'some severe punishment' – could hang over demonstration of political embitterment, this was because the summer of 1595 had produced around 13 insurrections and food riots around London. They had culminated in that explosion of popular insurrection known as the Apprentices' Riot of 29 June, when a crowd of a thousand or more apprentices, mixed with angry soldiery, tore down pillories, marched on Tower Hill, and drove back the watch.[10] In the aftermath, a very shaken Privy Council arrested five apprentices, then had them hanged, drawn and quartered. Martial law was imposed on 4 July. ('For now, these hot days, is the mad blood stirring', shivers a fearful Benvolio in *Romeo and Juliet* [III.i.4], written between 1595–96.) Anonymous seditious 'libels' were scattered about the city following the executions: a form of political incitation often composed or tossed into alehouses.[11] The government countered swiftly with a propaganda tract of its own, *A Student's Lamentation* (1595), which piously justified the apprentices' execution, and sought anxiously to dissuade disaffected youth from further protest. It also appealed for informers. 'If any trecherous insinuater goe about to intice you to insurrection: if any idle headed libeller scatter papers amongst you, winne never dying praise by detecting them.'[12] Demonizing allegedly idle and ungoverned under-class youth under the blanket term of 'apprentices', it prayed

> Lord roote them from this Citie and Suburbs, and put in the
> Magistrates heads to punish them with more and more severitie:
> for these and their companions are causes of all mutinies: and it is
> miraculous they have not long since wrought some great mischiefe.[13]

The later 1590s indeed saw, as Sharpe records, 'an intensification of the use of the death penalty' by assize judges, 'anxious to make examples'.[14]

In consequence, from July 1595, London's lower classes were squeezed between dearth-driven grievances and savage government reprisals, between malnutrition and martial law, as punitive authorities stepped up the watch for 'danger and disobedience in thine eye' (I.iii.16). It is essential, I would argue, to recall the extensiveness of that chilling machinery of surveillance surrounding labouring people, and the cor-relative dread of sudden betrayal, if we are to recuperate political struc-tures of feeling foundational to *1 Henry IV*.

The *Lamentation*, we saw, sought to entice youthful informants. The government, moreover, possessed already two espionage networks, headed, respectively, by Burghley and Essex: 'a hotch-potch of desper-ate Catholics, disbanded soldiers, failed priests, moonlighting mer-chants, and gentlemen-adventurers of no fixed abode'.[15] This 'shifting mass of freebooters' produced 'a culture of widespread informers', eager for cash reward, notes Breight. The term 'intelligencer', signifying a spy, was a coinage of the late sixteenth century. Paid informers were placed even in prisons like the Marshalsea, to play the role of fellow-prisoners; and *agents provocateurs* haunted the book stalls around St Paul's, seek-ing entrapment of religious malcontents.[16] Government men sprang surprise searches periodically on homes, alehouses and outbuildings, searching out criminals and anyone suspicious. Such 'general searches', observes Erickson, 'threw the city into panic . . . Any "unknown men" – those without certain employment or reliable friends or connections – were seized and locked in churches while the raid went on to its end'.[17] This kind of terrifying punitive eruption must clearly have impacted audience response when Bardolph rushes into the Eastcheap tavern crying 'O, my lord, my lord, the sheriff with a most monstrous watch is here at the door', and the Hostess ('O Jesu, my lord, my lord!') reports 'They are come to search the house' (II.iv.465, 469, 472). Welles's film, *Chimes at Midnight*, with its inrush of armed men and baying dogs on leashes, catches superbly the violence of such an incursion with the panicked fleeing it generated.

The governors of Bridewell, too, were vested with sweeping powers to search in London and Middlesex and with discretionary powers of punishment. In practice these powers were used against vagrants, disorderly servants, sexual offenders, and an assortment of other offenders against community norms, such as scolds, barrators, and drunks. The offenders were subject to short, sharp shock treatment of incarceration for average periods of a month and work discipline (beating hemp, scouring City ditches, dredging the Thames, and the like), punctuated by regular whippings.

Constables were instructed 'to make fortnightly searches of alleys for inmates', that is, illegal subtenants.[18] Godly reformism added a further dimension to punitive underclass surveillance, as officialdom sought to destroy the traditional culture of popular revelry by prosecuting men and women caught dancing, drinking, fornicating and even harbouring unmarried pregnant women.[19] Enforcing these new oligarchic values being imposed on London, churchwardens and their assistants seized moral offenders from alehouses or their homes for presentment to church courts. Churchwardens 'failing to present such reprobate cases might themselves be prosecuted.[20] In Southwark, from 1594, churchwardens were supplemented by members of the poor themselves, recruited as 'surveyors' and paid to expose among their fellows any harbouring inmates, presenting them to the wardmote inquest. Records show that they 'executed their offices with zeal, hustling inmates out of the parish . . . snooping into the morals of the poor, noting those who kept victualling' (i.e., alehouse keepers).[21] London aldermen had even issued orders earlier in the reign, presumably given only desultory implementation, that the poor 'were to be visited daily by a member of the vestry to determine whether they were working.[22]

Deeply alarmed by London's spirited youth culture – the two new Marshals of 1596 were to suppress 'any further distemperature that may arise by youth' – and obsessed with fear of incoming itinerant hordes, legislation of 1593 and 1598 ensured that 'whipping posts appeared all over London, and payments in accounts show that they were regularly used in ensuing years'.[23] Breight's characterization of 'the final two decades of Elizabeth's reign as a kind of McCarthyist era, frequently highlighted by dismemberment' would therefore seem particularly appropriate to the mid-nineties.[24]

'Trust nobody, for fear you be betrayed' Buckingham had counselled in *2 Henry VI* (IV.iv.57). 'Trust none', the departing Pistol would advise Mistress Quickly in *Henry V* (II.iii.42). 'I wonder men dare trust themselves with men' reflects Apemantus, the philosopher, in *Timon* (I.ii.42). Harassed by a near-ubiquity of invidious surveillance, and menaced by fears of surprise denunciation, caught between opposèd eyes and dread of an empty belly, the earliest spectators of *1 Henry IV* at the Theatre or the Curtain would have had little difficulty sympathizing with the position of those who had incurred the mistrust of the king:

> Suspicion all our lives shall be stuck full of eyes . . .
> Look how we can, or sad or merrily,
> Interpretation will misquote our looks (V.ii.8, 12–13)

From the world of whipping posts, hostile prying and embittered malnutrition, the poorer commons retreated to the refuge that seemed increasingly to be 'setting itself up as the stronghold of a populist community, beyond the writ of the ruling classes': the alehouse.[25] As historian Peter Clark recounts in his definitive study, labourers, small craftsmen, droves of young people, and during periods of economic distress, middling-level tradesmen and craftsmen too, went regularly to the alehouse: not only 'in search of alcoholic release', but because the alehouse increasingly provided a set of services which helped the poor survive.[26] Providing cheap food in small quantities, ale supplying vital nutrients to the malnourished, an outlet for poached or stolen consumables, and lodgings for poorer travellers, runaway servants and apprentices, not to mention entire families of vagrants, the 'victualling house' offered also news of local employment possibilities, as well as credit and pawnbroking in desperate years.[27] It became in fact a kind of alternative economic centre for poorer people, with unregulated sale of food, clothing, salt, candles and even forged passports.[28] Though its core constituency came from the lower half of society, merchants, yeomen, clergymen and gentlemen could also be found there: dropping in to enjoy the possible piping, fiddling, dancing, bowling, football, card games, seasonal entertainments, feasting and even plays that might be found there, as these pastimes, driven from churchyard and open streets by the new respectability, gradually relocated within its walls and yard.[29] Alehouses were often run by women, and alehouse brothels sprang up.[30] Political news and gossip were exchanged in the alehouse, and irreligious jesting, savoured. From the tippling house attacks both verbal and literal might come upon constables and bailiffs, and riots would be planned there.[31] Poaching bands would organize in the alehouse's provision of cross-class anti-authoritarian impulse.[32] Unsurprisingly, then, the alehouse accrued a reputation for brewing crime and sedition along with its ale; and in this bulwark against officialdom, disaffected speakers hoped, in the words (once again) of the drama's rebels, to 'keep aloof from strict arbitrament, | And stop all sight holes, every loop from whence | The eye of reason may pry in upon us' (IV.i.70–72). 'The communal world of the tippling den', concludes Clark, free of the involvement of the well-to-do, appeared to reinforce class solidarity among the lower orders. From here, or so it seemed, it was only a short step to the alehouse functioning as the command post in a war against church and state.[33]

In these 'nests of satan', alleged magistrates and the godly, 'idle and discontented speeches' proliferated.[34] 'When the drunkard is seated upon the ale-bench and has got himself between the cup and the wall' fumed John Downame [in 1613], 'he presently becomes a reprover of magistrates, a controller of the state, a murmurer and repiner against the best established government'.[35]

Yet for the young, the festive and the economically disadvantaged, the alehouse meant a heartland of animated fellowship and restorative goodwill in a society reneging on traditional neighbourly values and the old bonds of commensality. Ballads on alcoholic 'good fellowship' abounded in the period; and 'good neighbourliness', an imperilled social virtue, would be frequently celebrated there with flowing toasts.[36] Indeed, the sharper the suffering inflicted by outrageous food prices, aggressive officials and daily fear on the whipping streets, the more needed the refuge of human warmth, sympathetic class solidarity and roistering counter-abuse of governors and church, as harassed workers 'doffed the world aside | And bid it pass' (IV.i.96–97). In consequence, the rebels of *1 Henry IV*, opposing a king who was scaldingly abusive of underclass revelry ('Such poor, such bare, such lewd, such mean attempts, | Such barren pleasures, rude society', III.ii.13–14) and who had, furthermore, foregone his 'seeming brow of justice' in violating his populist promise to reform 'strait decrees | That lie too heavy on the commonwealth' (IV.iii.79–80), must thus have garnered, as alarmed 'strangers to his looks of love' (I.iii.288), a ready underclass sympathy missed by modern readers. The very spirit of the alehouse, dancing at the edge of the precipice in the dark heart of the dearth, would be caught, in a remarkable twist of character, by seigneurial Hotspur:

Doomsday is near; die all, die merrily. (IV.ii.135)

And here, once more, mapping the precise historical juncture of *1 Henry IV* recovers, I suggest, crucial political overtones: for at the point in time when the drama was written and first performed, alehouses were being suppressed by the authorities. Though alehouses were subject customarily to the scrutiny of mistrustful officials, Archer reports that the 1590s saw 'no less than nine orders for a general review of alehouse licences compared to just six in the previous thirty years'.[37] Further, although the dearth made alehouses more necessary than ever to the poor – 'for many members of the lower orders, unable to afford high food prices, a pot of beer at the alehouse served as their principal source of nutriment' – a government crackdown was now forcing many of them shut down in precisely these, the worst of the dearth years.[38] For, from 1594, the fear that alehouse brewing was diverting the barley necessary for cheap bread, compounded by the dread, from the summer of 1595, that the victualling house might spark further unrest after the recent seismic riots, combined to send, as it were, the sheriff's men to the door of all London alehouses judged by authority to be 'unnecessary'.[39] Capping the stinging new curb on dangerous popular tippling, in the summer of 1596 beadles were dispatched to every household in the capital to deliver the command that no apprentice be allowed out of doors, between August and Michaelmas.[40] This was the very period, of course, when scholars believe *1 Henry IV* was taking shape.

The implications for the drama, with its delighting central scenes of boozy anti-establishment bonhomie, are not hard to perceive. Martial law and the class cold war, the intensifying suppression of tippling dens and the domestic confinement of apprentices, must all have charged the experience of the drama's bibulous merrymakings, at least for the audience's numerous youths and groundlings, with an even more joyous relish, heightening exultation in the unsubjugated flourishing of this menaced underclass Elysium. For the site of the drama's antics is a distinctively low-raftered establishment, at least as much the alehouse as the tavern. Though specifically referred to as a tavern, and supplying wine, unavailable in the alehouse, it is redolent in several ways of the underclass fastness of the victualling house. It is run, it seems, by a poor woman,[41] has bawds in attendance, and prominently features both lower-class clientele and their slang ('I can drink with any tinker in his language during my life', I.iv.17–18). It stages ritualized drinkings – 'dyeing scarlet' and crying 'hem' (14–15) – of the kind that Clark notes to be taking root in the late-sixteenth-century alehouse.[42] Falstaff's humour is consistently irreligious, a mini-drama is initiated, and the whole atmosphere one of gamesome anti-authoritarian freedom. The real-life Gad's Hill robbers of the 1590s, as audiences may have known, stayed in alehouses.[43]

Finally, and centrally, the carousing scenery emphasizes popular bonds of good fellowship, become almost cultic. Welcomed heartily, Prince Henry, lusty, mischievous and quaffing, is baptized into the ranks as 'a Corinthian, a lad of mettle, a "good boy"'. Accepted with trusting gusto, he will 'command all the good lads in Eastcheap' (II.iv.11–14). Gadshill refers with like subcultural pride to 'Trojans that thou dream'st not of', men of prowess in undertakings 'for sport's sake' (II.i.67–69). In the play's sequel, Falstaff will be said to sup, still, with 'Ephesians'

(II.ii.128). Such fellows, moreover, are definitively disaffected, for Gadshill's Trojans 'pray continually to their saint, the commonwealth' (II.i.77–78): the latter term being a kind of code for underclass economic grievance. 'Communal drinking as a way of celebrating good fellowship', records Clark, 'took on distinct class overtones, more sharply defined by the plight of the lower orders. One commentator noted how poor customers at the alehouse "strive so after community . . . They think it some ease and comfort in misery to have companions".[44]

Literary criticism has spoken often of the inheritance by the new professional London theatres of the medieval legacy of carnival, with its celebrative spirits, its sense of popular liberation and holiday license. Location in the Liberties, beyond the writ of London's Puritan governors, must have consolidated the sense of transgressive release, as spectators wound their way in Bankside and other Liberties among whorehouses and gambling dens to the 'gamehouse' or 'playhouse': terms interchangeable for much of the sixteenth century.[45] The theatre's liberty was, in Steven Mullaney's phrase, 'at once moral, ideological, and topological'.[46] Critics, however, neither commonly note nor consistently apply in analysis of Shakespeare's scripts the clear and considerable consonance between the carnivalesque gamehouse and the alehouse. Not only did both institutions offer intervals of cathartic release from rule-governed normalcy through irreverent populist recreation; each was subject to denigration by city fathers as a gathering-place of the idle, unruly and disaffected, each associated with rioting in the mind of the authorities – at the first hint of gathering disorder, theatres were shut down – and each offered a cross-class bonding in an allegedly godless institution stealing minds away from churches. Furthermore, not only do the lower orders appear, as an encircling sea of groundlings, to have dominated responsiveness in the gamehouses, and not only were large numbers of apprentices regularly present in the audiences. Once gathered within the gamehouse walls, I would argue, notwithstanding the range of ranks spanned by audience members, the sentiment easily prevailed in that holidaying crowd of a collective solidarity with the oppressed commons as against the threatening rich. For as recent historians have noted, this defensively binaristic way of thinking was developing with the economic polarization in the late century, could be shared even by the relatively well-to-do, and was especially marked in times of crisis and resistance. Thus Keith Wrightson has noted in the sixteenth century 'a dichotomous perception of society' that, in disregard of 'the fine-grained (and highly contested) distinctions of the hierarchy of degrees' generated a language which 'regroup[ed] the English into two broad camps . . . cleaving society into the haves and have nots'.[47] Andy Wood argues our need to recognize 'the continuing willingness of contemporaries to conceive of a simple division between "rich" and "poor" . . . Plebeian definitions of social conflict worked within a dualistic perception of society.'[48] 'It is notable', observes Wood, 'that in the rebellions of 1536, 1537 and 1549, otherwise wealthy farmers identified themselves as part of a "poor commons", a "commonality", an "estate of poorality", or simply as members of something they called "The Povertie". Likewise, labouring people often mobilized the language of community in defining social conflict.'[49] Though normally prosperous townsmen might define themselves through distinction from their inferiors, they could present themselves, when resisting upper-class authority, as members of 'the poor' or the 'trewe comons'. Consequently, 'Precisely who constituted "the commons" or "the rich" could vary greatly'.[50] In the hungry crisis years of 1595–97, and in the anti-authoritarian conditions of the public amphitheatres, the 'trewe comons' and the 'estate of poorality', the groundlings and the galleried, could become one in irreverent festive community: 'for the poor abuses of the time want countenance' (I.ii.148).

'Out upon this half-faced fellowship!' (I.iii.208)

Into the tavern flavoured by the 1596 alehouse – precious, affectionate, and menaced – comes bouncing the prince in Act I, Scene ii, parading his identity as habitué of revels and beloved 'sweet wag' (134) from the first. At the same scene's close, following much familiar jesting, commitment to an armed robbery, and enrolment in further practical joking, he lingers as his fellows depart: and then steps out of the storyline to gaze on the 2000 or more commoners, delighting in all this behaviour, surrounding the stage. 'I know you all', he announces, in the sudden, very public, silence.

'Go to. I know you well enough' Falstaff will sneer at the hostess, Mistress Quickly, at Act III, Scene iii, line 234. The phrase evidently stung: 'No, Sir John, you do not know me, Sir John. I know you, Sir John.' Whether or not it was current in those years as an accusatory formula used by superiors – even associated, perhaps, with exposure of crime and the pounce of the buff jerkin (worn by an arresting officer) with whose mention the prince alarmed Falstaff (I.ii.41) – the phrase is evidently cold-eyed.[51] It proves, indeed, pivotal, as gamester Hal turns to – turns on – his amicable fellow revellers in the gamehouse, and reveals opposèd eyes.

> I know you all, and will, awhile, uphold
> The unyoked humour of your idleness.[52] (I.ii.183–84)

Idleness was, of course, precisely the accusation levelled against frequenters of the alehouse and the theatre by the employing classes and antitheatricalist tracts. A letter of the Lord Mayor to Lord Burghley in November 1594 deplored 'playes, beeing the ordinary places of meeting for all vagrant persons and maisterless men that hang about the City': an accusation frighteningly reiterated in July 1597 in a petition to the Privy Council for the closure of all playhouses.[53] Youth and commoners should be yoked, by profitable employment; once slipped out from its restraints, they effectively become, in their seditious liberty, a banding of masterless men. Apprentices, as we have seen, had been recently denied escape into unyoked humour for 5 months; and the *Student's Lamentation* had been specific in attributing the great riots to unoccupied indolence, which fashioned the 'idle headed libeller'.[54] Parliament would soon move to prohibit, in an Act of 1603, tippling or sitting drinking for more than 1 hour, even in a man's own township.[55]

In this denunciatory climate, Henry declares, in direct audience address, that he recognizes, and will uphold (that is, support) its unyoked idleness: but only 'awhile'. Royal support of theatre was indeed highly provisional at this point: the amphitheatres would not only be closed automatically at signs of riot or with a substantial return of plague, but, under regular assault by London's Mayor and Corporation as nurseries of crime, were sustained only by a royal 'upholding', which could not be relied upon. The theatres had been closed due to plague during 1592–94. They had just been shut down again, by order of the Privy Council, from July to October 1596, allegedly owing to plague; and from August 1596, Shakespeare's company lost the title and protective status of the Lord Chamberlain's Men, as that title passed to Lord Cobham. As a letter of September 1596 by Thomas Nashe reveals, this was now a time of worrying vulnerability to a vindictive city government: 'now the players . . . are piteously persecuted by the L[ord] Mayor and the aldermen, and however in their old Lord's time they thought their state settled, it is now so uncertain that they cannot build upon it'.[56] On their face, in Hotspur's phrase, was turned an eye of death (I.iii.143). On 28 July 1597, there came the worst possible command from the Privy Council: following staging of an allegedly seditious drama, not only was all playing to cease, but the theatres themselves were to be pulled down. It would turn out, with time, that nothing worse would ensue from this than another lengthy stoppage of playing: this one from July until about 10 October. But late 1596 through 1597 was clearly a period when both playwright and audiences knew their beloved playhouse to be, like the London underclasses faced down by Provost Marshals, under pressures akin to siege from hostile civic authorities. Without princely upholding, playhouses were doomed.

Lest we doubt the prince's words in this passage to be deictic – addressed, that is, to the encircling spectators, rather than referring only to characters within the fiction – we should note, what I have argued at length elsewhere, that the language of vapour, breath and air function frequently in Shakespeare as contemptuous reference by socially elite characters to the immediate playhouse ambience: an allegedly reeking audience.[57] Contemporaries often remarked, as Andrew Gurr records, the smells of the playgoers – artisan mouths debouching odour of onion and garlic, tobacco fuming from pipes. Gurr cites Marston sneering in 1600, for an exclusive Paul's audience, at the odour and sticky clothing of lower-class audiences – [here] 'A man shall not be choakte | With the stench of Garlicke, nor be pasted | To the barmy Jacket of a Beer-Brewer' – and Gurr notes Dekker's references to the groundlings simply as 'the stinkards'.[58] Shakespearean allusion to air, breath and cloud thus may underscore passages of deixis whose language may suddenly confront or affront adjacent spectators, in varied processes of teasing, class condescension, or structural antagonization. Rosalind is explicit in the epilogue to *As You Like It*: were she a woman she would kiss 'as many of you as had . . . breaths that I defied not' (Epilogue, 16). Sworn foe of underclass immoralism, Angelo in *Measure for Measure* despises 'foolish throngs' whose massing will 'stop the air' of any they would assist (II.iv.24–26). Cleopatra fears being 'uplifted to the view' of lower-class audiences – 'mechanic slaves | With greasy aprons'. 'In their thick breaths, | Rank of gross diet, shall we be enclouded, | And forced to drink their vapour' (*Antony and Cleopatra*, V.ii.205–09). Thus, the amiable 'Hal', sweet wag, becomes himself breathtaking, as he coolly informs the surrounding throng that although he will, awhile, uphold their idleness, 'when he please again to be himself', he will permit no longer 'base, contagious clouds | To smother up his beauty'. The groundlings, of course, were both metaphorically base, as underclasses, and literally so, as standing below the speaking prince. Theatres were denounced, among other things, for contagion, for spreading feared diseases. Soon, Henry announces, he will '[break] through the foul and ugly mists | Of vapours that did seem to strangle him' (I.ii.186–91). The first nine lines of Prince Henry's deixis have thus engineered a stunning transformation of his identity in both play and playhouse, one all the more marked in those jumpy months of dearth-driven sedition, intensive post-riot surveillance, and the roaming of deadly Provost Marshals. Henry's sudden accusation of 'I know you all', coming from a scion of supreme power, evokes the surprise menace of intruding authority, so familiar to the contemporaries of government searches, prying vestrymen, snooping surveyors, invasive churchwardens, and bloodied beadles at their whipping posts. Stepping out of the cloak of camaraderie donned for surveillance, 'Hal' chills into a blunt, authority figure, giving judgement on the apprehended. Startlingly revealed as a traitor to pretended good fellowship, he must also have evoked the contemporary figure of the alehouse spy. His seven succeeding lines then unleash a string of upper-class insults ('base contagious clouds') at the many hundreds of poorer playgoers massed below him.

From this point, the sneering pseudo-populist appears to turn inward, away from spectator engagement into the roomy chambers of his narcissistic dreaming. Yet even there, the echo of alien and estranging values persists. 'If all the year were playing holidays', Henry will add – and the phrase allows the meaning of 'holidays when we can watch plays' – 'To sport would be as tedious as to work' (192–93). The work ethic has found an evangelist within the gamehouse. Henry then happily anticipates throwing off a behaviour which he characterizes as 'loose' (196), and looks joyfully forward to his 'reformation, glittering o'er [his] fault' (201). 'Reformation', of course, was a primary category of yearning in the lexicon of Puritanism, extolled in its national campaign against the reprobate masses and their sinfully festive culture. Celebration, moreover, of a 'reformation' that triumphed astonishingly over a 'loose' or dissolute life was a familiar hallelujah of godly preachment.[59] That this reformation seeks to 'show more goodly' (202) sounds, in the loose conditions of Elizabethan language and pronunciation, suggestively like 'show more godly'.

The prince unveils a career strategy, then, aiming, in his own words, to 'falsify men's hopes' (199). Shakespeare has placed in his mouth a thoroughly estranging articulation of this scheme, first through a surprise deixis carrying overtones of insider betrayal; next, through class-denigration of audience members; and finally, through overtones of Puritan cant, which echo the eager agenda of a sworn foe to the playhouse, whose unyoked idleness he will only awhile uphold. That it is Puritan piety and the diction of its subculture that Falstaff endlessly and hilariously satirizes ('Why, Hal, 'tis my vocation, Hal, 'tis no sin for a man to labour in his vocation', I.ii.99–100) only accentuates the momentous alienation that Shakespeare has enforced here. Like his father, this prince has seemed initially 'a king of smiles' (I.iii.245), only to reveal 'Unkind usage, dangerous countenance, | And violation of all faith and troth' (V.i.69–70). There had been no trickery, we recall, no anti-populist subtext, in the rollicking Prince Henry of *The Famous Victories of Henry the Fifth*, a play which Shakespeare clearly knew. The madcap prince there suggested a Robin Hood figure, proud of his assaults on authority, as David Bevington has noted.[60] His abrupt conversion to respectability, at his father's death, came unforeseen by even himself.

The tavern-cum-alehouse setting of the carousing scenes thus generates powerful political connotations that render its enclave a very different affair from 'a child's world in which he need never grow up . . . the

fantasy of a timeless world of game'.[61] The prince's soliloquy, recognized
by editors as deictic, but not hitherto (to the best of my knowledge)
politicized, far from supplying a 'reassurance of the audience' that this
youth will forsake sin – as if the listeners lined prim pews at a St Paul's
sermon, tut-tutting at Falstaff's jests – and farther still from 'suggesting
his comprehensive sense of responsibility', compels in fact a jarring
alienation from this cozener, his turncoat 'dangerous countenance'
(V.i.69) forcing alarmed disidentification.[62] That this passage comprises,
aside from Falstaff's battlefield philosophy ('there's honour for you',
V.iii.32) the play's only deixis – certainly the prince's sole and unre-
scinded deictic turn – concentrates its negative force.[63] Thereafter, spectators have been driven into a suspicion-charged distantiation from this
antagonist of the commons, spurned into a guarded and defensive relation of judgement that will, in Brecht's essential phrase, think above the
action. The dignifying 'education' that so many modern critics see
resulting from the prince's sly slumming – as if fluent patois were his
aspiration – is thus actually gained by the audience, taught wary emotional detachment from the sham respect of wooing lords, whether Bull-
ingbrooke, Prince Henry, or the Earl of Essex ('wooing poor craftsmen
with the craft of smiles', *Richard II,* I.iv.27; compare *I Henry IV,* V.i.56).

Prince Henry's soliloquy, then, comprises a Shakespearean 'stagecraft secret': activated in the public amphitheatre, to whose performance conditions it is manifestly cued, its deixis will lie respectfully
dormant in performance at court. Sensitized by years of experience in
the volatile sensurround of the commoners' playhouse, the passage is
vintage Shakespeare: an expert's exercise in the theatrically invidious,
invisible to the censor's eye, but transformative of princely definition.

For it is in the *ensuing* scenes that we witness 'Hal' enveloped by
underclass warmth and welcome (a Corinthian, a good boy, etc.): a spectacle that consequently works, with a characteristically Shakespearean
density of tones, as an exposé, of callous lord and duped, naive commoners – a scene of not only laughter but of pathos. Henry's charm is
unflagging – more even than Milton, Shakespeare gives the devil his due
– but the spectators' unease is regularly reinforced by a series of alarms.
It is reactivated by the tellingly cruel joke on Francis, whose pointless-
ness is queried by Poins ('what cunning match have you made with this
jest of the drawer? Come, what's the issue?' II.iv.87–89). Disquiet is further preserved by a sense of overhanging threat, created in the motif of
being caught and hanged, that surfaces often in banter. Falstaff's 'There
lives not three good men unhanged in England, and one of them is fat
and grows old, God help the while!')[64] is converted by the prince from
shared laughter into a gallows humour, *ad hominem* and calculated to

disturb. 'And is not a buff jerkin a most sweet robe of durance?' demands the gloating prince. 'How now, how now, mad wag', splutters Falstaff, (I.ii.41-43). Similarly, when Bardolph claims that his glowing face signifies 'Choler, my lord, if rightly taken', the prince coolly jabs 'A halter, if rightly taken' (II.iv.314-15): precisely the fate which he will mete the flinching Bardolph when 'taken' in *Henry V*. When suddenly the Sheriff and the watch appear at the door, forcing solidarity to the acid test, the prince's good fellowship is immediately in doubt – despite nearly 500 preceding lines of bibulous bonhomie. Falstaff calls out anxiously – 'Dost thou hear, Hal? Never call a true piece of gold a counterfeit'. Clearly unsure of any loyalty, he bluffs 'If you will deny the sheriff, so; if not, let him enter. If I become not a cart as well as another man, a plague on my bringing up!' (II.iv.473-74, 477-79). Though Prince Henry opts to protect Falstaff at this point, the scene closes with him conducting a surprise search of his own, commanding the rifling of Falstaff's sleeping body: 'Search his pockets . . . What has thou found?' 'Nothing but papers, my lord.' 'Let's see what they be. Read them' (II.iv.511-14). The prince then confiscates the remainder for further study: 'What there is else, keep close; we'll read it at more advantage' (522-23). Preserving amid the humour the figure of intrusive surveillance, the 'sword and buckler Prince of Wales' (I.iii.229) silhouettes a sheriff's man.

Above all, the prince's rejectionist deixis suggests the answer to the perennial question of his authorially intended stature. Should we see in Henry's banishment of Falstaff and former friends a regretful maturity conceding *raison d'etat*, or a precalculation of Machiavellian *froideur*? Is Henry V, as the climax of the second tetralogy and the final instalment of Shakespeare's histories, the series' culminating definition of the ideal ruler, or the last nail in monarchy's coffin? So frequently pronounced unanswerable – Norman Rabkin famously compares the allegedly insoluble ambiguity of *Henry V* to cognitive psychology's duck / rabbit gestalt puzzle[65] – the question finds substantial answer in the relationship to his audience that we have seen Shakespeare design for his heir to the throne. Disambiguating the prince from his very first scene, Shakespeare's provision of an audience address that mingles the threatening with the sneering, superadding Puritan tones, explodes the exceptionalist theory of Henry. Positioning him in an intrusive externality to the good fellowship of alehouse and theatre, touching the nervy chord of traumatic surveillance, the passage functions to demote this faux-demotic peer to the level of other kings in Shakespeare's English histories: like Richard II, an exploiter of the commons, like Richard III and Henry IV, a monarch of machination. Last in a line of the untrustworthy and self-serving, he, too, is a *princeps* shown alien to the *populus* claimed to be his care.

As if to underscore the point, the prince's perspective then melds into the king's own scorn, as Henry IV storms onstage:

> My blood hath been too cold and temperate,
> Unapt to stir at these indignities,
> And you have found me, for accordingly
> You tread upon my patience. But be sure
> I will from henceforth rather be myself,
> Mighty and to be feared, than my condition,
> Which hath been smooth as oil, soft as young down . . . (I.iii.1–7)

The prince's suspended repudiation of the watching festive community has carried over into the king's overt threatening. The monarch's words will rapidly attach themselves, of course, to Worcester and the incipient rebels; but in the scene's opening seconds, the object of his anger depends entirely on the direction of his furious gaze, on the travelling of his opposèd eyes. Another stagecraft secret, this sequencing creates, I would argue, what one might term elisional deixis: a continuum-effect Shakespeare deploys elsewhere, in *Richard II* and *As You Like It*.[66] The king who will thunder against carnivalesque behaviours ('So stale and cheap to vulgar company' etc., III.ii.41; compare 13–15, 60–70), and who had opened the drama announcing his intention to levy further troops ('new broils | To be commenced in strands afar remote . . . Forthwith a power of English shall we levy', I.i.3–4, 22) – hardly a popular move among commoners bone-weary of war after more than a decade's impressment, and almost 100,000 men dispatched already overseas [67] – now brandishes in this passage 'the scourge of greatness' as Worcester, cringing, calls it (I.iii.11) against the community of commoners raked by his antagonistic gaze. It is just the voice with which the Privy Council will anathematize that space, on 28 July 1597:

> Her Majesty being informed that there are verie great disorders committed in the common playhouses . . . hathe given direction that not onlie no plaies shalbe used within London or about the citty . . . but that also those play houses . . . shalbe plucked downe . . . plucke downe quite the stages, gallories and roomes that are made for people to stand in, and so to deface the same as they maie not be ymploied agayne to suche use.[68]

Falstaff Banish plump Jack, and banish all the world.
Henry I do, I will. (II.iv.461–62)

'If manhood, good manhood, be not forgot upon the face of the earth, then am I a shotten herring' (II.iv.123–24)

Falstaff's role in *I Henry IV* as charismatic saboteur of chivalry's honour code ('can honour set to a leg?' etc., V.i.130–40) is highly self-evident and widely remarked, its exposition needless here. Likewise, his redolence of roast beef, his heartwarming unity with the feasting principle – 'How agrees the devil and thee about thy soul that thou soldest him on Good Friday last for a cup of Madeira and cold capon's leg?' (I.ii. 108–10) – is beyond all forgetting. With these two traits – 'Sack-and-sugar Jack', who likes not such grinning honour as Sir Walter hath (I.ii.107; V.iii.57–58) – a commodity of good names have been bought, in the playhouses at least. Yet this carnivalesque consummacy is rarely politicized.[69] Fashioned in the years of dearth, and flaunted before groundlings dreading malnutrition, the politics of girth become, I suggest, polyvalent. Falstaff is indeed associated, as Dover Wilson long ago noted, with chops and cutlets, ribs and guts, gravy and lard, Bartholomew pigs and the roasted Manningtree ox with the pudding in his belly: with an Eastcheap that is 'the London centre at once of butchers and cookshops'.[70] But we should recall, what would never have gone unnoticed by dearth-traumatized commoners, that it is 'advantage [that] feeds him fat' (III.ii.180). It is *Sir* John who is the embodiment of satiated appetite; and Shakespeare's portrayal of Falstaff, 'plying his audience with suggestions of the choicest food that London and Eastcheap had to offer'[71] – food currently spiralling ever further from mass reach in dearth-pumped inflation – evokes, simultaneously, plebeian appetency and patrician privilege. The spectacle of a gourmand flourishing amid hunger occasions both popular joy and popular offence.

In the climate of official hostility to youth-culture, Falstaff scores magnificently with the alehouse constituency. 'Younger folk frequently faced underemployment or unemployment; with time on their hands they drifted about, often ending up in the alehouse.'[72] The new Provost Marshals, we recall, aimed to contain 'any further distemperature that may arise by youth'.[73] 'Ah, whoreson caterpillars, bacon-fed knaves!' shrieks Falstaff at the 'grandjurors', 'They hate us youth. Down with them . . . What, ye knaves, young men must live', II.2.80–81, 84–85). Symptomatically, however, rhetorical solidarity and gregarious swilling notwithstanding, Falstaff's dining betrays commensality for a solitary self-glutting. His tavern reckoning ('Item, a capon . . . But one halfpennyworth of bread to this intolerable deal of sack?') is a matter of revelation to Poins and the prince (II.iv.515–23). Audience ambivalence towards the Knight of Eastcheap is sharply tightened from the onset of Act IV, Scene ii, as the colossus of gustatory gusto yields to the government's fraudulent officer plundering a vulnerable commons. 'I have misused the King's press damnably. I have got, in exchange of a hundred and fifty soldiers, three hundred and odd pounds' (IV.ii.11–13). In this, the period (1596–97) when some further 17,000 to 20,000 men were being sent abroad,[74] blown Jack brags of pressing 'a commodity of warm slaves' (IV.ii.70), and mocks their fears ('hearts in their bellies no bigger than pins' heads', 20–21). The devourer of cold capon now designates commoners as 'food for powder' (IV.ii.62).

Sir John Falstaff, then, turns out to be, like the honey-sweet prince, an unexpected and gloating betrayer of the nation's underclasses. 'The devil take such cozeners!': Hotspur's indignant language seems once again appropriate (I.iii.253). 'Proud Jack' (II.iv.11) evolves, after all, into a government man. King's son and gluttonous officer are textually linked in heartless exploitation of the commons: 'Francis, darest thou be so valiant as to play the coward with thy indenture and show it a fair pair of heels and run from it?' (II.iv.44–46) the Prince of Wales urges the tapster. Sir John numbers 'revolted tapsters' among his 'commodity of warm slaves' (IV.ii.27, 17).

The fat rogue's standing with the amphitheatre audience wobbles, I have suggested, on the constitutive ambiguity of graphic corpulence in time of dearth. *Romeo and Juliet*, another product of the dearth years, and perhaps of 1596, had likewise contrasted an insouciantly banqueting plenty enjoyed by the privileged classes with the plight of poor commoners, emblematic in the figure of the emaciated apothecary ('Famine is in thy cheeks, | Need and oppression starveth in thy eyes', V.i.69–70). Romeo had mocked his desperation ('Art thou so bare and full of wretchedness, | And fears't to die?', V.i.68–69), bullied him into illegal transaction ('My poverty but not my will consents', 75), praised his services ('O true apothecary, | Thy drugs are quick', V.iii.119–20), then betrayed him to the authorities ('here he writes that he did buy a poison | Of a poor pothecary', V.iii.287–88).[75] In both dramas, penned during a witch-hunt for treacherous agitators allegedly swarming among the idling underclasses, Shakespeare portrays, conversely, the pathos of commoners as victims: like Mistress Quickly and Doll Tearsheet, like Francis and the 'leash of drawers' to whom Prince Henry feigns sworn brotherhood (II.iv.6), they are threatless, hard working, good-natured, and betrayed.

'This . . . draws a curtain | That shows the ignorant a kind of fear | Before not dreamt of' (IV.i.73–75)

Summoned from 'vulgar company' and 'rude society' (III. ii. 41, 14) to the counsels of the king, the Prince of Wales in Act III, Scene ii enters a space of elite privacy. The stage fills with resplendent robes as king, prince, and lords cross the boards: but the attendant lords are commanded to depart in the scene's opening line. That collective exit leaves the two men very alone, heightening the sense of a separated 'private conference' (2) now to ensue in the palace chamber. We are in the secret heart of power. Only secure from other ears can the monarch tutor the prince.

Berating his son's behaviour, King Henry unfolds a clandestine art: the seizing of supremacy. Downward deference and rarity of appearance have proven the key to a cultic popularity: 'my state, | Seldom, but sumptuous, showed like a feast | And won by rareness such solemnity' (III.ii.57–59). Richard II, by contrast, who 'mingled his royalty with cap'ring fools' (63), forfeited 'extraordinary gaze' (78). The tutelage runs to 50 lines, in a vehement insistence marking its momentous importance.

Theatrically, however, like Prince Henry's bruising deixis to playhouse spectators earlier, this urgent passage functions, paradoxically, to induce audience apperception. King Henry's relentless assault on 'barren pleasures, rude society', upon 'shallow jesters and rash bavin wits', his horror of going 'To laugh at gibing boys and stand the push | Of every beardless vain comparative' (III.ii.14, 61, 66–67), infallibly reminds spectators, through force of iteration, of these alehouse-style ecstasies they have thoroughly enjoyed. That it is themselves who are being scorned produces more than simple estrangement of the monarch from playgoers' sympathy. The welter of insults works to position them, effectively, as rank outsiders – political eavesdroppers, listening in on secrets of state emphatically not intended for the likes of them.

The same effect, collective spectator self-consciousness as intimately observing outsiders, is stimulated by the contradictions of Henry's observations to which Shakespeare moves his playgoers. 'Not an eye | But is aweary of thy common sight' (III.ii.87–88) disastrously misjudges the hilarity of the skipping prince, the *verve railleuse* of his delighting jousts with Falstaff. Whatever the charged, suspicious ambivalence that Shakespeare sets up towards him, the prince is never wearisome. 'Being with his presence glutted, gorged, and full' (84) evokes Falstaff: who, enfeoffed to popularity, never induces drowsing eyes and eyelids hung down (69, 81).

Emphasizing the privacy of the conference and its sharp alterity to the gamehouse, rendering observation of this sequestrated domain a transgressive, one-way viewing, the passage interpellates the spectators as members of an alien constituency, spying upon *arcana imperii* – that strategic yoking of humours by high place. In the era of intrusive surveillance, Shakespeare has appropriated the empowering privy gaze, the probing by opposèd eyes, for his fellow commoners: supplying, here, precisely that potent, privileged inspection which power had sought to forestall through rarity of managed appearance. The intervention must have seemed startling, truly a matter of 'extraordinary gaze' (78): it was for the high to monitor the low, not the reverse. 'Great men have reaching hands', bragged Lord Saye in *2 Henry VI*: 'Oft have I struck | Those that I never saw, and struck them dead' (IV.vii.73–74). Hamlet will be enraged by the presumptuous counter-espionage of commoners, when Rosencrantz and Guildenstern seek, as he fumes, to 'pluck out the heart of my mystery . . . 'Sblood, do you think I am easier to be played on than a pipe?' (III.ii.336, 339–40). But *1 Henry IV*, with its systematic exposé of English state power – manipulation of the masses, a militarism feeding off bribery and dead pays, incrementally successful regicide, and the posturing ambition of the contemporary Earl of Essex plainly evoked in King Henry's populist wooings – is a work which 'Draws a curtain | That shows the ignorant a kind of fear | Before not dreamt of' (IV.i.73–75). Exposing to their survey the machinations of the great, radical Shakespeare becomes a tutelary intelligencer to the commons, furnishing, with theatrical genius, a revengeful reciprocation of class-surveillance.

Notes

1. All quotation of *1 Henry IV* is from the World's Classics edition, ed. David Bevington (Oxford: Oxford University Press, 1987). All other plays quoted from *The Norton Shakespeare* ed. Stephen Greenblatt, et al. (New York: Norton, 1997).
2. Curtis C. Breight, *Surveillance, Militarism and Drama in the Elizabethan Era* (London and New York: Macmillan and St Martins, 1996), p. 82.
3. Ian W. Archer, *The Pursuit of Stability: Social Relations in Elizabethan London* (Cambridge: Cambridge University Press, 1991), p. 8. Proclamation 'Prohibiting unlawful assembly under martial law', 4 July 1595, in *Tudor Royal Proclamations*, ed. P. L. Hughes and J. F. Larkin (New Haven, CT: Yale, 1969), no. 769, vol. 2, pp. 143, 83.
4. Corporation of London Record Office, Samuel Barton's Book, folio 46; cit. Archer, *Pursuit of Stability*, p. 9.
5. John Walter and Keith Wrightson, 'Dearth and the Social Order in Early Modern England' in *Rebellion, Popular Protest and the Social Order in Early Modern England* ed. Paul Slack (Cambridge: Cambridge University Press, 1984), pp. 108–28 (108).
6. Andrew Appleby, in *Famine in Tudor and Stuart England* (Stanford, CA: Stanford University Press, 1978), pp. 138–40.
7. Joyce Youings, *Sixteenth Century England* (Harmondsworth: Penguin, 1984), p. 270. Wheat prices rose from 17.61 to 36.56 shillings per quarter between 1592–94, and thence to 40.34 in 1595, and 47.61 in 1596, as R. B. Outhwaite, 'Dearth, the English Crown and the Crisis of the 1590s' in *The European Crisis of the 1590s* ed. Peter Clark (London: George Allen & Unwin, 1985), pp. 23–43, shows in his table on p. 28. Appleby, in *Famine in Tudor and Stuart England*, p. 6 details the price increases during these years of cereals eaten by the poor: rye, for instance, had risen by 1596 to 5.68 times its price in 1593.
8. Jim Sharpe, 'Social Strain and Social Dislocation, 1585–1603' in *The Reign of Elizabeth: Court and Culture in the Last Decade*, ed. John Guy (Cambridge: Cambridge University Press, 1995), pp. 192–211 (pp.198–99).

9. Letter reprinted in *Tudor Economic Documents* ed. R. H. Tawney and Eileen Power (3 volumes., London: Longmans,1924), Volume 2, pp. 339–46.
10. Roger Manning, *Village Revolts* (Oxford: Oxford University Press, 1988), pp. 204–05, 208–10; Archer, *Pursuit of Stability*, pp. 1–2.
11. Alison Wall, *Power and Protest in England 1525–1640* (London: Arnold, 2000), p. 136; Archer, *Pursuit of Stability*, p. 7.
12. Anon, *A Student's Lamentation*, Cr.
13. *A Student's Lamentation*, C3r.
14. Sharpe, 'Social strain', p. 202.
15. Charles Nichol, *The Reckoning: the Murder of Christopher Marlowe* (London: Picador, 1993), p. 115.
16. Breight, *Surveillance, Militarism, and Drama*, pp. 102–03, 49, 104–07, 150.
17. Carolly Erickson, *The First Elizabeth* (1983; rpt. New York: St Martin's Griffin, 1997), p. 357.
18. Archer, *Pursuit of Stability*, pp. 218, 244.
19. Eric Carlson, 'The Origin, Function, and Status of the Office of Churchwarden', in *The World of Rural Dissenters 1520–1725* ed. Margaret Spufford (Cambridge: Cambridge University Press, 1995), pp. 164–207 (174); David Underdown, *Revel, Riot and Rebellion: Popular Politics and Culture in England 1603–1660* (Oxford: Oxford University Press, 1985), p. 59.
20. In these culture wars, in some places outside London churchwardens chose not to present offenders to church courts. 'It was very tempting to report *omnia bene* in order to defend the community's liberty against the inquisitorial central power': Christopher Hill, *Society and Puritanism in Pre-Revolutionary England* (London: Secker and Warburg, 1964), p. 337; compare Carlson, 'Churchwarden', pp. 172–74, 200–06.
21. Archer, *Pursuit of Stability*, pp. 184–85, 219, 244.
22. Archer, *Pursuit of Stability*, p. 244.
23. J. Stow, *The Annales or Generall Chronicle of England* (1615), pp. 768–69, cit. Archer, *Pursuit of Stability*, p. 8; p. 244.
24. Breight, *Surveillance, Militarism, and Drama*, p. 51.
25. Peter Clark, *The English Alehouse: A Social History 1200–1830* (London: Longman, 1983), p. 156.
26. Clark, *English Alehouse*, p. 126.
27. Clark, *English Alehouse*, pp. 125–27, 137.
28. Clark, *English Alehouse*, pp. 137–39.
29. Clark, *English Alehouse*, pp. 123–32; see also pp. 151–57; Keith Wrightson, 'Alehouses, order and reformation in rural England, 1590–1660' in *Popular Culture and Class Conflict 1590–1914: Explorations in the History of Labour and Leisure* ed. Eileen Yeo and Stephen Yeo (Brighton, Sussex: Harvester, 1981), 1–27 (pp. 6–11).
30. Clark, *English Alehouse*, p. 160.
31. Clark, *English Alehouse*, pp. 157–59
32. Roger B. Manning, *Hunters and Poachers: A Social and Cultural History of Unlawful Hunting 1485–1640* (Oxford: Clarendon Press, 1993), pp. 55, 160, 166–67, 194.
33. Clark, *English Alehouse*, p. 157.
34. Archival quotations cited in Wrightson, 'Alehouses', p. 12.
35. J. Downame, *Foure Treatises Tending to Disswade all Christians* (1613), p. 88; cit. Clark, *English Alehouse*, p. 145.
36. Wrightson, 'Alehouses', p. 6.
37. Archer, *Pursuit of Stability*, pp. 208, 244–45. The trend would continue: in the sessions of 1601, 1604, and 1606, a remarkable 'twenty-five bills for the regulation of alehouses were introduced' into parliament: Underdown, *Revel*, p. 48.
38. Clark, *English Alehouse*, p. 167.

39. Wrightson, 'Alehouses', p. 11; Clark, *English Alehouse*, p. 172; Archer, *Pursuit of Stability*, p. 255.

40. Archer, *Pursuit of Stability*, p. 216.

41. In Part 2 of *Henry IV*, Mistress Quickly's establishment, like her role, is greatly enlarged. Though comically attempted self-embourgeoisment may underlie it, 'thou didst swear to me upon a parcel-gilt goblet, sitting in my Dolphin chamber, at the round table, by a sea-coal fire' (II.i.79–80) evokes the tavern or inn, not the humble alehouse.

42. Clark, *English Alehouse*, p. 156.

43. Clark, *English Alehouse*, p. 146.

44. Clark, *English Alehouse*, p. 156.

45. Louis Montrose, *The Purpose of Playing: Shakespeare and the Cultural Politics of the Elizabethan Theatre* (Chicago: Chicago University, 1996), p. 19.

46. Steven Mullaney, *The Place of the Stage: Liberty, Play and Power in Renaissance England* (Ann Arbor, MI: University of Michigan, 1988), p. 31.

47. Keith Wrightson, 'Estates, Degrees and Sorts in Tudor and Stuart England', *History Today* 37 (1987), pp. 17–22.

48. Andy Wood, 'Poore Men woll speke one daye: Plebeian Languages of Deference and Defiance in England c. 1520–1640' in *The Politics of the Excluded, c.1500–1850*, ed. Tim Harris (New York: Palgrave, 2001), 67–98 (pp. 74, 82).

49. Andy Wood, 'Fear, Hatred and the Hidden Injuries of Class in Early Modern England', *Journal of Social History*, 39:1 (2006), 803–826 (p. 812).

50. Wood, 'Poore men woll speke', p. 83.

51. Compare, perhaps, 'thou shalt know him for knave and cuckold' (*Merry Wives* II.ii.252), and 'knew me for a fool, a coward' (*Measure for Measure* V.i.494).

52. I have inserted the commas before and after 'awhile', for reasons the ensuing exposition makes clear.

53. Cited in E. K. Chambers, *The Elizabethan Stage* (Oxford: Clarendon Press, 1923), Volume 4, p. 317.

54. *Student's Lamentation*, C3r.

55. Wrightson, 'Alehouses', p. 11.

56. Thomas Nashe, letter to William Cotton, cit. Chambers, *Elizabethan Stage*, vol. 4, p. 319.

57. See my *Radical Shakespeare: Politics and Stagecraft in the Early Career*, forthcoming.

58. Andrew Gurr, *Playgoing in Shakespeare's London* (Cambridge: Cambridge University Press, 1987), pp. 38–39 and 45.

59. Compare Shakespeare's satiric presentation of excitable acclaim of 'reformation' by Jack Cade, discussed in Chris Fitter, ' "Your captain is brave and vows reformation": Jack Cade, the Hacket rising, and Shakespeare's vision of popular rebellion in *2 Henry VI*' in *Shakespeare Studies*, 32 (2004), 173–216 (pp. 182–88, 191–92).

60. David Bevington, 'Introduction', World Classics edition, p. 21.

61. Bevington, 'Introduction', pp. 56–57.

62. *The First Part of King Henry IV*, ed. Herbert Weil and Judith Weil (Cambridge: Cambridge University Press, 1997), pp. 10–12, 42; Bevington, 'Introduction', p. 60; Weil and Weil, p. 11.

63. The usual markers of deixis, plentiful in Henry VI, Richard III and Richard III, are otherwise absent in this drama. See *Radical Shakespeare*, chapters 3, 6 and 9.

64. II.iv.124–26; compare I.ii.56–69; I.ii.25–27; II.i.63–65; II.ii.14; II.ii.28.

65. Norman Rabkin, *Shakespeare and the Problem of Meaning* (Chicago: University of Chicago Press, 1981), pp. 33–62.

66. *Radical Shakespeare*, chapters 9 and 11.

67. Likewise the Princes' promise 'I will wear a garment all of blood' (III.ii.135) and the king's admiring line 'a hundred thousand rebels die in this' (III.ii.160) were more likely to repel than enthuse those knowing themselves potential cannon-fodder. Paul Hammer, *Elizabeth's Wars: War, Government and Society in Tudor England* (Basingstoke: Palgrave Macmillan, 2003) displays on p. 246 a table summarizing yearly figures for troop recruitment for service aboard from 1585–1602.

68. Chambers, *Elizabethan Stage,* p. 322.

69. François Laroque, for instance, in 'Shakespeare's Battle of Carnival and Lent: the Falstaff scenes reconsidered' in *Shakespeare and Carnival: After Bakhtin* ed. Ronald Knowles (Basingstoke: Macmillan, 1998), pp. 83–96, discusses a traditionally carnivalesque Falstaff as though festive revels were not under active prosecution in the last decades of the sixteenth century, and there were no dearth when the play was in composition.

70. John Dover Wilson, *The Fortunes of Falstaff* (Cambridge: Cambridge University Press, 1953), p. 26.

71. Wilson, *Fortunes of Falstaff,* p. 31.

72. Clark, *English Alehouse,* p. 127.

73. Stow, *Annales,* p. 769.

74. Hammer, *Elizabeth's Wars,* p. 246.

75. On class frictions and the impact of the dearth in this play, see my essay 'The quarrel is between our masters and us their men: *Romeo and Juliet*, dearth, and the London riots' in *English Literary Renaissance,* 30.2 (Spring 2000), 154–83.

CHAPTER SIX

New Directions: Falstaffian 'Gross Indecorum', 'Contrarietie', and Arrested Prodigality: Anachronism and Colliding Generational Sensibilities in *1 Henry IV*

Robert Hornback

Why was Falstaff funny? Much criticism about Falstaff focuses on his origins, including the significance of his original Shakespearean stage name, that of the historical Lollard rebel/martyr, Sir John Oldcastle, whose vestiges famously remain in the extant text via Prince Hal's jesting reference to him as 'my old lad of the castle' (*1 Henry IV*, I.ii.41). Given his initial association with this proto-Puritan Lollard, the character has sometimes been interpreted anachronistically as a full-blown Puritan. Other accounts of Falstaff's origins align him with the Lord of Misrule within the context of contemporary Puritanism, in the wake of the colourful 'Martin Marprelate' pamphlet war (1588–89) waged between the pseudonymous, carnivalesque Puritan Martin and the orthodox anti-Martinists. Still other literary and theatre historians have pointed to the marked influence of the morality play's comic Vice figure upon Falstaff's character. But, as David Ellis has impatiently declared, '[none] of these approaches tells us much about why he makes us laugh and provides so much comic pleasure.'[1] Nonetheless, much remains to be said about Sir John's origins precisely in order to shed light on why he was – and *is* – funny. Here I will investigate the generational conflict between the youthful Prince Hal and his father, King Henry (as well as the old knight Falstaff), through which Shakespeare refracts, to comic and satiric effect, both religious and aesthetic change.

1 Henry IV was written around 1596, a moment of hastening transition in theatrical and religious sensibilities. Notably, as Robert Weimann has demonstrated, traditional–popular performative modes were increasingly colliding with learned–elite neoclassical ideals. Falstaff bears the impress not only of this aesthetic debate but of a marked change in religious sensibilities among Protestants in the half century between the first exuberantly iconoclastic evangelical generations emerging in England after the 1520s and those of the post-1570s generation, when an equally zealous but very different ethos of Presbyterian–Puritan sobriety began to dominate English Protestantism.

In this context, 'old Jack' (II.iv.477) stepped forth as a profane and indecorous throwback, that is, as '*Old*-castle'. Indeed, he insistently recalled what we shall see was the prior dramatic allegorical personification of 'Old Custom', representing a corrupted older generation. Our own vestigial sense of him as laughably out of time and place, as indeed an incomprehensibly large fish out of water, still makes us laugh even today. Some recognition of Sir John as not just any fish but an extinct one – and as one therefore violating every rule of time, place, custom, and nature – remains key to our own sense of him as so incongruous as to be inherently laughable. That is all the more so as we delight in seeing this absurd figure not just improbably surviving but impossibly thriving, even feasting, against all odds. If so, we will see, debate about whether Falstaff was meant to represent a *contemporary* Puritan – rather than, as I will maintain, chiefly an outmoded type of evangelical – may be, to mix icthyological metaphor, a red-herring. What is ultimately certain is that the overt opposition between fat, aged Falstaff and the 'starveling' (II.iv.244) youth Hal stages a collision between new and old sensibilities.

Falstaffian Anachronism, 'Grossness', and 'Contrarietie' as Indecorum

One striking characteristic of the aged Falstaff is that he is, from his first entrance, represented as opposed to, oblivious of, or suspended in, time. Harold Bloom thus views the old knight as a 'defier of time' (not to mention 'law, order, and the state').[2] To offer but a few instances of this signature tendency, in his very first line, Falstaff betrays his obliviousness to time even in indifferently asking, 'Now, Hal, what time of day is it, lad?' (I.ii.1), prompting Hal's virtuoso, 11 line (2–12) rebuke, including the exasperated rhetorical question, 'What a devil hast thou to do with the time of the day?' (i. 6). Later, in battle, Hal likewise rebukes Falstaff with the equally rhetorical, 'What, is it a time to jest and dally now?' (V.iii.57). In *2 Henry IV* (1598), Falstaff will assert freedom from time's effects and claim, revealingly, to have sprung forth already old: 'My lord, I was born about three of the clock in the afternoon with a white beard, and something a round belly' (I.ii.181–83).[3] It is almost as if, in his mind, 'the chimes' are stuck irrelevantly striking the youthful revels 'at midnight' he invokes elsewhere in *2 Henry IV* (III.ii.214).

Other principals in the second tetralogy have, by contrast, a heightened awareness of time: in the second line of *1 Henry IV*, the weary king claims that now 'Find we a time for frighted peace to pant' (I.i.2), and later Hotspur reminds his men before battle that '[T]he time of life is short!' (V.ii.81) and, shortly before his death, defines life as 'time's fool, / And time, that takes survey of all the world, must have a stop' (V.iv.81–83). In the earlier *Richard II*, that dissolute king becomes aware, too late, of the import of time (e.g., he cannot 'bid time return' [III.ii.69] and learns, 'I wasted time, and now doth time waste me' [V.v.49]). Far from being an antagonist to time, Prince Hal in *1 Henry IV*, in the last line of his scene-ending soliloquy in Act I, Scene ii, announces his determination of 'Redeeming time when men think least I will' (l. 217). We will return to the significance of Hal's pledge about '*redeeming* time', but for now suffice it to say that the character note about Falstaff's oppositional relation to time will be key to understanding not only why he makes us laugh but why this character has such depth when reconsidered in an Elizabethan *milieu*.

Here we must take up the particular challenge this old knight presented to changing aesthetic sensibilities in the latter half of the 1590s. Shakespeare began to conceive the part of Sir John just as Sidney's neoclassical critique of that Renaissance English practice of 'mingling kings and clowns' was first printed in two rival editions – one authorized, one not – in 1595. The unauthorized printing of Sidney's *Defence* was handed over to the authorized publisher who sold these copies under a new title page along with his own edition, resulting in a relative flood of copies entering the market just before Shakespeare turned to *1 Henry IV*. Sidney had objected to

> these gross absurdities, how all their plays be neither right tragedies, nor right comedies, mingling kings and clowns not because the matter so carrieth it, but thrust in clowns by head and shoulders, to play a part in majestical matters, with neither decency nor discretion, so as neither the admiration and commiseration, nor the right sportfulness, is by their mongrel tragi-comedy obtained.[4]

That Shakespeare was quite familiar with Sidney's now newly topical criticisms is suggested when, especially in *1 Henry IV*, he seems determined to prove such views wrong-headed by showing his unique ability to obtain just the 'right' admiration and commiseration, while also making the comic 'sportfulness' integral to the contrasting 'matter' of the play.

Shakespeare must have written Falstaff partly as a tongue-in-cheek provocation against the strictures of neoclassical sensibilities. Joseph Hall's oft-cited objection in *Virgidemiarum* (1597) to the mugging popular clown who 'laughs, and grins, and frames his mimic face . . . . For laughter at his self-resembled show' (ll. 34–35, 44)[5] appeared in print immediately after Sir John had made his successful appearance on stage as the specific kind of self-consciously performing clown to whom Hall objects. Other details in fact recall the old knight's particular relationship with Prince Hal, since Hall's critique refers, oddly, to a 'hungry [hence thin or 'starveling' (II.iv.244)] youth' performing 'princely carriage' (ll. 19, 22) and then imagines a clown as 'justl[ing] straight into the prince's place' (l. 36), evidently responding specifically to the jostling familiarity of Shakespeare's odd couple in the Boar's Head Tavern. After all, whom else would readers have had in mind when now imagining a thin prince with a self-conscious comic performer?

More than any other Shakespearean clown, Sir John represented what George Whetstone, writing in his dedication to *Promos and Cassandra* (1578), had called 'a grose *Indecorum*'.[6] By palpably violating in his interactions with the prince every decorum of time, place, rank and what Whetstone referred to as the 'order of speech', Falstaff served as a medium for Shakespeare's most daring affront to neoclassical sensibilities to date. Shakespeare makes Falstaff's signature 'gross indecorum' extend to his saying or doing whatever would be most inappropriate – whether in a tavern, where his profane invocations of scripture and evangelical cant are inapt; or immediately before, during and after highway robbery; or in selecting soldiers, where he makes no attempt to conceal his disregard for others' lives; or on a battlefield, where he has a bottle of sack in lieu of a pistol in his holster, cheers on Hal in his fight with Hotspur like an exuberant fan at a wrestling match, and plays dead just before stabbing the obviously already deceased Hotspur, lugging his body around irreverently, and then improbably claiming credit for his death. For anyone seeking decorum, it would be inconceivable to imagine a character who could have been more of an affront.

Shakespeare might also have had Whetstone's complaint about '*grose* Indecorum' and Sidney's similar rebuke of '*gross* absurdities'[7] punningly in mind in an era in which 'gross' could mean 'bloated with excess, repulsively fat' (*OED* adj. 2) when he atypically wrote a role for the clown Will Kemp emphasizing abusive fat jokes – for example, Hal's references to this 'fat-witted' (II.ii.2), 'fat-kidney'd' (II.ii.5), 'horse-back-breaker' (II.iv.242), 'fat paunch' (II.iv.144), 'huge hill of flesh' (II.iv.243), 'tun of man' (II.iv.448), and 'whoreson round man' (II.iv.140) as being '*gross* as a mountain' (II.iv.226). Whether or not Shakespeare was literalizing hyperbolic neoclassical complaints against 'grossness' through the grotesque figure of 'plump Jack' (II.iv.479), he did defy the rising influence of neoclassicism in other ways.

Falstaff's embodiment of the aforementioned 'self-resembled show' – the old-fashioned performative mode first associated with the Vice, in which the actor remained self-embodied to the extent that he was never utterly submerged in the character, part, or play-world but rather performed *to the audience*, often via down-stage acting, asides and comical soliloquies – makes him one of Shakespeare's most overt throwbacks to the power of the supposedly outmoded tradition of the morality play. Even more than other parts written for Kemp, Falstaff is characterized as resembling the figure of the Vice which took to the stage over the first two decades of London's permanent theatres, and which Shakespeare had likely seen performed at Stratford in his youth. Falstaff himself threatens jestingly that he will beat the prince out of the kingdom with the Vice's conventional stage prop 'dagger of lath' (II.iv.137), and Hal refers to him as a 'Vice' (II.iv.453), as the personified 'grey Iniquity' (II.iv.454), as a 'villainous, abominable misleader of youth' (II.iv.462), and as 'that old, white-bearded Sathan' (II.iv.463). Significantly, Shakespeare's evocative amalgam of the Vice is 'grey' and 'white-bearded', for as Robert Weimann noted, for Shakespeare, 'the Vice was the *old* Vice', as with Feste's reference 'Like to the old Vice' (*Twelfth Night*, IV.ii.120) and Speed's remark 'Your old vice still' (*Two Gentleman of Verona*, III.i.284). Thus, for Shakespeare, the 'old Vice' was a self-conscious anachronism, but the morality play was a powerful dramatic reference still, as we shall see later in his ironic treatment of the figures of wayward Youth and aged Counsellor.

Related to such aesthetic anachronism is Falstaff's embodiment of yet another long-ignored concept inspired by 'the old Vice', that of 'contrarietie'. Here too, Falstaff reflects Shakespeare's ironic meditation on aesthetics of the then relatively new-fangled neoclassicists. The *Oxford English Dictionary* defines 'contrarietie' as 'Opposition of one thing to another in nature . . . ; diametrical difference, repugnancy, contrariness' (*OED* 1); 'disagreement, discordance, discrepancy, inconsistency' (*OED* 2); '*Logic.* Contrary opposition' (*OED* 5). As Weimann has observed, Sidney's *Defence* objects to theatrical 'contrareitie', not merely for mixing kings and clowns, but also 'delight' and 'laughter', which 'in themselves . . . have as it were a kind of contrarietie'.[8] Both Shakespeare and Sidney would have encountered contrariety in such moral plays published in the mid-Elizabethan period as the anonymous *Tide Tarrieth No Man* (1576), where we find the ironically named Courage the Vice speaking of 'Courage contrarious', and a stage direction in Thomas Lupton's *All for Money* (1577) requiring improvisation mistaking words:

'*Here the vyce shal turne the proclamation to some contrarie sence at everie time all for money hath read it*'.[9] Contrariety, then, was one thing that had made the Vice funny, and so it remains, we must recognize, with the Vice-descendant Falstaff, who often plays 'the old vice still'.

Falstaff indeed embodies within his wide circumference extraordinary diametrical oppositions, discrepancies and inconsistencies to the point of making him a grotesquely comical paradox, a walking oxymoron.[10] J. Dover Wilson had some sense of this when he wrote that 'Falstaff is a bundle of contradictions. He is not only Riot but also Repentance'. Though Wilson limited the degree to which Falstaff is extraordinary in this regard by prefacing these remarks with the qualifying phrase, 'Like all great Shakespearian characters, . . . '[11] Falstaff's palpably absurd or 'gross' embodiment of contradictions (encompassing, but hardly limited to, hypocrisy) is far from typical of Shakespeare's greatest characters. Instead, much of the outrageous humour in this inherently laughable figure centres upon the uniquely ridiculous juxtaposition of otherwise mutually exclusive opposites, many of which he himself or Hal call attention to, for he is 'not only witty in [him]self, but the cause that wit is in other men' (*2 Henry IV*, I.ii.8–9); at once conscienceless – blithely moving 'from praying to purse-taking' (*1 Henry IV*, I.ii.103) – and troubled by a longing to repent (the latter earning him the nickname 'Monsieur Remorse' [I.ii.113]); a 'reverent Vice' (II.iv.453) quoting scripture and moralizing self-righteously in a tavern; a sanguine melancholic, lusty yet impotent, lumbering yet improbably capable of moving 'nimbly, with . . . quick dexterity' (II.v.236), and the paradoxical embodiment of perpetual carnival as if 'all the year were playing holidays' (I.ii.204).

The contrariety that has the most bearing on Falstaff's anachronism – itself inherently involving perception of contrasting sensibilities – is the fact that this aged man (by his own disingenuous count being of an 'age some fifty, or by'r lady inclining to three score' [II.iv.418–19]) maintains an incongruous self-identification with youth. David Ellis, noting Falstaff's 'absurd pretensions to youth', observes that, '[t]hroughout both plays, Falstaff's main concern is to defy nature and assume that being old and fat is no natural bar to intimate friendship with two young men about town' (Ellis, pp. 87, 86, respectively). In this comic mode, he speaks contemptuously of 'the rusty curb of old father antic the law' (I.ii.61), and, most absurd of all, during the robbery, Falstaff feigns hot-headed youth in crying out, '[B]acon-fed knaves! they hate us youth. Down with them!' (II.ii.84–85) and 'What, ye knaves, young men must live!' (90–91). The impression given by Falstaff's bizarre self-association with the timeless theme of rebellious youth versus the censorious restrictions imposed by law and aged authority is thus one of a grotesquely arrested adolescence. So insistent is Falstaff upon acting young that Hal aptly characterizes him as 'the latter spring' or 'All-hallow'n summer' (I.ii.158–59), as if he were some fantastic allegorical personification of arrested time. Here, Shakespeare self-consciously plays upon contrariety as a rhetorical figure, evoking the hilarity of Falstaff's essential untimeliness, but also his unique ability to make different sensibilities collide with remarkable vitality – and eloquence.

Early Evangelical Misrule, 'Jangling', and Theatricality

The prolonged identification of the carnivalesque Falstaff with his own (albeit fictional) youth some half century before his anachronistic appearance c. 1596–97 raises the spectre of misrule that had expanded half a century before, oddly enough, during the zealous reign of Edward VI (1547–53), when royally sponsored entertainments at court were dominated by raucously iconoclastic anti-papist revels.[12] Whereas the carnivalesque iconoclast Falstaff embodied topsy-turvy sensibilities that late Elizabethan Puritans fiercely rejected, Edwardian evangelicals like court Lord of Misrule Sir George Ferrers, acting as a semi-professional stage clown, had indulged in highly theatrical and irreverent religious humour, including, in 1552–53, one performance of a comic Pope as Antichrist, with an Apocalyptic, anti-papist coat of arms reading, '[T]he serpente with sevin heddes . . . is the chief beast of myne armes . . . my worde is *semper ferians* . . . [or] always feasting or keeping holie daie'. The polemical/satirical Lord of Misrule here appeared alongside 'fooles, *friers and suche other*', one wearing 'a Vice's co[a]te . . . of *white and redde damaske figured with goulde churche worke*', that is, a Roman Catholic clerical vestment.[13] Such iconoclasm is consistent with Imperial ambassador Jehan Schyfve's account of misrule, in a letter dated 18 January, 1551–52, which observed that Ferrers offered a crude burlesque of religious processions and of the ritual blessing of the Eucharistic monstrance: 'They paraded through the Court, and carried, under an infamous tabernacle, a representation of the holy sacrament in its monstrance, which they wetted and perfumed in most strange fashion, with great ridicule'.[14] Though the point of evangelical appropriation of misrule was to stereotype Catholicism as carnivalesque, radical Reformation movements, whenever they emerged, were invariably stereotyped as advocating misrule. So it was that Thomas More could already compare his opponent William Tyndale to 'an abbote of mysrule in a Christmas game'.[15] The Reformation was further associated in Tudor traditionalists' polemic with youthful misrule. As Susan Brigden has shown in her classic essay, 'Youth and the English Reformation',

Protestantism was said to allow carnivalesque 'license to turn upside down the established order.'[16]

Whereas many critics have remained skeptical about the relevance of Falstaff's Oldcastle/Lollard origins to his carnivalesque embrace of licensed law-breaking because it defies a contemporary Puritan's censorious typology, Falstaff's original status as a *proto*-Puritan is not at all at odds with Shakespeare's deployment of the related tropes of anachronism and misrule in the play. That is, Falstaff would have been recognizable as an instantiation of a hardly forgotten, however anachronistic, type. He would not have been radically dissimilar to a good number of reform-minded men who came of age at mid-century while being inspired with the spirit of evangelizing misrule. Shakespeare himself must have had some familiarity with the type of the aging evangelical associated with performative iconoclasm, for famous versions survived into his own day, including the iconoclastic yet knightly Lord of Misrule Ferrers (d. 1579). Yet another was Thomas Lever (d.1577), a leader of the Elizabethan Puritan movement who, according to the 'St John's College Register of Inventories' in 1548–49, appeared as the Lord of Misrule at Cambridge University[17] in riotous entertainments drawing on an inventory of costumes that included 'fooles coote[s]', 'a fooles dagger of wodd', 'A silk gold cap with a cockes hed in ye crown', and also items hinting at mock-religious processions, such as 'A miter', 'iij shildes . . . two with [superstitious] red draggones', 'ii black develles cootes with hornes', two 'steple capp[s]' (bishops' hats?), and 'ii past[e] hates'.[18]

In terms of interpreting Falstaff, at issue here is what Patrick Collinson has characterized as 'the depth of the gulf now opening up between the old and the new religious sensibilities' in the Elizabethan period.[19] Like the semi-professional clown Ferrers, who performed a riotous 'dronken Maske' of 1551–52 before thousands in London upon 'a grett skaffold in Chepe hard by the crosse' where 'my lord dranke',[20] Falstaff's own anachronistic motto for his carnivalesque performances in an Eastcheap tavern might similarly be '*semper ferians*' or 'always feasting'. Perhaps most obvious here are what Collinson discusses as

> the changing attitudes of religiously minded Protestants to alehouses, inns and other places of popular resort. At first, they were at home in such places, where they argued points of theological difference [and scriptural interpretation] with their opponents (the phenomenon called by contemporaries 'jangling').[21]

Critics from Alfred Ainger and J. Dover Wilson through Naseeb
Shaheen and Kristen Poole have noted a 'frequent resort to Scriptural
phraseology' in Falstaff's idiom, and even as the *Henry IV* plays include
54 references to drinking, 'more than a seventh of the total . . . in
Shakespeare',[22] Falstaff does quite a bit of jangling at the Boar's Head
Tavern in *1 Henry IV*. In fact, he single-handedly accounts for 26 of the
50-plus biblical references identified in the play, including citations of
the parables of Dives, Lazarus, and the prodigal son; the books of
Genesis, Exodus, Psalms, Proverbs, and 1 and 2 Samuel; the Gospels of
Matthew, Mark, and Luke; and Paul's first and second letters to the
Corinthians and first letter to the Thessalonians.[23] Consider the following instances: 'Thou knowest in the state of innocency Adam fell, and
what should poor Jack Falstaff do in the days of villainy? Thou seest I
have more flesh than another man, and therefore more frailty'
(III.iii.164); 'slaves as ragged as Lazarus in the painted cloth' (IV.ii.25–26);
'you would think that I had a hundred and fifty totter'd prodigals lately
from swine-keeping, from eating draft and husks' (IV.ii.33–35); 'I never
see thy face but I think upon hell-fire and Dives that liv'd in purple; for
there he is in his robes, burning, burning' (III.iii.40–43).

What I want to emphasize here is that long-standing debate about
whether or not such rhetoric made Falstaff represent a modern Puritan
or whether he himself instead intentionally satirized them perhaps
misses the central fact that Sir John was represented as godly in a
decidedly 'jangling', old-fashioned way. Not for nothing does Hal's page
in *2 Henry IV* liken 'the Boar's Head tavern, where Falstaff resides, to
the meeting place of 'Ephesians . . . of the old church' (II.ii.150): that is,
to the 'primitive church' evangelicals emulated.[24] Whereas moderns
tend to think of Protestantism in terms of later ideals of sobriety, during
the earlier tradition of scriptural 'jangling', so the critical commonplace
goes, the Reformation was won early on in the pubs. Collinson thus
observes that under Mary the protestant congregation gathered at tav-
erns such as the Swan at Limehouse, the Kings Head at Ratcliffe, the
Saracens Head at Islington, and the like, where it was not unheard of for
the fellowship of 30 to consume 3 or 4 'pots' of beer each before attending to the scripture.[25] Zealous late-Elizabethan Puritans, however, found
such socializing profane. One Puritan writer, Collinson notes, indeed
claimed that anyone godly venturing into a drinking house immediately
'doth thinke he cometh into a little hell'.[26] The throwback Falstaff instead
spends time in the Boar's Head Tavern moralizing about the damnation
of *others*.

The tremendous gulf between new and old Protestant sensibilities is
equally evident in Falstaff's oft-noted theatricality. In contrast to the
famed late Elizabethan Puritan anti-theatricality, earlier evangelicals

such as the playwrights John Bale and that 'father of English comedy'[27], Nicholas Udall, advanced their calls for Reformation via the comic. As Collinson argues, under Mary, 'Gardiner and other conservative bishops were pilloried in "all sorts of farces and pastimes".'[28] So tied to the drama were early evangelicals that at Coventry Marian martyr John Careless regularly starred in the traditional Corpus Christi plays.[29] The afore-mentioned student of theatrical misrule Lever, archdeacon of Corpus Christi, did not suppress the cycle plays there, which continued until 2 years after his death. But when Lever's generation of Protestants died, so too did their evangelical tolerance for theatre, religious or otherwise. Whereas Abbot Feckenham of Westminster, speaking in Elizabeth's first parliament, could still assume Protestant polemical theatricality when he railed against the 'preachers and scaffold players of this new reli-gion'[30], by the late 1570s and 1580s, many evangelicals had already turned against even religious theatre as handled in 'filthie playes and enterludes'.[31]

In marked contrast to such ever-rising Puritan antipathy to the drama by the end of the century, appearing on stage in 1596–97, Falstaff embraced an old-fashioned play in declaiming, 'I must speak in passion, and I will do it in King Cambyses' vein' (II.iv.386–87), evoking a work from three decades earlier, mixing history with allegorical figures from the old morality play tradition (e.g., Diligence and God's Justice). When printed in 1569 it was advertised as *A lamentable tragedy mixed full of pleasant mirth, containing the life of Cambyses King of Persia, from the beginning of his kingdom unto his death, . . . and last of all, his odious death by God's Justice appointed.* Falstaff's model is therefore, character-istically, outdated, as is his desire for an improvisational 'play extempore' (II.iv.280). Shakespeare has, once again, made Falstaff an unmistakable throwback, for his sensibilities are laughably at odds with most Elizabethans of any stripe, let alone contemporary puritans.

The Un-Prodigal Son: Irony and the Pre-Reformation Morality Play

Though allusions to the pre-Reformation morality play have long been noted in *1 Henry IV*, Shakespeare's ironic handling of this tradition has heretofore not been recognized. Critics have instead tended to speak of Hal in terms of the parable of the prodigal son and derivative conven-tional plays such as *The Interlude of Youth* (c. 1513–20), in which, as Wilson pointed out, the titular everyman is seduced by the Vice Riot, who, like Falstaff, commits robbery on the highway, jests with his young drinking companion on the subject of hanging, and spends time with him in a tavern (while in the company of Pride and Lechery).[32] King

Henry therefore speaks allegorically in claiming that '[R]iot and [D]ishonor stain the brow | Of my young Harry' (I.i.85–86). Ellis argues further that a number of ostensibly authoritative characters invite this same 'reading' of the play in terms of the prodigal son paradigm, that of a rebellious youth who lacks respect for his father and his patrimony, wastes his inheritance, falls into dissolution, suffers extreme degradation, then experiences a reformation, followed by reunion with a forgiving father.[33]

The temptation is to read such allusions uncritically. Samuel Johnson, writing in his 1765 edition of Shakespeare's works, was perhaps the first critic to voice such an interpretation when he concluded,

> The moral to be drawn from this representation is that no man is more dangerous than he that with a will to corrupt hath the power to please; and that neither wit nor honesty ought to think themselves safe with such company when we see Harry seduced by Falstaff.[34]

Among modern critics, Wilson, above all, fleshed out this dominant reading of Hal as 'not only the youth or the prodigal' but as 'the young prodigal *prince*', further maintaining that

> [N]ever, for a moment, did [Shakespeare] twist [the story of the Prodigal Son] from its original purpose, which was serious, moral, didactic. Shakespeare plays no tricks with his public. . . . Prince Hal is the prodigal, and his repentance is not only to be taken seriously, it is to be admired and commended. Moreover, the story of the prodigal . . . ran the same course as ever and contained the same three principal characters: the tempter, the younker, and the father with property to bequeath and counsel to give.[35]

Recently, Ervin Beck found the paradigm's application so self-explanatory a fact that he merely lists '*Henry IV, Parts 1* and *2* (Prince Hal)' as one of six plays in which 'Shakespeare, in fact, used the archetypal story'.[36] It has thus long appeared that Hal's progress toward kingship corresponded to the archetypal pattern of prodigally-inspired morality plays in which, according to Fiona Dunlop, the youthful protagonist's temporary fall from grace is 'often represented by the child's choice of an evil counselor rather than a good one as his guide for the life ahead'.[37] It is just such contrariety that Wilson had in mind in invoking a contrast between 'the tempter' and the upright father with 'counsel to give'.

Yet, the seeming contrariety of foils has a curious habit of collapsing in Shakespeare, never more so than in the elaborate similarities Shakespeare establishes between the supposed opposite counsellors, Falstaff and King Henry. If Falstaff is meant to recall the Vice, Henry only ironically resembles virtuous figures of the morality play world. In both parts of *Henry IV*, he self-consciously evokes a typical Virtue character serving as the wise, moral councillor to Youth, particularly the figure of Conscyence, since he dispenses much stern remonstrance in Act III, Scene ii, to the supposedly wayward Hal for indulging 'lewd desires' and 'barren pleasures' among 'rude society', making him 'degenerate' (ll. 14–16, 128). But Henry's final advice is not really morally 'good', and his own flawed conscience renders his moral posturing ironic.

Just as Falstaff represents one variety of religious anachronism, Henry, who likens his majesty and authority to that of 'a robe pontifical' (III.ii.56), is associated ironically with archaic notions of pilgrimage and penance linked to the 'Old Faith', Catholicism. Henry seems to want his penance for ordering the murder of King Richard II to be a proverbial 'two-for', serving the ends of 'policy' as well as conscience, since he announces a scheme to end the civil war his usurpation incited by leading an expedition to the Holy Land in an amalgam of medieval pilgrimage and Crusade (I.i.19–27). Thus, like Falstaff, Henry presents the persona of one ostentatiously *wanting* to be moral, as in the case when he remarks, 'there thou mak'st me sad, and make me sin | In envy . . . ' (I.i.78–79). Significantly, it is someone else who *makes him sin*, for elsewhere he seems not to fully acknowledge his own culpability, as when he tries to make Hal feel guilty, proclaiming, 'I know not whether God will have it so | For some displeasing service I have done', concluding that perhaps the prince is 'mark'd | For the hot vengeance, and the rod of heaven, | To punish my mistreadings' (III.ii.4–5, 9–11). Of course, the Vice-like Falstaff is similarly associated with would-be repentance, earning him that colourful epithet, 'Monsieur Remorse' (I.ii.113). Like Henry, he cannot bring himself to repent, because he blames others for his weakness: 'Well, I'll repent, and that suddenly, while I am in some liking. I shall be out of heart shortly, and then I shall have no strength to repent. . . . Company, villainous company, hath been the spoil of me' (III.iii.4–10). Rather than contrariety, a remarkable doubleness between the two 'Vicious' figures therefore becomes apparent in Falstaff's deflating performance as King Henry in the 'play extempore' at the tavern in Act II, Scene iv, when the old knight burlesques the king's self-congratulatory moralizing with a cushion as his crown and a dagger for his sceptre.

Consistent with doubleness, both old father-figures would seem to have been plump, that is, physically similar. For example, Worcester provokes Henry in Act I, Scene iii, by reminding him that the Percy family 'Have holp to make [him] so portly' (l. 13). Though 'portly' could suggest something like 'stately', it also meant 'fat' or 'corpulent', as Falstaff is a 'goodly portly man, i'faith, and a corpulent' (II.iv.422). Worcester thus later again taunts a king who had boasted that his presence showed 'like a feast' (III.ii.58) in terms of eating and portliness in asserting that, 'being fed by us', a Gargantuan Henry 'Grew by our feeding to so great a bulk' that the Percy clan cannot come near him 'For fear of swallowing' (V.i.59, 62–63). Interestingly, tradition has always maintained that Burbage, who must have played the mature part of King Henry, not the thin boyish prince, was plump, for, just as Henry is 'portly', so is another of Burbage's roles, Hamlet, 'fat, and scant of breath' (V.ii.87), having 'foregone all custom of exercises' (II.ii.296–97). Dwelling on fattening, Hamlet muses, 'we fat all creatures else to fat us, and we fat ourselves for maggots: your fat king and your lean beggar is but variable service' (IV.ii.21–24). More than did Kemp, Burbage's physique invited the opposition of fat and lean.

If a plump Burbage played an old, fat King Henry, he might have physically resembled the padded Kemp playing Falstaff (who is described as 'sweet creature of *bombast*' [II.iv.327], i.e., cotton padding), so that the two – appearing together only once in Act V, Scene i, before the battle at Shrewsbury – actually mirror each other in arms. The play invites just such a staging/reading. Fretting before battle, Falstaff urges his friend with 'Hal, if thou see me down in the battle and bestride me, so; 'tis a point of friendship' (V.i.121–22), prompting Hal's jest, 'Nothing but a Colossus can do thee that friendship' (123–24). Shortly thereafter Hal actually has the opportunity to 'bestride' his portly father in defence against Douglas, since at V.iv.38 ff. the stage direction reads: '*They fight; the king being in danger, enter* PRINCE OF WALES'. Hal then interjects, 'Hold up thy head, vile Scot, or thou art like | Never to hold it up again!' (IV.iv.39). It is clear here that the king is what Falstaff feared he would be, that is, 'down in battle', because Hal is determined to stop Douglas from looking down on and killing his now endangered father. The stage action thus invites Hal to essentially stand over his father, recalling the prior 'Colossus' imagery. What is clear is that the paradoxically *immoral Virtue* and the so-called 'reverent Vice' do not remain contraries at all but instead become, especially at Shrewsbury, doubles – fat, old, anachronistic, hypocritical, self-deluded, bombastic and cowardly.

Thus, for all the consensus about the conventional Youth/Prodigal morality play reading,[38] it does not finally square with the characters or plot we encounter in the play. Contrary to the conventions for the youthful protagonist of traditional moralities, Hal is never actually seduced, never indeed misled, never in fact in need of any repentance; nor does he squander his patrimony 'prodigally'. As Ellis frames the scenario at work here, '[F]rom the beginning of *1 Henry IV* Hal is presented as *already a reformed character*, far too clear-sighted and in control of his actions to be "misled" by Falstaff'.[39] Hal instead announces at the end of his stunning second-scene soliloquy his plot to falsify a disreputable image, a kind of disguise, in order to stage his own eventual stunning 'reformation':

> By so much shall I falsify men's hopes,
> And like bright metal on a sullen ground,
> My reformation glitt'ring o'er my fault,
> Shall show more goodly and attract more eyes
> Than which hath no foil to set it off. (I.ii.211–15)

As much or more a foil than that other Harry, Harry Percy, the prince himself presents the mask or 'vizard' of a Prodigal that will allow his feignedly wild, 'loose behaviour' (I.ii.208) to serve as a 'sullen' background or past for the final spectacular unmasking of his already extant 'bright' and 'redeemed' self, which will then appear to be 'glitt'ring o'er [his *seeming*] fault'. Of course, the reading of Hal as a sincere 'prodigal prince' does not account for his pragmatic hoodwinking of his self-deluded father-figures. Thus, when in *2 Henry IV* the Lord Chief Justice asserts, 'You have misled the youthful Prince', Falstaff offers a correction whose accuracy we cannot deny: '[T]he young Prince hath misled me' (I.ii.143–44). Even Wilson observes with some bemusement, 'In this play of the Prodigal prince it is Hal who should rightly exhibit moods of repentance', so that 'it seems quite illogical to transfer them to Falstaff, the tempter'.[40] Consistent with his self-identification with youth, in a remarkable inversion of youth and age, it is Falstaff who serves as an *arrested* prodigal (and it is in fact he who invokes the biblical story).

Likewise contrary to the wayward prince of the popular source play *The Famous Victories of King Henry the Fifth* (prior to 1587), Hal does not wish to participate in robberies, does not ever do so, and in fact goes so far as to pay back the stolen money, 'with advantage' or interest (II.iv.547). Ellis thus finds Shakespeare '[d]isinclined to show a Hal who is at any point authentically dissolute'.[41] Shakespeare's self-conscious alteration of his source is all the more pronounced in light of the fact that *Famous Victories* 'lacks a Vice figure' and instead 'locat[es] vice in young Hal, who later undergoes a St Paul-like transformation'.[42] By contrast, far from repenting, Shakespeare's anything-but-madcap prince repeatedly 'sounds a faint but persistent note of moral disapproval' about Falstaff's character.[43] Ironically, then, Hal takes on part of the plot function of the charismatic Vice, disguising his true nature and announcing his scheme to the audience, even as he disapproves of traditional moral vices. Hal is thus what we might perhaps understand as a censorious 'Anti-Vice', inverting audience expectations.

The Influence of the Post-Reformation Morality Play: New Youth Paradigms, New Ideology

While Shakespeare self-consciously alludes to old traditions of the morality play, he also draws upon other, Edwardian, dramatic models. In an attempt to influence the boy-king and the youthful population of England, Edwardian evangelical dramatists looked to the Bible for precedents of youths who rebelled against the traditions of foolish elders for good ends. They found there the figure of the boy-king Josias, who reformed the idolatrous practices rampant under his father, as well as the predestined youth Jacob, who tricked his older reprobate brother Esau out of his inheritance and used disguise (goat's skins) to dupe his blind old father Isaac into believing him to be the rougher Esau in order to receive his blessing. Such biblical models gave rise to new Reformation-era dramatic treatments of generational conflict. Edwardian morality plays such as *Lusty Juventus* and *Nice Wanton* (both c. 1548–50) illustrate that when 'the Reformation rendered the values of elders synonymous with those of the corrupt faith, the youthful protagonist might be encouraged to cast aside the values of his elders'.[44]

The paradigms of youth during the Reformation had indeed changed in ways that inform Shakespeare's treatment of generational conflict via Hal's ironic brand of rebellion against his corrupted elders. Compared to the paradigms of pre-Reformation generations, where youths had been represented as 'essentially sinful' and elders as respectable moral authorities, by mid-century, traditionalists could inveigh that children were now making 'a merry mockery of their parents', with one imagined monologue running, 'My father is an old doting foole and will fast upon fryday . . . . But you shall se me of another sorte, I warraunt you. For I wil neuer folowe . . . nor walke in the papysticall pathes of my parents'.[45] Brigden notes that Protestant anti-papist polemic actually 'attack[ed] paternal authority', whether that of the Pope, of priests ('ghostly fathers'), or of the actual fathers of Catholic households.[46]

The extant mid-century predestinarian court play, *Jacob and Esau*, with its duping of the similarly blind old patriarch, Isaac, at the expense of the blustering, hot-headed twin, Esau, prefigures the often comic Harry Percy/Hotspur (a twin or double Harry to Harry Monmouth/ Hal[47]). The now-lost play *Old Custom* (c. 1548–50) alludes to the same biblical story, and the storyline in both Protestant plays mirrors Hal's pragmatic hoodwinking of two essentially blind old father-figures.

Interestingly for a reexamination of Hal's pragmatism, such drama reflects the Edwardian 'policy' of John Dudley, earl of Warwick, duke of Northumberland, who 'took great pains with the [young] king's political education, recruiting the services of . . . one of the clerks of the privy council', who was enlisted 'to help by introducing the king to political essays, along Machiavellian lines'.[48] Dudley also favoured court plays that promoted a new pragmatic ethos of justified, elect Protestant self-interest. In fact, he is noted for having owned a copy of *Old Custom*, listed in an inventory of his documents; this Edwardian court play pitted 'Virtue', 'Zeal', and the youthful 'Hunger of Knowledge' versus the evidently hoodwinked Catholic 'Old Blind Custom'.[49] The marriage of Machiavelli and Calvinist predestination in such drama was an extreme extension of a new religious ideology justifying some calculated self-interest, both spiritual and monetary. If the overthrow of the corrupt father-figure in Calvinist drama is sympathetic to Machiavellian pragmatism, Shakespeare arguably underscores this linkage when he alludes to Edwardian models in the *Henry IV* plays.

Notably, Hal's 'reformation' occasionally seems to be imbued with Calvinist-inspired ideology, as after the plotting to dupe Falstaff at Gad's Hill when he promises in the concluding couplet to his I.ii soliloquy, 'I'll so offend to make offence a skill, | Redeeming time when men think least I will' (209–10). Hal is here not just restoring the relevance of time in opposition to the un-timely Falstaff (though he is certainly doing that as well), for critics have also recognized an echo here of St Paul's Epistle to the Ephesians: 'Take hede therefore that ye walk circumspectly, not as fooles but as wise, | Redeeming the time: for the days are evil' (5:15–16).[50] In this scripture, the word 'redeeming' was widely interpreted as an economic-spiritual metaphor, since the marginal gloss in the Calvinist Geneva Bible offers the following interpretation: 'Selling all worldlie pleasures to b[u]y time . . . In these perilous days & crafte of the adversaries, take hede how to b[uy] again the occasions of godliness, which the world hathe taken from you'. Time is thus commodified as something bought for a good/spiritual end. Shakespeare might have found the same allusion to St Paul treated in similar fashion in *Lusty Juventus*: 'Saint Paul unto the Ephesians giveth good exhortation, | Saying, walk circumspectly, redeeming the time, | That is, to spend it well, and not to wickedness incline'. The lines here paraphrase 'redeeming the time' in overtly economic terms ('to spend it well').[51] Shakespeare, too, plays on Paul's Epistle in an economic sense. Though several meanings of 'redeem' found in the *Oxford English Dictionary* are possible, including 'To buy back' (*OED* 1), 'To ransom, liberate, free . . . from bondage' (*OED* 3), 'To rescue, save, deliver' (*OED* 4), particularly relevant here is 'To free (mortgaged property), to recover . . . by payment

of the amount due' (2a.). Hal has, after all, already been using such connotations, as in pledging that he will 'pay the debt I never promised'
(I.ii.202).

The language of debt pervades *1 Henry IV* in ways that typically sound
crass rather than spiritual: 'The King will always think him in our debt'
(I.iii.286); Hal has had to pay Falstaff's 'reckoning many a time' to the
hostess at the Boar's Head Tavern (I.ii.47) so that the latter must admit,
'I'll give thee thy due, thou hast paid all there' (I.ii.51); Hal finds in
Falstaff's pockets in II.iv what he later identifies as 'tavern-reckonings'
(III.iii.158); the loot taken at Gad's Hill 'shall be paid back again with
advantage' or interest (II.iv.528); Falstaff 'will give the devil his due'
(I.ii.119); by contrast, he 'owest God a death' but insists, "Tis not due yet;
I would be loath to pay him before his day' (V.i.126–28). Above all, the
rhetoric of economics is evident in Hal's extended elaboration of the calculating metaphor of Hotspur being 'but [his] factor' or business agent,
who will '*exchange*' glories for indignities (III.ii.145) and labours 'To
engross up glorious deeds on my behalf; | And I will call him to so *strict
account* | That he will *render* every glory up . . . Or I will tear *the reckoning*
from his heart' (III.ii.147–52). Whereas the New Testament story of the
prodigal son used wealth as a spiritual metaphor, Shakespeare's handling
of religio-economic rhetoric seems to literalize the potential 'redeeming'
of debt metaphor so that the economic here often seems seedy, selfish,
and ruthlessly pragmatic. Such grotesque literalization may therefore
have sounded an ironic note in lines that potentially invoke Calvinist
ideology.

In this way, ultimately, Shakespeare offers neither a straightforward,
traditional Youth morality play consistent with the prodigal son paradigm nor a simple endorsement of Hal's Machiavellian tendencies or his
sense of his own elect justification, but rather a richly ambivalent,
remarkably witty and satirical exploration of the ever-widening gulf
between new and old generational sensibilities. Falstaff's 'gross' embodiment of pre-neoclassical sensibilities, particularly of the indecorous
'mingling [of] kings and clowns' and the 'contrariety' of the medieval
Vice and Vice-descendant clowns of the Elizabethan stage, like his
enactment of a 'jangling', anachronistic religious ethos that was at once
iconoclastic, carnivalesque and theatrical, demonstrates just how resonant such subsequently oxymoronic sensibilities had once been.
Indeed, however extinct those sensibilities may be today, they continue
to remain viable on stage, where Falstaff's gross indecorum, contrariety,
anachronism and arrested self-identification with youthful prodigality
continue to be vital sources of laughter. In the end, *1 Henry IV* affords
to readers and audiences extraordinary ambiguity and ambivalence,

weighing the costs and benefits of cultural transition by poising the undeniable satisfactions of the rational pragmatism potential in a new ethos against the loss of a sympathetic vitality discernible in the now seemingly irrational incongruity of the old.

NOTES

1. David Ellis, *Shakespeare's Practical Jokes: An Introduction to the Comic in His Work* (Lewisburg, WV: Bucknell University Press, 2007), p. 84.
2. Harold Bloom, *Shakespeare and the Invention of the Human* (New York: Riverhead Books, 1998), p. 305.
3. Giorgio Melchiori interprets this enigmatic statement as referring to 'the time when performances in public theatres began' in *The Second Part of King Henry IV*, The New Cambridge Shakespeare edition (1989; rpt.: Cambridge: Cambridge University Press, 2007), p. 26.
4. Philip Sidney, *Apology for Poetry*, ed. H. A. Needham (London, 1931), pp. 54–55.
5. Robert Weimann, *Author's Pen and Actor's Voice: Playing and Writing in Shakespeare's Theatre* (Cambridge: Cambridge University Press, 2000), p. 101.
6. Quoted in *Narrative and Dramatic Sources of Shakespeare Volume Two: : The Comedies 1597–1603*, comp. by Geoffrey Bullough, 8 vols. (London: Routledege and Kegan Paul, 1958), p. 443.
7. Sidney, *Apology*, p. 54.
8. Weimann, *Author's Pen*, p. 10.
9. Weimann, *Author's Pen*, p. 10.
10. Some awareness of this character note is evident in Edward Elgar's 1913 symphonic portrait *Falstaff*, Symphonic Study in C minor, Opus 68). Elgar wrote that 'Falstaff is really the mad, pathetic mixture of contrarieties in us all'. Michael Kennedy, *The Life of Elgar* (Cambridge: Cambridge University Press, 2004), p. 136.
11. Wilson, *The Fortunes of Falstaff* (Cambridge: Macmillan Co., 1944), p. 32.
12. See Albert Feuillerat, (ed.), *Documents Relating to the Revels at Court in the Time of King Edward VI and Queen Mary* (Louvain, 1914), pp. 20, 22, 194, 255–58, 5–6, 26, 49.
13. Feuillerat, *Documents Relating to the Revels*, pp. 89–90, 97; emphases added.
14. Royall Tyler, (ed.), *Calendar of Letters, Despatches, and State Papers. Relating to the Negotiations Between England and Spain* (London: David Nutt, 1914), 10: 444.
15. St Thomas More, *The Confutation of Tyndale's Answer*, in *The Complete Works of St Thomas More*, ed. L. A. Schuster et al. (New Haven, CT: Yale University Press, 1973), volume 8, p. 42.
16. Susan Brigden, 'Youth and the English Reformation', in *The Impact of the English Reformation 1500–1640*, ed. Peter Marshall (London: Arnold, 1997), (p. 56).
17. Alan H. Nelson, (ed.), *REED: Cambridge* (Toronto: University of Toronto Press, 1989), in 2 Volumes, 1: 159–60.
18. Nelson, *REED*, 1: 159.
19. Patrick Collinson, *From Iconoclasm to Iconophobia: The Cultural Impact of the Second Reformation* (Reading: University of Reading, 1986), p. 13.
20. John Gough Nichols (ed.), *The Diary of Henry Machyn, Citizen and Merchant-Taylor of London, From A.D. 1550 to A.D. 1563* (London: British Library,1848), pp. 13–14.
21. Collinson, *From Iconoclasm to Iconophobia*, p. 9.

22. Wilson, *Fortunes of Falstaff*, p. 16; Buckner B. Trawick, *Shakespeare and Alcohol* (Amsterdam: Rodopi, 1978), p. 11.
23. Naseeb Shaheen, *Biblical References in Shakespeare's History Plays* (Newark, DE: University of Delaware Press, 1989), p. 137; Alfred Ainger, *Lectures and Essays*, Volume I (London: Macmillan, 1905), p. 142; Kristen Poole, *Radical Religion from Shakespeare to Milton: Figures of Nonconformity in Early Modern England* (Cambridge: Cambridge University Press, 2000), p. 35.
24. Grace Tiffany, 'Puritanism in Comic History: Exposing Royalty in the Henry Plays', *Shakespeare Studies*, 26 (1998), 256–87 (p. 265).
25. Collinson, *From Iconoclasm to Iconophobia*, p. 9.
26. Collinson, *From Iconoclasm to Iconophobia*, p. 9.
27. Edwald Flügel, ed., *Ralph Roister Doister*, in *Representative English Comedies*, gen. ed., C. M. Gayley (New York: Macmillan, 1903), Volume I, pp. 98, 99.
28. Collinson, *From Iconoclasm to Iconophobia*, p. 10.
29. Collinson, *From Iconoclasm to Iconophobia*, p. 11.
30. *Proceedings in the Parliament of Elizabeth I*, vol. 1, 1558–1581, ed. T. E. Hartley (Leicester: Leicester University Press, 1981), p. 31.
31. Philip Stubbes, *Anatomy of Abuses in England in Shakspere's Youth AD 1583*, ed. F. J. Furnivall (New Shakespeare Society, n.s.s. iv, vi, xii. 1877–82), pp. 140–43.
32. Wilson, *Fortunes of Falstaff*, pp. 18–19.
33. Ellis, *Shakespeare's Practical Jokes,* pp. 99–100.
34. Samuel Johnson, 'Notes from The Plays of William Shakespeare (1765)', *Henry The Fourth Parts I and II. Critical Essays*, ed. David Bevington (New York and London: Garland, 1986), pp. 7–8; 8.
35. Wilson, *Fortunes of Falstaff*, pp. 23, 21.
36. Ervin Beck, 'Terence Improved: The Paradigm of the Prodigal Son in Early English Renaissance Comedy', *Renaissance Drama* 6 (1973), 107–22 (p. 107).
37. Fiona S. Dunlop, *The Late Medieval Interlude: The Drama of Youth and Aristocratic Masculinity* (Woodbridge, Suffolk: York Medieval Press in association with Boydell and Brewer, 2007), p. 26.
38. For notable exceptions, see A.C. Bradley, 'The Rejection of Falstaff', in *Oxford Lectures on Poetry* (London: Macmillan, 1909) and Ellis, *Shakespeare's Practical Jokes,* pp. 99–101.
39. Ellis, *Shakespeare's Practical Jokes,* p. 100; emphasis mine.
40. Wilson, *Fortunes of Falstaff,* p. 33.
41. Ellis, *Shakespeare's Practical Jokes,* pp. 101–02.
42. Melchiori, *Second Part of King Henry IV*, p. 11; Alan Lutkus, 'Sir John Falstaff', in *Fools and Jesters in Literature, Art, and History: A Bio-Bibliographical Sourcebook*, ed. Vicki K. Janik (Westport, CT: Greenwood, 1998), pp. 176–84 (p. 178).
43. Ellis, *Shakespeare's Practical Jokes,* p. 99.
44. Pamela M. King, 'Minority Plays: Two Interludes for Edward VI', *Medieval English Theatre*, 15 (1993), 87–102 (p. 88).
45. Dunlop, *Late Medieval Interlude*, p. 33; John Christopherson, *An Exhortacion to All Menne to Tke Hede and Beware of Rebellion* (London, 1554), sig. Tii^v; cited in Brigden, 'Youth and the English Reformation', p. 56.
46. Brigden, 'Youth and the English Reformation', p. 64.
47. For an analysis of Hotspur as Hal's double see John Kerrigan, '*Henry IV* and the Death of Old Double', *Essays in Criticism* 40.1 (1990), 24–53.
48. David Loades, 'Dudley, John, duke of Northumberland (1504–1553)', *Oxford Dictionary of National Biography*, (Oxford: Oxford University Press, 2004); online edn, May 2005 [www.oxforddnb.com/view/printable/8156, accessed 20 December 2007].

49. See Albert Feuillerat, 'An Unknown Protestant Morality Play', *Modern Language Review*, 9 (1914), 94–96; Paul Whitfield White, 'Patronage, Protestantism, and Stage Propaganda in Early Elizabethan England', in *Patronage, Politics, and Literary Tradition in England 1558-1658*, ed. Cedric C. Brown (Detroit: Wayne State University Press, 1991), p. 123.

50. See D. J. Palmer, 'Casting off the Old Man: History and St Paul in *Henry IV*' (1970), in *Henry The Fourth Parts I and II. Critical Essays*, ed. David Bevington (New York and London: Garland Publishing Inc., 1986), pp. 315–35. Palmer's essay informs subsequent discussion throughout this paragraph.

51. Palmer, 'Casting off the Old Man' p. 319.

CHAPTER SEVEN

New Directions: 'By Shrewsbury Clock': The Time of Day and the Death of Hotspur in 1 *Henry IV*

Brian Walsh

Shakespeare had multiple sources for *1 Henry IV*, and while there is no consensus among scholars about the precise constellation of materials he employed, the primary wellsprings were probably Holinshed's *Chronicles* (1587), the anonymously-authored play *The Famous Victories of Henry V* (ca. 1587) and Samuel Daniel's *Civil Wars* (1595).[1] In this chapter, I explore a particular innovation of *1 Henry IV* in relation to its theatrical model, the *Famous Victories*: the unprecedented inclusion of Hotspur in the dramatic rendering of Henry V's life. The inclusion of the Percy rebellion, and of the Hotspur character in particular, alters the theatrical experience of the Prince Hal/Henry V story by extending the amount of time it takes to tell that story, so much so that it cannot be done in a single play. This move reveals to audiences that the temporal shape of history can always be recast. Further, I suggest that there is a connection here between temporal manipulations and factual ones. Through Falstaff's involvement in the disputed details of Hotspur's death near the end of the play, *1 Henry IV* comments on the ways that such acts of reshaping time can call attention to other kinds of inflections of the historical record, and so alerts audiences to the instability of historical knowledge. Shakespeare, throughout the play, calls attention to theatrical performance as an activity that depends in part on its conspicuous distortion of time, and the play's ending braids the distortion of time with the distortion of historical events. *1 Henry IV* thus stages how dramatic form can contribute to the development of a critical historical consciousness.

Enter Hotspur

The Percy family and their revolt had certainly always been a part of the historical materials covering the reign of Henry IV, and it was Daniel who adjusted the age of Hotspur to make him a foil to the Prince of Wales.[2] But for Elizabethan playwrights and playgoers, the *Famous Victories* provided a paradigm for putting the history of Henry V's life on stage without recourse to the involvement of the house of Northumberland. It depicted the career of Henry V, starting with his days as a reckless young prince and covering the death of the king, Henry V's invasion of France, his victory at Agincourt, and the subsequent show of fealty by the French king years afterward. One of Shakespeare's chief interventions in his own version of the story about the decline of Henry IV and the rise of his son was his modulation of the pace of this story. Rather than covering Hal's rise to the throne and subsequent foreign conquest, *1 Henry IV* instead concentrates on the period of the rebellion led by the Percy family. This concentration on an internal, rather than an external, struggle for sovereignty has a number of political implications for questions of national unity and monarchial succession in the 1590s.[3] I will explore here what this addition says about historical representation more broadly, especially historical representation in the theatre.

The American comedian Steven Wright, known for his deadpan delivery style and the inversions of common sense he inflicts on common phrases, used to tell a joke about a map of the United States he just purchased: 'it's actual size'. The joke unsettles the basic functionality of a map: such objects are delineations of space that work because they are radical reductions of what they represent. A map orients us through a miniature rendering of a locale, so that we can navigate or merely get a sense of an immensely larger whole. History plays that cover any amount of time greater than the length of a performance likewise work through a kind of temporal reduction, so that the minutes and hours that make up the duration of a history play come to stand for larger slices of the time span it represents, which itself is but one slice of the totality of the past. No history play can ever be actual size, and so each always involves intense acts of temporal compression and sleight of hand in order to produce an experience of the past within the time allotted for a stage play.

To take one small example of this from *1 Henry IV*, Hal at one point announces the time of day, speaking of 'this present twelve o'clock at midnight' (II.iv.92–93). This is shortly before Falstaff enters the tavern to take his rhetorical lumps over the actual beating he took during the Gad's Hill caper. After the exchange about the Gad's Hill jest blows up in Falstaff's face, he demands they change the subject and perform a little play. The Sheriff, looking for the men who robbed the travellers, comes knocking as this is happening. He proclaims that it is 'two o'clock' in the morning (II.iv.512). Shakespeare maps a false temporality onto the objective time of a performance-in-progress. The 'two hours traffic' in the tavern world – from midnight to two – perhaps takes 25 minutes or less to play.[4] It demonstrates with particular clarity how the passing of time *within* the play is out of sync with the real time *of* the play in performance. To posit that more time has occurred during the span of a play than the audience can themselves detect is to impress upon audiences that time is among the conceptual materials that dramatic poets machinate to suit their aims.

This is not a surprising or unique occurrence. Shakespeare's dramaturgy is not, of course, troubled with the so-called 'unity of time'; rather, it regularly exploits various forms of 'double time'.[5] Indeed, the flagrant manipulation of temporality on the Elizabethan stage more broadly was enough of a convention that it could be derided by Sidney and others. As Sidney writes in the *Defence of Poetry*:

> Now, of time they [dramatists and players] are much more liberal: for ordinary it is that two young princes fall in love; after many traverses, she is got with child, delivered of a fair boy; he is lost, growth to a man, falls in love, and is ready to get another child; and all this in two hours' space: which, how absurd it is in sense, even sense may imagine.[6]

Audiences were clearly more tolerant of the temporal aesthetics of most plays than Sidney. That the 'theatrical time' of a play – that is, the time expenditure of an actual performance – frames the representation of these alternate, fantastic time schemes that emerge within the dramatic fictions offered on stage was surely axiomatic by the time Shakespeare called attention to it in the Prologue to *Henry V* where the chorus promises to turn 'th' accomplishment of many years|Into an hour-glass' (*Henry V*. Prologue.30–31).

If we assume that the text of the *Famous Victories* as we have it accurately records what was designed as a single play – and it should be noted that some scholars have questioned this – that play would have presented the narrative of Hal's base youth to his triumph at Agincourt in one performance.[7] Elizabethan playgoers at a performance of *1 Henry IV* during its initial run may have thus had certain expectations about which accomplishments would be stuffed into the hourglass governing the play they were about to watch, and at what kind of pace it all would happen. Playgoers on the way to the play we now call *The First Part of*

Henry IV had in all probability no idea that a *second* part, much less a third, were coming in which further aspects of Henry's life would be enacted.[8] Both the *Famous Victories* and *1 Henry IV* feature early scenes of the prince hanging around a disreputable crew of robbers, and it would have been reasonable to expect that this new play would also present a structure that would round out the prince's early, self-promised 'redemption' with his triumph over the French at Agincourt. Falstaff, who banters with Hal in the prince's first scene, had his analogues in the *Famous Victories*, split between the clown Derrick and Sir John Oldcastle, the jocular companion to the prince and Falstaff's original namesake, who eventually recedes from view in that play. Playgoers familiar with *The Famous Victories* would surely be able to intuit that however much fun Shakespeare's Hal is going to have with Falstaff/Oldcastle at the expense of his responsibility to his family's royal position, he would assume the mantle of a glorious hero, while the clown figures and those, like Oldcastle and others in the *Famous Victories* who assist him in a robbery, would eventually have to fade away somehow.[9]

But the road Shakespeare's Hal takes to his new destined glory is more winding than that taken by the prince in the older play. *1 Henry IV* ends well before Agincourt and the French villains it offers in contrast to Henry's new found heroism. The climax at the Battle of Shrewsbury fixes the initial stirrings of Hal's princely mind as a response to the defence of his father's crown, rather than to the death of his father, as happens in the *Famous Victories*, and it is this shift that allows Hotspur to enter the story.

Shakespeare did not invent Hotspur, but he did help to remake this figure in the popular imagination when he chose to represent him in his play as the antagonist of the young Prince of Wales and, following Daniel's example, the generational equivalent of Hal. Critics have long understood that this move makes artistic sense, as it heightens the dramatic tension of the story. The prince must seek to gain his father's love and trust against the example of a preferred pseudo-son. This younger Hotspur serves as a kind of alternate self for Hal, one he must both emulate and defeat.[10] Young Percy exists on the margins of *Richard II*, but bursts into *1 Henry IV* with a *tour de force* speech that asserts he will be a major presence in the play, as both challenger of his king and as the reigning champion of English ideals of honour. Shakespeare's decision to plot his play so that it would include this rival figure and conclude at Shrewsbury creates dramatic space for Daniel's nemesis version of Hotspur to emerge and, more importantly, to expand on stage.[11]

The compact *Famous Victories of Henry V* moves rapidly through the prince's ascension to the throne and toward his triumph at Agincourt, without mention of the Percy rebellion. In the second scene, the carrier

Derick enters, complaining that he has been robbed. The culprit is Cuthbert Cutter, one of the prince's loose companions, who soon enters and is arrested. When he is brought to trial before the Lord Chief Justice, the Clerk of Office announces that the robbery took place 'the twentieth day of May last past, in the fourteenth year of our Sovereign Lord, King Henry the Fourth' (IV.18–20), that is, in May 1413. If we take that as the rough starting point for the play's action, and plot it to the closing scene, in which King Henry promises he will marry the French princess 'the first Sunday of next month', an event that took place in June 1420, we can date the play's ending as occurring in May 1420. From the end of Henry IV's life, through the Battle of Agincourt in 1415, through this postscript on his marriage settlement, the play covers about seven years.

1 Henry IV on the other hand begins with news from the Battle of Humbleton Hill, which took place in September 1402, and ends at the Battle of Shrewsbury, which happened in July 1403. Shakespeare thus slows down the pace considerably, so that audiences who had seen in the earlier play the representation of time moving along multiple years from scene to scene are here confronted with a dilation of time within a single year. It is still an outrageous act of temporal legerdemain to purport that the events of a year can be covered in an afternoon of theatre, but relative to the *Famous Victories* it is economic. Of course, we cannot assume early modern audiences to have been as sensitive to these temporal markers as later critics tend to be. It is most certainly true that most in Shakespeare's audience would not have had the dates for Henry's marriage to Princess Katherine or for the battles of Agincourt, Humbleton Hill or Shrewsbury easily at hand. But my emphasis isn't so much on the particular years being scrutinized, as on the general amount of time being represented in each play. The mere fact that the action of the *Famous Victories* runs from Hal's time as prince to the announcement, when he is years into his kingship, of his impending marriage clearly indicates a different span than that of *1 Henry IV*, in which he begins and ends as Prince of Wales. Some elements of the chronological precision I've just outlined – the years 1413–1420 versus the years 1402–1403 – may in fact have been blurred in the minds of playgoers, so that, failing to have those dates in mind, it would be difficult to gauge that the latter play is supposed to begin at a much earlier moment than the former. And this reinforces my larger point, for if that is the case, the similar early scenes involving the prince and his tavern companions in each play would give audiences the impression that *1 Henry IV* is more or less starting at the same place as the *Famous Victories* – the prince's errant youth – and would, like its predecessor, end with his kingly triumphs.

But the play cannot end there because of the presence of Hotspur. Every moment Hotspur remains undefeated in *1 Henry IV* suggests to an audience familiar with the older play that the apotheosis of Hal as the ideal English king is being further deferred, and that his story, as presented here, is being given a more diffuse temporal shape. This deferral creates tension around Hotspur's presence, for he blocks the prince's progress and the desired climax of Agincourt. When Hotspur will die and what place that death will hold in the play – whether it will serve as the end or as a turning point in the course of its enactment – is left in suspension for much of the first half. It is only as the play goes on that it become clearer that Hotspur's death will serve as a climax.

This sense of Hotspur as slowing down the pace of the history being told in *1 Henry IV* is a structural component of his characterization. Nearly all of his scenes in some way or another convey his wordiness. His style of speaking dilates the play through his extended speeches and rants. For instance, in the scene with his father, Northumberland, and his uncle, Worcester, after their family has been berated by King Henry, Hotspur's garrulous disposition is highlighted. His series of complaints and execrations upon the king are followed by a series of protestations from Worcester and Northumberland:

Worcester:	Peace, cousin, say no more (I.iii.186)
Northumberland:	Imagination of some great exploit
	Drives him beyond the bounds of existence
	(198–99)
Worcester:	He apprehends a world of figures here
	But not the form of what he should attend
	(208–09)
Worcester:	You start away
	And lend no ear to my purposes (215–16)
Worcester:	Hear you cousin, a word (225)

The impatience of the older men finally reaches a new pitch:

Worcester:	Farewell, kinsman. I'll talk to you
	When you are better tempered to attend.
Northumberland:	Why, what a wasp-stung and impatient fool
	Art thou to break into this woman's mood,
	Tying thine ear to no tongue but thine own!
	(232–36)

But even this reprimand cannot stop him from launching into another long attack on King Henry. When Hotspur finally claims 'I have done', Worcester responds ironically: 'Nay, if you have not, to it again; |We will stay your leisure' (253–54).[12]

Hotspur's penchant for unlimited speech is underlined to such an extent early in the play that it suggests Shakespeare wants audiences to be aware of the fact, throughout the rest of the play, that when Hotspur talks, he is taking up a lot of time, further deferring his defeat and the eventual triumphs of Henry V. Even his amusing deflation of Glendower, where he stands as the hard-headed rationalist and the Welshman as the insufferable windbag, is itself a bit of an extravagant rhetorical perform-ance (see III.i.24–34). His claim towards the end of the play that 'I pro-fess not talking' is surely a laugh line soaked with dramatic irony (V.ii.91). That Hotspur dies in mid-sentence, his linguistic excess lim-ited only by mortality, is one of Shakespeare's grimmer jokes.

This death comes well into a performance of *1 Henry IV*, quite close to its end. It marks the dénouement of the theatrical experience of his-tory the play offers, and gives way to an ending in which Hal is still Prince of Wales, King Henry still reigns, and Agincourt nowhere in sight. The play then, as we have said, offers a different experience of the story of Henry V's youth and development than had previously been available on the popular stage. David Scott Kastan, in his useful book *Shakespeare and the Shapes of Time*, offers a compelling way to assess how this change comments on historical representation in the theatre. Kastan discusses the Shakespearean history play's generic specificity in terms of the impossibility of a play being 'actual size' in the ways dis-cussed above. He writes that a history play's 'beginning and end demand to be considered only as arbitrary boundaries'. Each history play repre-sents a 'mere episode carved from the continuum of human time'.[13] Kastan's insight is an important starting point for the conclusions I want to draw from the fact of Hotspur's presence in *1 Henry IV*, and the ways that this presence warps the shape of the history of Henry V's life pre-sented in the *Famous Victories*. For, if we see that any history play is presenting, again in Kastan's words, 'a mere segment of an on-going temporal process', we can then focus that observation further to see how each segment can itself be segmented.[14] Thus, the rhythm of temporal-ity in the conception of the past can be constantly modulated. This is true of all historical representation, no species of which can ever detail the full totality of the past, but the point is driven home in particular ways in the theatre. This is because theatre is itself an experience in time, and so, as Kastan and others have argued, as an artistic form bears a special relationship to history.[15]

To subject history to theatrical performance is to bring the past into being in the present.[16] This 'being' is, of course, a simulacrum of the 'real' past. Performance of history proffers a three-dimensional experi-ence of the past that gives audiences an opportunity to imagine that they have a preternatural perspective, that they can see and hear what happened in a different spatio-temporal reality than the one they now occupy. But there were enough factors in Elizabethan playing conditions that rendered a full immersion in this illusion of access to the past impossible.[17] Today, sitting in modern theatres, usually darkened and insulated against outside noise, it may be easier for audiences to accept the fantasy of a gaze that can pierce the 'dark, backward and abysm of time'.[18] But when we stay mindful of the fact that Elizabethan plays in the popular theatres took place out of doors, in natural light, we remember that during the performance of a play in such conditions the fact of being always in the present of the theatre was palpable. The waning of sunlight, subtle or extreme changes in temperature, as well as the ringing of bells from churches nearby, to name a few prominent factors, would have worked on playgoers' minds and bodies to impress on them that experiencing the movement of time in the present as a performance progresses is a central aspect of attending the theatre.[19]

Beyond simply undermining the efficacy of theatre as a time machine, though, the conditions of theatrical performance may have prodded Elizabethans to see history as always a negotiation between the present and the traces of the past available at any given present. Since the actors on stage playing figures from the past were obviously of the time and place of contemporary London, history plays could contribute to a consciousness of history in which there is constant awareness that the past cannot exist independent of the human effort to make it legible. The fact that history plays, like all plays, take place in 'real time' heightens audience awareness of the past–present dialectic that is at work in this brand of history making.[20] In the *Famous Victories*, the playwright and players had brought a certain experience of past time to the stage, one in which the performance marked out a long duration of history from the prince's youth to the time of his maturity as king. By compressing that duration, dilating a smaller section, and populating it with other figures and events from the past, Shakespeare's play suggests a temporal 'nesting doll' potential for historical representation in the theatre. Performing history is an opportunity to posit new pockets of past time, so that the totality of the past comes to seem like a series of discrete, modular segments that can be shortened, lengthened and combined variously.

Opposing God's transcendence to the limited human experience of time, Thomas Browne remarked in the seventeenth century that 'the created world is but a small parenthesis in eternity'.[21] Shakespeare shows through his revision of the *Famous Victories* in *1 Henry IV* that human time itself can be understood as a series of parenthetical moments and that, when its events are set forth, there is no obvious duration. Where to place the, as it were, 'upright curves' to mark each temporal parenthetical unit's beginning and ending in performing the past is a decision the dramatic playwright makes to manipulate and vary an audience's sense of the rhythm of the past.

Enter Falstaff

The 'nesting doll' potential of historical representation would seem to be a wholly positive thing for playwrights always in search of material, for audiences always in search of new shows, and especially for those playgoers who more specifically always sought deeper encounters with the past. Awareness of this potential, though, can also help to inculcate a critical consciousness of history making. Within *1 Henry IV*, Shakespeare creates a sense of the nesting doll effect and alerts audiences to some disturbing implications of it when Falstaff outrageously boasts that he killed Hotspur after the two men had fought for a 'long hour by Shrewsbury clock' (V.iv.148).

The context for this line is familiar, but a quick summary may nonetheless be useful. While Hal and Hotspur duel, Falstaff enters to watch. The Douglas confronts him, and Falstaff falls and feigns death. Hal kills Hotspur, pronounces a brief, ambivalent eulogy for him and one for Falstaff once he notices his apparently dead body.[22] Hal exits, and Falstaff leaps up to deliver his oration on the virtues of 'counterfeiting'. He cautiously sticks Hotspur in the thigh with his sword, and picks up the corpse. Hal and his brother John of Lancaster then enter. Both princes are surprised to see the fat knight is alive, standing with Hotspur's body slung over his shoulder. It is here that Falstaff claims he was simply out of breath, as was Hotspur, and that they both rose 'at an instant' and 'fought a long hour by Shrewsbury clock'. Hal immediately expresses disbelief at Falstaff's claim to have killed Hotspur: 'Why, Percy I killed myself' (V.iv.144). The audience knows, of course, even better than Hal that Falstaff's assertion that he killed Hotspur is a lie. They have seen Falstaff timidly stab the corpse and formulate his plan to claim credit for slaying him. The dilation of time in his rhetoric – a '*long* hour by Shrewsbury clock' – surely adds to the comedic hyperbole of Falstaff's absurd boast that he fought with Hotspur at all. But the status of this boast and its relation to the creation of historical knowledge is, in this moment, more than just a joke. It is also a problem that invites critical speculation on the death of Hotspur in the historical record and on the process of historical production more broadly.

Falstaff's speech on 'counterfeiting' clearly raises questions about theatrical performance and its relation to reality; indeed, his characterization as a whole, and his seeming 'resurrection' in this scene, have been described by many critics as metadramatic.[23] His claim about the duel by 'Shrewsbury clock' is especially interesting in metatheatrical terms. Falstaff here appropriates a dramatic narrative technique that, as we have noted, Shakespeare employs elsewhere in this play: the sudden positing of a time span that is out of sync with that of the performance itself. In the example explored above, 2 hours are purported to have taken place in the tavern during a much shorter interval of objective time. Other instances of time bending occur in *1 Henry IV*, often when there is a claim to some time expenditure that is difficult to gauge precisely but that gestures at some fictive expense of time that must be taken by audiences as a fact of the world they are seeing unfold.[24]

When Falstaff claims that he and Hotspur fought for a 'long hour' he opens up a new span of time and makes a claim for its reality, as if asking Hal, as he returns to the ground where Hotspur had expired, to retrofit his own sense of time passing to accommodate this. This replicates the work of the history play itself, as seen throughout *1 Henry IV* when Shakespeare asks audiences to retrofit their own experience of time passing in the theatre to accommodate the time that is said to have passed within the world of the play. And, remarkably enough, Hal seems poised to accept the warping of time proffered by Falstaff. As we have seen, the prince is initially incredulous at Falstaff's claim: 'Why, Percy I killed myself'. But Hal's amusement at his old friend wins out: 'Come, bring your luggage nobly on your back. |For my part, if a lie may do thee grace, | I'll gild it with the happiest terms I have' (V.iv.156–58).

The suggestion here is that Falstaff will gain credit for killing the great warrior Hotspur, and that Hal, poised to become the next king and, in effect, the arbiter of official discourses such as state histories, will perpetuate, even 'gild' this version. Audiences here witness the potential for factual legerdemain alongside the temporal legerdemain we have discussed. It is a move that anticipates the infamous moment of insidious legend-making Shakespeare later depicts in *Troilus and Cressida*, when Achilles' followers slay Hector, and are then ordered to go announce that Achilles alone did it.[25] Playgoers see Hal kill Hotspur, and they see Hal and Falstaff collude to disseminate a different story entirely, one that is supposed to have taken place in an hour whose status is impossible to assess. Is it, as it seems, a lie, like Falstaff's claim to have killed Hotspur, or is it one of the many putative hours that audiences must accept have passed before their eyes without their knowing it, an hour when Falstaff lay counterfeiting and Hotspur a corpse? This is a compelling question, but almost everything in the play about Falstaff suggests that the 'hour' has the same epistemological status as Falstaff's arithmetic about the robbers he encountered at Gad's Hill.

Falstaff invents a historical action, that he killed Hotspur. In order to support this claim, he invents as well an hour in which he accomplished that action. For Shakespeare, the larger framework of the play itself involves a connection between time and fact bending. By compressing the time frame of the *Famous Victories*, he can dilate the presentation of Henry V's youth. This greater focus, made possible by a new construction of the dramatic shape of the Henry V story, opens up factual lacunae that need to be filled. Some of these gaps are filled in *1 Henry IV* by facts from the historical record about the Percy rebellion. Otherwise, they are mostly plugged with the invented specifics of the legendary riots of the prince among his low-life cronies, acts that exist in the shadowlands of myth and historicity, in the historical past of the play's putative setting and the present tense of Elizabethan theatrical comedy and clowning. The death of Hotspur on the battlefield at Shrewsbury is a truth the play must account for. But as depicted in *1 Henry IV* this action is not less 'unhistorical' than the prince's chicanery at Gad's Hill. For there was no agreement about how Henry Percy actually died at Shrewsbury. Holinshed, in his *History of Scotland*, says he was slain by the king, while later in the portion of his *Chronicles* on English history that Shakespeare likely consulted, we read that Hotspur was killed by an 'other on his part, incouraged by his [King Henry's] doings'.[26] Daniel merely notes that Hotspur is killed, as does even John Harding, the early chronicler who claims to have been present at the battle and might have been in a position to know more details.[27]

Shakespeare's portrayal of Hotspur's death at the hands of Hal is one attempt to create a detailed version of a cause for the known effect of Hotspur's death.[28] It is an action that Shakespeare invented within the particular time frame he employed to pace his play. When Falstaff contends that he killed Hotspur, the audience knows that this is absurd according to the version of history they have just seen; but it also works to make precisely the point that what they have seen is one *version* – Shakespeare's version – of the story. Hal's victory over Hotspur is posited as history, and Falstaff's claim becomes, within the play world, a counterfactual. The existence of this counterfactual, though, unsettles any confidence that Hal really did defeat Hotspur as the play would have it, for it demonstrates how fragile and elusive any firm sense of the truth of historical particulars can be. Historical events prompt competing claims about their particulars, and what's more, in this case, the prince is willing to lend credibility to Falstaff's story. This willingness arises, it would seem, because he is amused by the idea, and this suggests that in the vision of the past Shakespeare presents, the facts of what really happened may always be subject to the whims of those who produce historical discourses, and perhaps also to what an audience wants to receive.

Falstaff's assertion, in other words, aligns the cultivation of history and historical consciousness generally with the way that such historical work is done in the theatre. Both depend on human labour in the present to posit a past reality, and both need an audience to grant it some form of, to adapt a term from speech-act theory to describe linguistic efficacy, 'uptake'.[29] When Hal first sees Falstaff standing with Hotspur's corpse, he asks: 'Art thou alive, or is fantasy |That plays upon our eyesight?' (V.iv.134–35). Falstaff's claim that he 'fought a long hour by Shrewsbury clock' with Hotspur is a fantasy that seeks to play upon the *mind's* eye of the historical imagination, an audacious attempt to invent a cause for the death of Hotspur. This attempt to fabricate historical material *within* the play puts the larger project of the play to posit the events of the past under scrutiny. It alerts audiences to the potential for the falsification of the past in a way that can't help but rebound on its own performance of history on the popular stage.[30] The kind of mendacity practiced by Falstaff is not the inevitable consequence of staging the past. But the play highlights that this is a likely threat to the reliability of all historical narratives that emerge in the context of a medium where time frames can be compressed or stretched variously to create room for more people and events to be enacted. Once seen in the theatre, a space where the constructed nature of historical knowledge is laid bare, this insight can amount to a larger critical consciousness of historical knowledge. The critical historical consciousness that the play inculcates is based on awareness that manipulations of time create space for the manipulation of facts, and that such acts of historiographical engineering are what make enactments of the past pleasurable and potentially fraught enterprises.

Exit Audience

When Falstaff, in his first scene early in the play, asks for the time, the prince's hilarious, scathing, rhetorically brilliant response makes clear that he regards the question itself as a kind of joke.

> What a devil hast thou to do with the time of the day? Unless hours were cups of sack, and minutes capons, and clocks the tongues of bawds, and dials the signs of leaping-houses, and the blessed sun himself a fair hot wench in flame-coloured taffeta, I see no reason why thou shouldst be so superfluous to demand the time of the day. (I.ii.5–11)

Hal's retort implies that Falstaff exists not according to seconds, minutes or hours, but according to the ebb and flow of his appetites and their fulfillment, not to mention their deferred costs, all of which are legible in the reckoning that he keeps in his pocket and that he never intends to pay: 'Item: a capon . . . 2s.2d' (II.iv.522). Falstaff is excessive in all things, 'out of all compass' as one of his friends notes (III.iii.21). But for Prince Hal it is the fat knight's pretence to time-consciousness that is downright 'superfluous'. Falstaff, it would seem, is not only out of all compass. He is, at least according to those around him, outside of time as well.[31]

But this, of course, is simply Falstaff's fantasy, one that is temporarily allowed him by those who indulge his wish to live apart from timely pressures.[32] The plot of *1 Henry IV* demonstrates that he lives in a time-bound world where obligations and responsibilities catch even him up, no matter how much he resists them. He might prefer to be home in bed, but he is nonetheless present at Shrewsbury, however ignominious his behaviour there. Beyond this, the physical performance of the play itself reveals that the character, and the actor who plays him, are subject to an even more unyielding time scheme, that which governs the professional theatre. As *Love's Labour's Lost* reminds its audience, works in the theater have a strict temporal delineation: 'twelvemonth and a day', or, indeed, any extended period beyond a few hours, is 'too long for a play'.[33]

Playgoers who step into the theatre might wish to, like Falstaff, enjoy a fantasy of living aloof from time, but they are as restricted by the time limits of a performance as the players are. Insofar as playgoers may have fantasized that time at the theatre could amount to a world of *otium*, we can see the audience at the playhouse where *1 Henry IV* was first performed as being targeted in Hal's famous charge 'I know you all, and will a while uphold |the unyoked humour of your idleness' (I.ii.185–86). While James Hirsh, in his recent book on the Shakespearean soliloquy, is sceptical that Shakespeare ever really intends audience address in such moments, the 'you' being addressed here is obscure.[34] Hal's 'you all' surely achieves a complicated conflation of the Eastcheap drinkers who have recently left the stage and the diverse crowd in the theater still privy to the prince's words.[35] One sixteenth-century anti-theatrical writer noted that 'playes . . . ought not to be suffered to prophane the Sabboth day in such sportes, and much lesse *to lose time on the dayes of trauayle* (travail)'.[36] Plays interrupted the work day and theatres could appear to be dens of idleness for those who attended them, but for those theatrical labourers who wrote for and performed in them, time was their limit but also a primary material of their medium. And for those in the crowd, the apparent physical idleness of theatre-going is complicated by the intellectual and sensory engagement they perform in watching and listening. *Experiencing* time in theatre is in its way such a form of engagement as well. As the theatre theorist Herbert Blau has argued, for audiences 'the drama itself is an extended meditation on the idea that whatever it is we're perceiving has already passed us by'.[37] The experience of history in this setting allows an extended meditation on the ontology of the past and the ways that its existence can be brought forth in various shapes and sizes.

This meditation contributes to a critical consciousness of history, for Falstaff's final charge at the end serves as a commentary on the larger practice of dramatic historiography being performed. *1 Henry IV* demonstrates how, from the totality of the past, the dramatic historiographer can contract and dilate time frames in creative ways that allow audiences to experience the rhythms of history differently.[38] The re-setting of the dramatic shape of the Henry V story allows for a closer look at the details of the king's youth, but also calls attention to the status of historical representation as artifact, as the work of a dramatist in setting that pace and, perhaps just as clearly, in limning those details in novel or idiosyncratic ways. This revelation suggests that the awareness of history gleaned from theatre, and perhaps history at large, may always be composed of and haunted by Falstaffian 'long hours by Shrewsbury clock'.

Notes

1. On sources for *1 Henry IV*, see Geoffrey Bullough, *Narrative and Dramatic Sources of Shakespeare Volume Four: Later English History Plays* (London: Routledge and Kegan Paul; New York: Columbia University Press, 1962) pp. 155–248. See also David Scott Kastan, (ed.) *King Henry IV Part 1* (London: Thompson Learning, 2002), pp. 339–44 for a more recent overview of the play's known and probable sources. All quotations from *1 Henry IV* in this chapter are taken from this edition and will be cited parenthetically in the text. All other Shakespeare quotations are taken from *The Riverside Shakespeare*, 2nd edition, ed. G. Blakemore Evans, et al. (Boston: Houghton-Mifflin, 1997).
2. On Daniel's portrait of Hotspur as a precedent dramatic foil to Hal, see Bullough, *Narrative and Dramatic Sources*, 166–67, 174.
3. See, for instance, Kastan in *Shakespeare After Theory* (New York and London: Routledge, 1999) on the play's depiction of the political pursuit of national 'one-ness'.
4. This is a very rough guess based on Alfred Hart's estimate that about 176 words per minute might have been spoken on the stage. The scene in question contains approximately 3, 479 words. Of course, Hart's method is an inexact metric, especially for a scene with ample opportunity for physical play and clowning not recorded in the published texts. See Hart, 'The Time Allotted for Representation of Elizabethan and Jacobean Plays', *Review of English Studies* 8 (1932) 395–413, especially 404.
5. There is a long tradition of criticism that tackles this issue of 'double time' in Shakespeare. The term was coined by John Wilson in his odd and fascinating meditations on Shakespeare in two pieces titled 'Dies Boreales', *Blackwood's Edinburgh Magazine*, 66: 409 (1849), 620–54, and 67: 414 (1850), 481–512, which take the form of fictional dialogues about issues and problems in Shakespearean drama, mainly in *Macbeth* and *Othello*. The phrase 'double time' appears in the 1850 essay, p. 512. Wilson is mainly concerned with how these plays alternate between what he calls 'long' and 'short' time. For instance, in *Macbeth*, the events from the murder of Duncan to the murder of Macduff's family seem to take place in the 'short' time, perhaps a few weeks based on textual clues. But simultaneously to this, Shakespeare also posits a 'long' time, seen in the language of Lenox and others, during which Scotland

languishes under Macbeth's tyranny. The origins and subsequent development of the concept is usefully discussed by Zdeněk Stříbrný in 'The Genesis of Double Time in Pre-Shakespearean and Shakespearean Drama', in *The Whirligig of Time: Essays on Shakespeare and Czechoslovakia*, ed. Lois Potter (Newark, DE: University of Delaware Press, 2007) pp. 79–97. Steve Sohmer, in *Shakespeare and the Wiser Sort* (Manchester: Manchester University Press, 2007) reads, with wildly varying degrees of success, some infamous time cruces in Shakespeare as a sign that Shakespeare was alluding to the Julian/Gregorian calendar debate in sixteenth-century Europe. Irwin Smith, in 'Dramatic Time versus Clock Time in Shakespeare', *Shakespeare Quarterly* 20:1 (1969) pp. 65–69, discusses a form of double time where the stated time of the stage action is out of sync with the objective time of the performance, and so lays the groundwork for what I am doing here.

6. Philip Sidney, *A Defence of Poetry*, ed. J. A. Van Dorsten (Oxford: Oxford University Press, 1966), p. 65–66.

7. Griffin, *Playing the Past: Approaches to English Historical Drama, 1385–1600* (Woodbridge: D.S. Brewer, 2001) p. 58, note 48, and p. 88, suggests this might be the case. He is following the argument to this effect put forth by John Dover Wilson, 'The Origins and Development of Shakespeare's *Henry IV'* *Library*, new series XXIV 1:2 (1945), pp. 9–10. There is some circumstantial support for this idea but no definitive evidence. We do know that another Queen's Men's play, *The Troublesome Reign of King John*, goes out of its way on its title page to call itself a two-part play, when there is no reason to think it in fact was. Scott McMillin and Sally-Beth MacLean argue that this was a 'printer's device' in apparent imitation of the success of the two-part *Tamburlaine* publications. If it is true that there was something to be gained by having a play known as a two-parter, then the publisher of the *Famous Victories* would have had incentive to note if it was a two-part play on its title page. See McMillin and MacLean, *The Queen's Men and Their Plays* (Cambridge: Cambridge University Press, 1998) p. 88.

8. There has been considerable debate over the question of Shakespeare's intentions in writing what we today consider a historical tetralogy. Whether Shakespeare intended to write a sequel to *1 Henry IV* or not is unknown, though, and, likewise, it cannot be known for certain whether audiences would have expected a sequel. Kastan in his edition of *1 Henry IV* concisely surveys the critical controversies on this topic, pp. 17–23. See Paul Dean, 'Forms of Time: Some Elizabethan Two-Part History Plays', *Renaissance Studies*, 4:4 (1990), pp. 410–30 for a discussion of how the two-part play structure could inflect historical time. Mable Buland specifically speaks of the double time of *1 Henry IV*, in particular of the various time spans of the Hal and Hotspur plots, in *The Presentation of Time in the Elizabethan Drama* (New York: Henry Holt, 1912) pp. 103–04.

9. For Oldcastle's participation in the opening scene's robbery, see 'The Famous Victories of Henry V', in *The Oldcastle Controversy*, ed. Peter Corbin and Douglas Sedge (Manchester: Manchester University Press, 1991) scene 1, 25–36. Quotations from the *Famous Victories* come from this edition.

10. On some implications of the age shift see, for instance, Kenneth Muir, *The Sources of Shakespeare's Plays* (New Haven, CT: Yale University Press, 1978) p. 97 and John Kerrigan, '*Henry IV* and the Death of Old Double', *Essays in Criticism* 40:1 (1990): pp. 24–53, esp. p. 42, and Ricardo Quinones, *The Renaissance Discovery of Time* (Cambridge: Harvard University Press, 1972) p. 330. The change helps also to make an array of political points. If Hotspur represents some notion of a fading chivalric code and Hal some notion of a new Machiavellian approach to leadership, the

dynamics of a struggle between them are quite different if that struggle is set up as one *between* generations or *within* a generation.

11. I admire, but do not accept, Harold Jenkins's ingenious argument that Shakespeare intended to tell a longer version of Henry V's story in *1 Henry IV*, at least up until his coronation, in a single work, but had to shift his intention during the composition when he realized he had too much material he wanted to cover. See Jenkins's *The Structural Problem in Shakespeare's 'Henry The Fourth'*, (London: Methuen, 1956), and Kastan's rebuttal in *1 Henry IV*, pp. 20–21. In his debunking of Jenkins, Sherman Hawkins reminds us that the Dering manuscript in the Folger Shakespeare Library actually conflates Shakespeare's *1* and *2 Henry IV* in precisely the way Jenkins thought Shakespeare had intended. See Hawkins, 'Henry IV: The Structural Problem Revisited', *Shakespeare Quarterly*, 33:3 (1982), 278–301.

12. See David Quint, 'Bragging Rights: Honor and Courtesy in Shakespeare and Spenser', in *Creative Imitation: New Essays on Renaissance Literature in Honor of Thomas M. Greene*, ed. David Quint, Margaret W. Ferguson, G. W. Pigman III, Wayne A. Reborn (Binghamton, NY: Medieval and Renaissance Texts and Studies, 1992), pp. 405–14 for a useful analysis of Hotspur's distinctive language and self-assertions that, in the context of changing historical relationships between the monarchy and the aristocracy, appear laughable.

13. Kastan, *Shakespeare and the Shapes of Time* (Basingstoke: Macmillan, 1982), pp. 50, 51. Each of these quotations is referring to a specific play – *Henry V* – but they reflect Kastan's argument about the Shakespearean history play more generally.

14. Kastan, *Shakespeare and the Shapes of Time*, p. 24. This is, of course, in distinction from the medieval cycle plays which, as Kastan points out, attempt to dramatize all of human history, from the creation to the final judgment.

15. In addition to Kastan's book-length exploration of this, see, for instance, Tom F. Driver, *The Sense of History in Greek and Shakespearean Drama* (New York: Columbia University Press, 1960) and Paul Dean, 'Shakespeare's Historical Imagination', *Renaissance Studies* 11:1(1997) 27–40. Stříbrný, 'The Genesis of Double Time' p. 79, and Kastan, *Shakespeare and the Shapes of Time*, p. 175, note 10, both credit G. E. Lessing for his seminal articulation of this concept in his 1766 essay *Laocoön*. See also Griffin, *Playing the Past*.

16. Paul Dean adapts a phrase of Michael Dummett's to assert that Shakespeare 'bring[s] about the past', p. 28.

17. In her brilliant discussion of anachronism in the history plays, Phyllis Rackin notes that the representation of Hal's tavern world as a kind of Elizabethan analogue by itself ensures that 'the historical world never takes on the illusion of full presence'. See *Stages of History: Shakespeare's English Chronicles* (Ithaca, NY: Cornell University Press, 1990), p. 138.

18. *Tempest*, 1.2.50.

19. As an example of this last phenomenon, see when Hodge compares the way that his coins 'jingle' like 'Saint Mary Overy's bells' in Thomas Dekker's *The Shoemaker's Holiday*, ed. Robert Smallwood and Stanley Wells (Manchester: Manchester University Press, 1979), Scene 7, lines 26–27. The play was performed at the Rose, which sat close to St Mary Overy's, today known as Southwark Cathedral. This line was certainly a knowing reference to the playgoers about a sound they were likely to hear on occasion at the Rose.

20. I elaborate on these points in my book *Shakespeare, The Queen's Men, and the Elizabethan Performance of History* (Cambridge: Cambridge University Press, 2009).

21. Thomas Browne, *Christian Morals* (London: Rivingtons, Waterloo Place, 1863) p. 141.

22. Kastan, *King Henry IV,* p. 331, notes that in modern productions it is common for Hal to deliver his eulogy over Falstaff jokingly, fully aware that the fat man is really alive. This makes for a funny scene in productions, but as Kastan also says, there is hardly textual warrant for this interpretation.
23. See, for instance, James L. Calderwood, *Metadrama in Shakespeare's Henriad: 'Richard II' to 'Henry V'* (Berkeley, CA: University of California Press, I979), and Hugh Grady, 'Subjectivity between the Carnival and the Aesthetic', *The Modern Language Review,* 96.3 (2001), 609–23.
24. Hotspur in a scene with his wife announces his intention to leave Kate 'within these two hours' (2.3.34–35) creating anticipation that a countdown has begun, a countdown that is left in suspension when Hotspur exits without acknowledgement of how much time is supposed to have passed. Later Hotspur once again creates anticipation that he will leave after the expiration of a by now familiar, fixed amount of time: 'I'll away within | these two hours' (3.1.257), and again it is never made clear whether those two hours are supposed to have been accomplished or not when the scene ends. The audience are given an indication how much time has passed among the conspirators beyond what they themselves witness occurring on stage when Hotspur complains of Glendower that he 'held me last night at least nine hours | In reckoning up the several devils' names | That were his lackeys' (III.i.152–54). One of the stranger occurrences is in the 'carrier scene', when one of the carriers claims it is four in the morning, then, oddly, a few moments later reports that it is 'two o'clock' (II.i.1;31). On that, see Kastan, *King Henry IV,* note on p. 186.
25. *Troilus and Cressida*, V.viii.13–14.
26. See Kastan, *1 Henry IV,* p. 329, note.
27. See Martha Tuck Rozett's essay (Chapter Eight) for a modern novelist's revision of Shakespeare's invention of Hotspur's death. Daniel does indicate that Hotspur encountered Hal in combat, but does not claim Hal killed him. For Daniel on Hotspur's death, see Book III of his *The first fovvre bookes of the ciuile wars between the two houses of Lancaster and Yorke* (London: Simon Waterson, 1595) p. 64. For Harding, see *The chronicle of Iohn Hardyng*, Sir Henry Ellis, ed., Richard Grafton's edition of Harding (London: Rivington, 1812) p. 361. See also Robert Adger Law, 'Structural Unity in the Two Parts of *Henry the Fourth*', *Studies in Philology*, Vol. 24, No. 2 (Apr., 1927), pp. 223–42 pp. 228–29 for a claim that Shakespeare may have mistaken Holinshed's syntax and believed that the *Chronicles* named Hal as Hotspur's killer.
28. See Dean, 'Shakespeare's Historical Imagination', p. 37.
29. On 'uptake' see J. L. Austin, *How to Do Things with Words* (Cambridge: Harvard University Press, 1975) p. 117.
30. See Robert C. Jones, *These Valiant Dead: Renewing the Past in Shakespeare's Histories* (Iowa City, IA: University of Iowa Press, 1991) pp. 100ff on the fudging of history in this scene.
31. For an elaboration of some similar points about this exchange, see Elliot Krieger's '"To Demand the Time of Day": Prince Hal', in *Modern Critical Interpretations: William Shakespeare's Henry IV, Part 1,* ed. Harold Bloom, (New York: Chelsea House Publishers, 1987) pp. 101–08.
32. Harold Bloom calls Falstaff a 'defier of time' in *Shakespeare and the Invention of the Human* (New York: Riverhead Books, 1998), p. 305, and this is accurate in terms of Falstaff's self conception, not in terms of how he actually exists.
33. *Love's Labour's Lost*, V.ii.868–69.
34. James Hirsh, *Shakespeare and the History of Soliloquies* (Madison, NJ : Fairleigh Dickinson University Press, 2003). See pp.199–221. He briefly mentions Hal's speech on p. 220.

35. Hotspur, as a critique of Hal, is also perhaps alluding to playgoers as corollaries to the tavern dwellers when he speaks of the Prince and his followers as 'the nimble-footed madcap Prince of Wales, | And his comrades that daffed the world aside | And bid it pass' (VI.i.93–95).
36. Geoffrey Fenton, quoted in E. K. Chambers, *The Elizabethan Stage Volume Four* (Oxford: Oxford University Press), vol. IV, p. 195, emphasis added.
37. Herbert Blau, *Sails of the Herring Fleet: Essays on Beckett* (Ann Arbor, MI: University of Michigan Press, 2000), p. 123.
38. See Dean, 'Shakespeare's Historical Imagination', pp. 39–40, for a riff on how Shakespeare's approach to history anticipates some twentieth-century philosophies of time as a 'continuum of durations'.

CHAPTER EIGHT

A Survey of Resources

Martha Tuck Rozett

Part I of *Henry IV* is among the most frequently taught of Shakespeare's plays, not only because of the enduring popularity of Falstaff, but because it is arguably the most of accessible and most brilliantly constructed of the history plays. As much a comedy as a history play, it can readily serve as the midpoint of a course on Elizabethan Shakespeare. *1 Henry IV* is the only play by Shakespeare included in the widely used *Norton Anthology of English Literature*, and it seems very likely that generations of college students in British literature survey courses have studied the play as part of the grand sweep of literary history from *Beowulf* to Milton and beyond.

When I teach *1 Henry IV* in a course devoted to the comedies and history plays my college students will already have read three comedies, typically *The Taming of the Shrew*, *The Merchant of Venice*, and *Much Ado about Nothing*. Thus they will be familiar with dramatic conventions, with Shakespeare's use of multiple plotlines and locations and with strategies for decoding complex poetic language. If they attended the first class of the semester, they will also have heard a lecture on the precursors of Shakespearean comedy, accompanied by a one-page diagram that provides a basic vocabulary of terms like 'mystery cycles', 'fertility rituals', 'St. George and the Dragon', 'Lord of Misrule', 'morality play', 'Roman comedy' and so forth. The middle section of the course often begins with *Richard II*, in which case the first scene of *1 Henry IV* will seem very much like a continuation of the historical events of the earlier play. When I begin with *Richard III* instead of *Richard II*, students need an overview of the two tetralogies and, with the assistance of genealogical charts, a rundown on the kinship networks and the claimants to the throne. The two-page chart in the *Riverside Shakespeare* that begins with Edward III is very useful for this purpose. After three or four class sessions devoted to *1 Henry IV* I spend a few moments with the rejection of Falstaff at the end of Part II and then move on to *Henry V.* The semester usually ends with a return to comedy (this is especially effective in the spring semester when the snows melt in upstate New York and the world becomes green again).

There are many ways to teach *1 Henry IV* and many opinions about how to do so. Indeed, the abundance of teaching editions, essay collections, texts accompanied by critical and contextual apparatus and other material that make up the Shakespeare industry can be daunting to the teacher in search of useful resources. I have gathered together some of the better known ones (both in and out of print) which I will discuss briefly along with some of the ways in which I approach the play in my own classroom.

Essay Collections

Some academic and public libraries will still have copies of the 'Twentieth Century Interpretations' collections of critical essays, published by Prentice Hall and long out of print. The volume on *1 Henry IV* (1970) edited by R. J. Dorius is a useful little book. In just over 100 pages, it includes a dozen excerpts from some of the most famous readings of the play by A. C. Bradley, William Empson, Northrop Frye, Derek Traversi and others. Many are quite short, but like other excerpts in edited volumes, they could lead the reader to the works from which they were taken. This collection is worth consulting if only for its longest selection, C. L. Barber's chapter on *1 Henry IV* in *Shakespeare's Festive Comedy* (a shorter excerpt is included in the Norton Critical Edition). Barber's book remains, 50 years after its first appearance, one of the most interesting approaches to the play, in my opinion. Its thesis, that Shakespearean comedy dramatizes 'the need for holiday and the need to limit holiday' (Rpt in Dorius, 51) works especially well for *1 Henry IV*. Barber's larger project of exploring 'the likenesses of comedy to [folk] ritual but [also] the differences, the features of comic form which make it comedy and not ritual' (51–52), provides students with a way into the play that is interdisciplinary and very appealing. He employs the folklore paradigm of 'the carrying off of bad luck by the scapegoat of saturnalian ritual', (64) citing James G. Frazer's *The Scapegoat*, the classic work on the subject, to show how Prince Hal frees himself from the sins of Henry IV's and Richard II's reigns through a dramatic structure that moves from participation in Falstaff's misrule to rejection of him (65). This participation is not simply Prince Hal's; it is also the audience, or reader's, for as Barber explains, our participation in Falstaff's clowning misrule is 'repeatedly diverted' to the laughter appropriate to comedy, even as we recognize that Hal must free himself of the scapegoat and become 'a king in whom chivalry and a sense of divine ordination are restored' (65).

Dorius also includes a 23 page excerpt from A. R. Humphreys's introduction to the 1960 Arden edition of *1Henry IV*, retitled 'The Unity and Background of *Henry IV, Part One*'. Humphreys follows the lead of J. Dover Wilson in warning against 'too much moralizing' and suggests that Henry IV's career 'proclaims less that God punishes deposition than that the king must rule' (Rpt in Dorius, 24–25). An excerpt from John Danby's *Shakespeare's Doctrine of Nature: A Study of King Lear* (1949) depicts Hal as 'a machiavel of goodness . . . [who] equips himself to be good in accordance with the terms of the State he will ultimately govern'. According to this 'refined machiavellism', 'technique is the thing, let the ends look after themselves', and by turning away from Falstaff, who is Appetite allegorized, Hal turns to Power, which 'was needed in the Tudor world to centralize, organize, canalize, concentrate, and sometimes curb Appetite' (Rpt in Dorius, 94). Teachers looking for patterns that are less allegorical than Danby's might employ Humphrey's discussion of the 'parody relationship' among parts of the play, such as 'the Falstaff-Hal burlesque (II. iv) and the king's genuine reproof (III.ii)' (Rpt in Dorius, 20). I introduce the concept of literary 'parody' when teaching *1 Henry IV* to undergraduates and then ask them how it helps to explain Shakespeare's juxtaposition of the comic double robbery and the Percys' plot to carve up the kingdom after helping King Henry 'steal' it from Richard II. The motif of parody comes up again with the parallel between the duplicating men in green buckram and the identically dressed 'kings' on the battlefield at Shrewsbury in Act V.

Another collection of essays, more comprehensive than Dorius's, is David Bevington's *Henry the Fourth Parts I and II: Critical Essays* (1986) in the Garland Shakespearean Criticism series. Bevington begins with eighteenth century essays on the play and its characters, including the well-known (Johnson, Coleridge and Hazlitt) and the less well-known (Corbyn Morris, Elizabeth Montagu). These are followed by early twentieth century critics, ranging from G. B. Shaw to A. C. Bradley to Mark Van Doren, Dover Wilson, E. M. W. Tillyard and others. The collection concludes with seven selections from the 1970s and early 1980s. There is a substantial, 25 page excerpt from Maurice Morgann's 'Essay on the Dramatic Character of Sir John Falstaff' (1777). Many subsequent commentaries on Falstaff refer to this 'defence' of Falstaff against imputations of cowardice.

If I were devoting an entire semester to *1 Henry IV* I might assign W. H. Auden's engaging and provocative essay, 'The Prince's Dog' (1948), reprinted from *The Dyer's Hand and Other Essays*. Like a dog, Falstaff 'loves Hal with an absolute devotion' for Hal is the 'son he has never had', and he believes that his love is returned. Auden's Falstaff will think he understands Hotspur, since anger and fear are emotions he can understand, and he will not understand why the audience and the rebels are shocked when Prince John 'tricks [the rebels] into disbanding their army and then arrests them . . . '(Rpt in Bevington, 166–67). For Auden, Falstaff is 'the Unworldly Man' in contrast to Hal, 'who represents worldliness at its best'; he 'radiates happiness as Hal radiates power', and 'this untiring devotion to making others laugh becomes a comic image for a love which is absolutely self-giving' (178).

For a more recent, but similarly thesis-driven essay, one could assign Robert N. Watson's psychoanalytic chapter on the Henry IV plays in *Shakespeare and the Hazards of Ambition* (1984), which Bevington reprints in full. Watson sets out to 'study the evolution of filial identity' in 'a systematic, Freudian way' (387), but he does so in an eminently readable fashion as he traces the plays' recurrent motif of ambition. This essay deals as much with Part II as with Part I, and so raises the question many a teacher of Shakespeare confronts: Should one assign both plays, or given the constraints of time, only Part I? This would depend, clearly, on whether the course is devoted entirely to the history plays, or to a mix of genres.

Critical Editions

Many teachers will be familiar with the series of critical editions published over the years by Bedford St. Martin's Press and W. W. Norton. The Norton Critical Edition of *1 Henry IV* has been in existence since 1962; the third edition, edited by Gordon McMullan, appeared in 2003, weighing in at 474 pages, including 94 pages devoted to the text of the play with glosses and notes at the foot of each page. The 'Contexts and Sources' section includes 17 pages from Peter Saccio's *Shakespeare's English Kings: History, Chronicle and Drama* (1977), an exceedingly useful account of the history behind all of Shakespeare's history plays. McMullan's excerpts include a few paragraphs from the early chapters on the two tetralogies, followed by a 'sketch [of] the main lines of fifteenth-century history' (168) beginning with Edward III, which takes the reader quickly through the history chronologically, before turning to events involving Henry Bullingbrook, the Percys, and Prince Hal in *Richard II* and *1Henry IV*. Saccio's lively and straightforward prose, unencumbered by notes, will prepare students for the Norton's 30 pages of selections (in original spelling) from Edward Hall's *Union of the Two Noble and Illustrious Families of Lancaster and York*, Raphael Holinshed's *Chronicles*, Samuel Daniel's *The Civil Wars*, and the anonymous play *The Famous Victories of Henry the Fifth*.

After writing a first draft of this chapter, I assigned the Norton edition in a course designed to teach critical reading and writing to English majors. My students read McMullan's chronologically arranged excerpts from John Dryden, Samuel Johnson, Elizabeth Montagu and Maurice Morgann, followed by longer excerpts from John Dover Wilson's *The Fortunes of Falstaff* (1943) and Arthur C. Sprague's 'Gadshill Revisited' (1953). My objective was to engage them in a critical conversation about Falstaff's influence on Hal, using the loaded words 'cowardice', 'valour' and 'honour'. Because Sprague refers to all of his predecessors and many other critics as well, I used his essay as a model for an assignment that asked students to develop and defend their own readings. We also read excerpts from C. L. Barber and from Michael Bristol's *Carnival and Theatre* (1985), which builds upon Barber's ideas about misrule and holiday, but with an emphasis on the political implications of the 'Battle of Carnival and Lent', in which Falstaff, 'like Carnival, is an ambivalent and grotesque figure', and Hal, his 'Lenten antagonist', is associated with 'civil policy' and 'abstemious social discipline' (Rpt in McMullan, 363, 365).

One of McMullan's longest selections is a 19 page excerpt from Stephen Greenblatt's essay 'Invisible Bullets', (originally published in 1985 in *Political Shakespeare: New Essays in Cultural Materialism*, ed. Jonathan Dollimore and Alan Sinfield), which was so influential in the heady early years of New Historicism. Greenblatt approaches *1 Henry IV* obliquely, by way of Marlowe's alleged references to Thomas Harriot and atheism in the Baines letter, and thence to 'Machiavellian anthropology' which posits 'religion as a cunning imposition of socially coercive doctrines' upon simple people (Rpt in McMullan, 289). This is one of the essays in which Greenblatt sets forth his theories about subversion and containment, which he eventually applies to a reading of Hal as a 'conniving hypocrite' (296). For Greenblatt, Hal's 'characteristic activity is playacting' and accordingly, theatricality is 'one of power's essential modes' (300). This essay would be appropriate for graduate students, as would David Scott Kastan's intriguingly titled essay ' "The King Hath Many Marching in His Coats" or, What Did You Do in the War, Daddy?' (1991), reprinted from the politically inflected collection *Shakespeare Left and Right*. Kastan deals with issues of power and the blurring of the distinction between Richard II's legitimate rule and Henry IV's usurpation (344), with references both to his contemporaries (Greenblatt and Robert Weimann, among others) as well as to Shakespeare's contemporaries, such as Florio and Sidney and to the political philosophies of

Hobbes, King James I, and less well-known sixteenth- and seventeenth-century writers; students working with primary sources could use this as a model. Both graduates and undergraduates, left to their own devices, would probably choose to read an excerpt from an interview with Gus Van Sant and a couple of pages of his screenplay of *My Own Private Idaho* (a 1991 film that loosely parallels the Hal/Falstaff relationship), followed by part of Susan Wiseman's essay on the film.

In keeping with the approach of the Bedford Texts and Contexts series, Barbara Hodgdon has assembled a range of fifteenth- and sixteenth-century documents with the aim of inviting an 'intertextual reading which decenters the play' (ix). While many teachers assign excerpts from Hall and Holinshed to students, the Bedford edition goes much further: its 270 pages of contextual materials, accompanied by six chapter introductions that organize the readings topically, provide enough reading to fill the better part of a semester. The old spelling and complex syntax are daunting for most undergraduates, so it is perhaps just as well that the excerpts are seldom longer than five or six lightly annotated pages. Like other volumes in the Bedford series, this one invites readers to speculate about Shakespeare's reading, a subject about which we know so much less than we would like.

I might assign the excerpts Hodgdon includes from 'An Homily Against Disobedience and Willful Rebellion', after reminding students that attendance at Sunday church services where the homilies were read was compulsory – which means that we can assume that Shakespeare's audience brought to the playhouse a familiarity with these injunctions against rebellion. The author of the homily conflates many kinds of undesirable behaviour under the heading of rebellion: if 'all sins possibly to be committed against GOD or man be contained in rebellion', then rebels can be persons who break their oaths to their prince, like the Percy faction, but they can also be drunkards or gluttons whose unthrifty impulses predispose them to 'rebellion, whereby they trust to come by other men's goods unlawfully and violently' (176). The homily, in effect, points out that the parallels between the portrayal of the Percys and the denizens of the Tavern world were not simply Shakespeare's dramatic invention; they were central to the way in which the Elizabethans thought about rebellion.

Falstaff's and Hal's memorable exchanges of insults in *1 Henry IV* prompted Hodgdon to include an excerpt from Thomas Dekker's *Of Lantern and Candlelight* which deals with the language of canting. Dekker begins with a mock-scholarly account of the linguistic disorder associated with the Tower of Babel and then turns to the Tribes and Regiments of Rufflers, Upright-men, Rogues, Abraham Men, Swadlers, Doxies, and so forth, a 'strange people' who speak 'a Language (proper only to themselves) called *canting* . . . . [which] none but themselves should understand . . . . ' (251–53). Some songs follow, both in the language of cant and translated or 'Englished'.

No collection of this kind would be complete without Machiavelli, and Hodgdon includes three and a half pages from *The Prince*, preceded by a one and a half page introduction advising readers that Machiavelli's ideas are 'less a literary or historical source for Shakespeare than a cultural locus for ideas of statecraft that trace through his plays' (309). The next paragraph warns against 'reductive interpretations of Machiavelli's thought'. There are references to the 'Machiavel', the Vice and the Senecan villain (309–10), but nothing that specifically directs the reader to view Hal or Henry IV or the Percy faction as the kinds of princes Machiavelli discusses in chapters XV and XVIII. A less well-known treatise from Shakespeare's time is Sir William Segar's *Honor Military and Civil* (1602). Hodgdon includes a one and a half page excerpt, which includes lists describing the 'office and duty' of every knight and gentleman:

> To avoid sloth and superfluous ease.
> To reverence Magistrates and converse with persons of honor.
> To eschew riot and detest intemperance.
> To prefer honor before worldly wealth, and be both in word and deed just and faithful. (336–37)

Like the homily, this is less a realistic description of gentlemanly behaviour than it is an ideal to which the English were instructed to aspire to.

Hodgdon devotes her final chapter (43 pages) to Falstaff and the Oldcastle controversy, with selections from Foxe's *Acts and Monuments* (better known as 'The Book of Martyrs'), from Holinshed, and from *The True and Honorable History of the Life of Sir John Oldcastle*. The introduction ranges widely, from *The Merry Wives of Windsor*, to Lollardry, to the Marprelate tracts, to the actor Richard Tarlton, to performance history from the mid-seventeenth century onwards. Her readings of lines from the play in the context of Oldcastle's martyrdom remind the reader that 'Given the lack of written evidence, such a history must always be conjectural: it is difficult to know precisely the range and nature of spectators' responses' (354). I should note in passing that most of the teaching editions devote some attention to Sir John Oldcastle, the implications of Shakespeare's appropriation of his name, and the textual history of the play. In my three or four 80-minute classes devoted to *1 Henry IV*, there never seems to be enough time for discussion of these topics, but I can envision doing so in a course that focuses on fewer plays.

Teaching Editions

Some years ago I reviewed the three major one-volume editions for *Shakespeare Quarterly* (48:4, Winter, 1997): *The Norton Shakespeare*, edited by Stephen Greenblatt, Walter Cohen, Jean E. Howard and Katharine Eisaman Maus; *The Riverside Shakespeare*, edited by G. Blakemore Evans (2nd ed.); and *The Complete Works of Shakespeare*, edited by David Bevington (updated 4th ed.). I consulted students and colleagues about various aspects of the three texts, starting with the physical appearance of text and notes on the page. Many readers prefer the way the Norton edition marks unfamiliar words with a small superscript circle and a gloss on the right margin; these glosses are easier to find than those in the Riverside or Bevington editions, which are given at the foot of the page and identified by line number. Bevington includes line numbers only when they are required to direct readers to a glossed word or phrase, which means that they do not occur at regular intervals of five or ten, as they do in most editions. Because of its format, the Norton tries to keep glosses to single word equivalents or very short phrases, while longer footnotes provide additional information and explanations. The Bevington edition is known for its ability to make sense of difficult syntax, which students find helpful, although some teachers may want their students to do this kind of interpretive work on their own. All three editions attempt to help students envision the action by augmenting the original stage directions with added directions in brackets, a practice common to all teaching editions. Of the three the Riverside contains the fewest editorial stage directions, which makes the reading experience less disrupted (Rozett, *Shakespeare Quarterly* 466–68).

I have used the Riverside for many years in upper-level undergraduate courses, although frequently students will bring other editions to class, which leads occasionally to discussions of textual variants and editorial choices. Although I don't assign the Riverside introductions to each play, some of the students read them on their own. Herschel Baker's introduction to *Henry IV, Parts 1 and 2*, written for the original 1974 edition, begins by addressing the relationship between the two plays and remarks upon the 'growing tendency to regard to regard Part 2 as a necessary conclusion, not an unplanned sequel, to Part 1' (1974 edition, 842). Baker uses phrases like 'stunning innovation', 'triumph of the form', and 'polyphonic structure' and 'contrapuntal presentation' to describe the 'persistent duality' that informs the Henry IV plays, setting scenes and speeches against each other to illustrate the 'various techniques of juxtaposition, inversion, and antithesis' (844–45). His emphasis on the plays' structure includes the parallel between the king and Falstaff in their relationship to Hal: 'the father standing for convention, duty, and control and his surrogate for disorder, crime, and license. Similarly, Hal and Hotspur form another pair of corresponding but contrasting types . . . '(844). The introduction continues in this vein in when describing 'our' relationship with Falstaff:

> If Falstaff, incapable of intellectual torpor and indifferent to the curbs that shackle most of us, represents the lawless ease and freedom that every man desires and most men never find, he also represents destruction. An example of the way that Shakespeare forces us to trade our routine, clear-cut misconceptions for the interlocking ambiguities of knowledge, he is both wholesome and malign: he amuses and instructs us by exposing fraud and folly, but he appalls us by annihilating all sense of order. (846)

Jean Howard's introduction to the play in *The Norton Shakespeare*, written nearly a quarter century after Baker's, reflects New Historicist developments in Shakespeare scholarship. Her second paragraph discusses the political geography of England and the 1569 Northern Rebellion in which the Percy family participated in an attempt to depose Queen Elizabeth and replace her with Mary Queen of Scots (1997 edn, 1147). Howard emphasizes the way Shakespeare sets his play simultaneously in the early fifteenth century and in his own time, through contemporary references to the commercial culture of the early modern England in the tavern scenes, and the 'problem of control' posed by Ireland in the 1590s (1148–49). Two of the introduction's eight small-print pages are devoted to Falstaff's derivation from Sir John Oldcastle and the fact that his descendent, the seventh Lord Cobham, oversaw the licensing of play in 1596–97, when *1 Henry IV* was first performed. Howard explains that although the Norton edition is based on the Oxford text, she and her fellow editors decided to use the name 'Falstaff' rather than 'Oldcastle' because to 'undo' an act of censorship 'creates new erasures in the textual and cultural history of the play' (1153). The introduction contains a brief discussion of the link between the rebels and their wives and daughters, a theme she explores at greater length in her chapter on the second tetralogy in *Engendering a Nation: A Feminist Account of Shakespeare's English Histories* (1997).

Large one-volume Shakespeares are cumbersome and expensive; hence many teachers prefer to use small paperback editions of each play, of which there are many. The best known in the United States are the Pelicans, the Signet Classics, and the Folgers. The Oxford School and Cambridge School editions are used mostly in the United Kingdom; according to the publisher's publicity material, the Oxford School edition of *1 Henry IV* is intended for the 11- to 14-year-old school children in England for whom the play is a set text. Most of Shakespeare's plays are available in the Oxford World Classic editions, the New Cambridge editions and of course, the Arden editions, which contain more extensive notes and attention to textual issues than the others. Since all are readily accessible, I will discuss only three here.

Humphreys' introduction to the first Arden edition of *1 Henry IV* has been replaced in the 2002 (third series), edited by David Scott Kastan. Kastan includes points he had made in ' "The King Hath Many Marching in His Coats" . . . ' although his 130 page introduction ranges far more widely, in keeping with the Arden format. Starting from the premise that we can read *1 Henry IV* either 'from above', because we value 'the polished and composed over the boisterous and robust', or 'from below', like the groundlings who 'filled the playhouse yard, characteristically demanding something more immediately engaging . . . . ' (35), he argues against viewing the play's politics 'from above'. Critics as different as Tillyard and Greenblatt, he observes, proceed from the assumption that Shakespeare subordinates 'comedy to history, demotic energy to aristocratic control, copiousness to coherence . . . ' (35). Hence, in the story of Hal's progress toward the throne the comic scenes are reduced to 'antimasque', a reading that fails to take into account the way Falstaff 'speaks to and for' the spectators in the yard (38). I might note in passing that the Olivier film of *Henry V* splendidly evokes Falstaff's popularity among the groundlings with the hoots and cheers that accompany the first mention of his name in those opening scenes designed to represent a performance at the Globe. A reading 'from below', says Kastan, challenges and contests authority, as containment gives way to carnival, and 'Falstaff rules' (38). He concludes that the play can be read both ways: Falstaff's 'unruly energies' are both 'triumphant' and 'banished', for 'plays mean differently at different times . . . their politics always newly created within different conditions of representation . . . ' (39–40). Like other historicists, Kastan places *1 Henry IV* firmly in the context of 'the ideological configuration and political repression' of Elizabeth Tudor's reign, and concludes that 'How we understand the politics of the play depends, then, on how much we allow Falstaff to undermine the political drive to unity'. Put simply, he asks, 'is order a positive or negative value in the play?' (43). The reader can have it both ways, though I remind my students that the directors and actors generally have to make choices.

The royalties from the Folger editions help support the Folger Shakespeare Library in Washington DC, which is one good reason to assign these inexpensive paperbacks. There are also other reasons for using them in an introductory class. Each volume has an introduction entitled 'Reading Shakespeare's Language' adapted to the individual play, with examples taken mostly from the first couple of scenes. The section on 'Shakespeare's Sentences', for instance, addresses the issue of placement of subject and verb:

> In *I Henry IV*, we find an inverted subject-verb construction in King Henry's '*Find we* a time: (1.1.2) as well as in his 'a power of English *shall we levy*' (1.1.22). Prince Hal's 'Yet herein *will I imitate the sun*' (1.2.204) is another example of inverted subject and verb. (xxi)

Each Folger edition also includes a section on wordplay and one on implied stage action. I have assigned the introduction as students begin reading to help them become oriented to Shakespeare's syntax. The Folger's notes are on facing pages in the same sized print as the playtext. Hence the reader can move through the text reading the right hand side only or else move back and forth between the glosses on the left, where words or phrases are printed in bold and identified by line number and then glossed. The student puzzled by the language in Falstaff's soliloquy on honour, for example, can read a half page of notes that gloss the expressions 'prick me off', 'mark me for death', 'suffer' and 'allow' with longer explanations for 'scutcheon' and 'catechism' (94). The left hand pages also contain three sentence summaries of each scene and occasional illustrations taken from contemporary woodblock prints, though too often they are rendered blurry by being so radically reduced in size. The editors of the series, Barbara Mowat and Paul Werstine, have included a seven page appendix entitled 'Historical Background: Sir John Falstaff and Sir John Oldcastle', which quotes from Holinshed but also places the debate about Oldcastle's supposed heresy and treason in the context of modern depictions of Falstaff in Branagh's and Van Sant's films.

An essay entitled 'A Modern Perspective' by a well-known Shakespeare scholar follows each play, written specifically for this edition and its intended audience. They differ considerably in approach, but I have found them to be clearly organized around a main point and suitable for introductory college courses. Alexander Leggatt's essay on *1 Henry IV* focuses on the play's 'twists' or reversals, its 'unreliable narratives' (245) and 'deceptive images' (247), cautioning against a reading that reduces the play to 'simple dichotomies' (252) – a useful contrast to the mid-twentieth century allegorical readings by Auden and Danby. Most of the 14- page essay is devoted to Falstaff and Hal, but interestingly, Leggatt includes long paragraphs on Lady Percy and Lady Mortimer. That is unusual for a short essay on this play, and very helpful in classrooms where minor characters can easily be overlooked. Like other Folger volumes, this one concludes with a section entitled 'Further

Reading', consisting of 17 annotated entries, a general bibliography common to all the volumes, and finally, a brief 'Key to Famous Lines'.

The New Cambridge edition of *1 Henry IV* edited by Herbert and Judith Weil (1997) is a more substantial paperback than the Folger, with a 60-page introduction. Its extensive footnotes, some filling half the page, constitute a running commentary that includes textual variants, OED citations, theatre history and references to other plays. As I remarked in my review article on the three major one-volume editions, there are times when the notes tell students more than they need to know and by so doing, slow down the reading process. An example of this tendency is a gloss on the word 'termagant' which takes the reader to the Termagant or Mahound character in the miracle plays, to Hamlet's line about 'o'erdoing Termagant' in the advice to the players, and to Jean Bodel's French thirteenth-century play which contains a 'Termagaunt'. For scholars, though, the notes are admirably comprehensive, with references to editions of the play dating back to Samuel Johnson, to the Quarto and Folio variants, and with plenty of historical details, such as the dates and locations of the three battles in which Hotspur fought against members of the Douglas clan (148).

In their introduction, Herbert and Judith Weil map out a three-movement structure in *1 Henry IV* which teachers might find useful as an organizing principle, particularly if, as I do, they teach the play in three class sessions. The first movement focuses on 'the drama of moral choice', ending with Hotspur's leave-taking from Lady Percy in II.3, while the second movement climaxes with Falstaff's line 'Banish plump Jack, and banish all the world' and ends in Act III (9–15). In the third movement, the Weils observe, 'Falstaff's resemblance to King Henry becomes more obvious', foreshadowing the motif of death and decline in Part II (16). The synopses of each movement include references to the play's critical reception, some contextual information, such as brief explanations of mystery and morality play conventions and references to the critics and to staging. A 20-page stage history with illustrations begins with information about the Globe and the acting companies and concludes with British productions from the 1980s and 90s.

The Garland Bibliography

Like the bibliographies in teaching editions, the 1994 Garland Annotated Bibliography of *Henry IV Parts 1 and 2*, compiled by Catherine Gira and Adele Seeff, remains a useful research tool despite the fact that it is not up to date. This volume contains over 1500 references, some as long as a full page. The entries are arranged topically and chronologically in categories titled 'Criticism', 'Sources and Background', 'Textual

Studies, Bibliographies, and Dating', 'Editions', 'Stage History, Performances, and Film', and 'Adaptation, Influence, and Synopses'. There is a
useful index that allows the reader to search, for instance, for the entries
that mention Prince John of Lancaster or search by the name of a
scholar. The index entry on Language is one and a half columns long, so
that one can locate articles on puns and quibbles, say, or disease imagery.
Other forms of cross-referencing are similarly helpful. For example, the
synopsis of Maynard Mack's introduction to the Signet edition of
1 Henry IV quotes Mack quoting Tillyard and then refers to item 31,
Tillyard's classic 1944 study, *Shakespeare's History Plays*. The page-long
summary of that book includes short quotes and sends the reader to
item 758, Dover Wilson's *The Fortunes of Falstaff*. That summary, in
turn, refers us to A. C. Bradley, in an entry that lists the collections in
which 'The Rejection of Falstaff' has been reprinted.

The bibliography contains separate sub-sections on Falstaff in four
of the six major sections, and the reader who pursues this line of inquiry
can find delightfully obscure essays like item 968, 'Shakespeare and
Orthopedics' in the *Journal of Surgery, Gynecology and Obstetrics* (1969),
which 'Argues that Shakespeare's description of Falstaff reflects the
poet's knowledge of Crook's *Anatomy* (London, 1615)' (Gira and Seeff
368). The follies of academe are very much on display, such as an article
published in 1952 dedicated to the proposition that Shaw's Captain
Bluntschli in *Arms and the Man* is a 'pale imitation' of Falstaff (533). I
cannot imagine a less convincing comparison.

Although the Garland bibliography was published in 1994 the most
recent entries date from the mid- to the late-1980s in each category;
there are only a handful of entries more recent than 1985. A sequel
would be welcome, but unlikely to occur in these straitened times. The
volume is most useful in directing readers to classic works of Shakespeare
scholarship that might not show up in a subject word library catalogue
search, such as item 750, Enid Welsford's 1935 study *The Fool: His Social
and Literary History*, which contains a reference to Falstaff as the highest development of the 'great primal joke of the undignified nature of
the human body' (289), or item 767, Lily B. Campbell's 'Epitaph on
Falstaff: The Problem of the Soldier' in her 1947 study *Shakespeare's
Histories: Mirrors of Elizabethan Policy*.

Pedagogical Resources

The teaching of Shakespeare's plays is a burgeoning sub-field in
Shakespeare studies. No organization has been more energetic in encour-
aging creative approaches to engaging secondary school students with
Shakespeare than the Folger Library's Teaching Shakespeare Institute,

the sponsor of summer workshops for teachers. Under the general editorship of Peggy O'Brien, the institute has issued three large format volumes entitled *Shakespeare Set Free*, each devoted to two plays. The one on *Hamlet* and *Henry IV Part 1* (1994) contains several essays written specifically for this volume, including one by Louisa Foulke Newlin entitled 'Nice Guys Finish Dead: Teaching Henry IV, Part 1 in High School'. Newlin notes that 'interestingly . . . my students often prefer Hotspur to Hal' but adds that they identify more with the latter and like the way the play is in part about the process of growing up (25).

I tested this hypothesis with an exam question that encouraged students to trace the Hal whom Henry IV despairs of at the end of *Richard II* to the king of *Henry V*. Many of the essays were disappointing, describing Hal as a 'frat boy', 'a selfish brat', a 'screw-up' who just wants to have fun and lacks discipline, a kid influenced by the crowd he hangs out with, an adolescent who will disobey his parents and do as he pleases, a well-off young man with few cares who finds himself suddenly in line for the throne and is ordered by his father to 'shape up'. These are readings characteristic of the naïve first readers I described in my book *Talking Back to Shakespeare* (1994), who often grasp at anything that seems to correspond with their own lives, disregarding both the artifice of theatre and the historical differences between past and present. Because it was not one of the passages the exam question cited as a starting point, surprisingly few mentioned Hal's soliloquy in II.ii, arguing instead that he underwent an unanticipated transformation later in the play. The more alert students did quote from the soliloquy, which I always discuss in detail on the first day and return to again as we move through the play.

Despite a confusing opening page or two which might deter teachers from reading further, Stephen Booth's essay in *Shakespeare Set Free* entitled 'The Coherences of *Henry IV, Part 1* and *Hamlet*' is useful for its discussion of 'patterns that do not usually call any attention to themselves . . . [but that] give a play its essence . . . ' (34). Booth points out that 'it is hard to find a character in *Henry IV, Part 1* who is not like or likened to the others'; one example is the 'incidental likeness between Hotspur and Falstaff in their shared tendency to become overheated' just as they are both mocked for 'uncontrolled volubility' (36–37). A less obvious pattern of likenesses is the repeated motif of horses. Booth reports that *1Henry IV* has 38 references to horses, in contrast to an average of 8 references in Shakespeare plays taken as a whole (38). Students might enjoy finding all the horse references using word search computer concordances that make it easy to do so; this could lead to other uses of concordances to trace language patterns.

Another pattern Booth mentions is the concept of time. When teaching the play I like to trace references to time, beginning with the first speech, in which the king longs for 'a time for frighted peace to pant' (I.i.2) and then, in the next scene, with Hal's comic riff on 'hours as cups of sack and minutes capons, and clocks the tongues of bawds . . . ' (I.ii.7–8; all quotations are from the Riverside edition). Characters are constantly looking forward and backward in time: Richard, who recognized at the end of his life that 'I wasted time, and now doth time waste me', is invoked repeatedly by the king, Prince Hal, and the Percys. In III. ii.144ff, Hal promises his father that 'the time will come | That I shall make this northern youth exchange | His glorious deeds for my indignities'. Hotspur, dying, calls himself 'time's fool', and adds that 'time | that takes survey of all the world, | Must have a stop' (V.iv.81–83). As the play draws to an end, Falstaff makes his exit vowing to 'purge and leave sack' (V.iv.164–65). We know, however, that he will not. Falstaff remains forever fixed in time, while Hal, as he promises in the play's most famous couplet, will fulfill his promise to 'so offend, to make offence a skill, | Redeeming time when men think least I will' (I.ii.216–17).

The main portion of each *Shakespeare Set Free*'s 'Innovative, Performance-Based Approach' consists of a 24 lesson unit on each play. The units were created by a consortium of high school teachers who have used this approach with 15- to 18-year olds in their respective schools. The volume includes handouts, writing projects, and a sequence of performance exercises that lead students through the play and culminate in a performance. The first handout is an illustrated cast list grouping the characters in the Court, among the Rebels, and in the Tavern Crew. The second is a 'Fifteen Minute *Henry*' that runs through the plot using short quotes interspersed with plot summary. The third launches students on long-term assignments such as preparing a research report on the play's performance history or designing costumes for a production. All of this takes place on Day 1. On Day 2 the students begin with II.ii; then, on Day 3, they return to Act I. The *Shakespeare Set Free* approach has students performing scenes and keeping logs from the very beginning. It isn't clear how much of the play they actually read and when they do the reading, since they are kept very busy with a variety of activities and assignments during the 24-day sequence. While teachers might not follow this unit slavishly, there are ideas here that could readily be incorporated into a more conventional curriculum. Undoubtedly, the last decade's advances in technology and the availability of internet resources in secondary school classrooms have introduced variations on this student-centered, performance-based approach. Since 1998, the Folger Library's website (www.folger.edu) has included free online lesson plans and a large collection of images that teachers can use. There are, of course, hundreds of other online resources on Shakespeare, far too many to list here; and besides, any survey would almost immediately become out of date. I'll note only the MIT (Massachusetts Institute of Technology) Shakespeare site, which I encourage students to use when they download sections of text to use for staged readings or adaptations.

Teaching Shakespeare Today: Practical Approaches and Productive Strategies (1993), edited by James E. Davis and Ronald E. Salomone, is now out of print, but I have used some of the essays it contains to good effect when teaching teachers to teach Shakespeare. The only essay devoted specifically to *1 Henry IV* is entitled 'If Only One, Then *Henry IV, Part 1* for the General Education Course', by Sherry Bevins Darrell. She argues that because this play is at once a comedy, history and tragedy; because it treats important themes such as duty, education, fathers and sons, failed communication between men and women, holiday, cynicism versus idealism; because it contains heroes, wastrels, battles and a lord of misrule; because the dialogue and soliloquies are filled with imagery and distinctions among social classes through alternations between prose and poetry – for these reasons and more, *1 Henry IV* 'will teach your general ed students more about Shakespearean drama than any other single play' (269).

Rewriting Shakespeare

The premise of my book *Constructing a World: Shakespeare's England and the New Historical Fiction* (2003) is that historical fiction can help us understand the past in ways that conventional history books do not, and that the 'constructed worlds' of extensively researched and innovative historical novels can prompt new readings of Shakespeare's plays in unexpected ways. A chapter subtitled 'The Henriad with and without Falstaff' deals with two historical novels: Edith Pargeter's *A Bloody Field by Shrewsbury* (1972) and Robert Nye's *Falstaff* (1976). Pargeter (who also wrote historical mysteries under the name Ellis Peters) chose Hotspur as the protagonist of her novel; this is a mature Hotspur restored to his rightful age, two years older than King Henry IV. Hotspur serves as friend and mentor to the young Hal, here portrayed as a sober and self-controlled young man who attends conscientiously to his duties as Prince of Wales. By excluding the comic world of the tavern and its most famous denizen from her story, Pargeter shifts the emphasis to the political tensions between the English and the Welsh and gives larger roles to the women behind the men – both historical, like Lady Percy and the king's wife Joan of Navarre, and invented. She also re-envisions the story's ending in ways that call attention to Shakespeare's use of his sources. As I observed in my book,

Hotspur's death is the climactic event in *A Bloody Field by Shrewsbury*, just as it is the climactic event of *1 Henry IV*. Saccio, following Bullough [the compiler of the multi-volume *Narrative and Dramatic Sources of Shakespeare*] and others, observes that 'an ambiguous sentence in Holinshed makes it possible to suppose that Hal killed Hotspur', although Hall, Holinshed's source, is not ambiguous on this score and modern historians assume that Hotspur was killed by an unknown combatant (Saccio 51; Bullough 4:164). Pargeter makes use of this ambiguity to challenge Shakespeare's dramatization of the event, replacing it with an intensely tragic climax that is consistent with her portrayal of the two friends (*Constructing*, 151).

Nye's comic novel appropriates elements of *1 Henry IV* and indeed, the entire Shakespeare canon, quite differently. His fictional Falstaff's stream-of-consciousness ramblings, presented in 100 short chapters addressed to the reader (as 'Sir' or 'Madam' or 'Reader') constitute metafictional commentaries on early modern literature and culture, mixed with colorful and irreverent bawdry. Speaking through his protagonist, Nye mocks the business of interpreting Shakespeare, even as he extrapolates from the scenes in which Falstaff appears, endowing him with an expansive 'life'. Like many of the historical novels I discuss in *Constructing a World*, Nye's *Falstaff* creates a context for reading Shakespeare, with descriptions of fourteenth-century London and a powerful chapter on the Black Death, for example. Interestingly, neither Pargeter nor Nye gives Prince Hal a particularly large or interesting role. While I doubt that most teachers of Shakespeare will be able to incorporate two long novels into their course syllabi, they might find that their own readings of Shakespeare are unsettled by the questions about history and character these novelists implicitly pose. I have, however, assigned them to graduate students, who are more likely to know the history behind the plays and who 'get' the allusions and unmarked quotations. Some good seminar paper and dissertation topics have emerged from these excursions.

Films and Performance

No overview of resources available to teachers would be complete without mention of the venerable BBC/Time-Life series of all 37 plays, a project begun in the late 1970s. These films make fewer textual changes or omissions than most film versions of Shakespeare's plays, which makes it easier for students to follow the text as they watch. In *King Henry IV, Part I*, directed by David Giles, with Anthony Quayle as Falstaff, the cast inhabit their period costumes and settings and deliver their lines with a consistency that is often missing in other film treatments. Several scenes from Orson Welles's *Chimes at Midnight* (1965), a fascinating black-and-white composite of scenes from the entire Henriad, with the focus on Welles as a wonderfully enormous and unrepentant Falstaff, are now available on Youtube (hitherto, this film was frequently unavailable). My students in the critical reading and writing course compared excerpts from the two films and read discussions of these and stage performances in the Norton edition; an excerpt from Barbara Hodgdon's *The End Crowns All: Closure and Contradiction in Shakespeare's History* (1991) contained an especially good discussion of Welles's film.

In my experience, showing a 10 or 15 minute excerpt from a film can bring the play to life for students who have never seen Shakespeare performed onstage. It will also guide them as they plan and rehearse the short staged readings I always include as optional assignments in my college classes. Critical cruxes that elude us when reading, difficult syntax that needs unpacking, and embedded stage directions that are easily overlooked all come into focus and demand attention when students are responsible for preparing a scene to perform in class. I suspect that after the term is over the staged readings will be what students remember best; certainly, they have been among the high points of my teaching career.

Bibliography

Bevington, David, ed., *Henry the Fourth, Parts I and II: Critical Essays* (New York and London: Garland Publishing Inc., 1986)

Bristol, Michael, *Carnival and Theatre* (London: Routledge, 1985)

Bullough, Geoffrey, ed., *Narrative and Dramatic Sources of Shakespeare Volume Four: Later English History Plays* (London: Routledge and Kegan Paul, 1962)

Danby, John, *Shakespeare's Doctrine of Nature: A Study of King Lear* (London: Faber & Faber, 1949)

Davis, James E. and Ronald E. Salamone, *Teaching Shakespeare Today: Practical Approaches and Productive Strategies* (Urbana, IL: National Council of Teachers of English, 1993)

Dekker, Thomas, *Of Lantern and Candlelight* (London: J. Busbie, 1608)

Dorius, R. J., *Twentieth Century Interpretations of Henry IV Part One: A Collection of Critical Essays* (Englewood Cliffs, N.J.: Prentice-Hall, 1970)

Evans, G. Blakemore, ed., *The Riverside Shakespeare* (Boston: Houghton Mifflin, 1974)

Gira, Catherine and Adele Seeff, *Henry IV Parts 1 and 2: An Annotated Bibliography,* Garland Shakespeare Bibliographies Vol. 26. (New York: Garland Publishing, 1994)

Greenblatt, Stephen, et al., eds., *The Norton Shakespeare* (New York: W.W. Norton, 1997)

Hall, Edward, *Union of the Two Noble and Illustrious Families of Lancaster and York* (London: Richard Grafton, 1548)

Hodgdon, Barbara, ed., *The First Part of King Henry the Fourth: Texts and Contexts* (Boston: Bedford Books, 1997)

Kastan, David Scott, 'The King Hath Many Marching in His Coats: Or, What Did You Do in the War, Daddy?' *Shakespeare Left and Right*, ed., Ivo Kamps (London: Routledge, 1991)

— ed., *King Henry IV Part I* (London: Arden Shakespeare, Thompson Learning, 2002)

McMullan, Gordon, ed., *1 Henry IV: A Norton Critical Edition, 3rd edition* (New York: W. W. Norton & Co., 2003)

Mowat, Barbara A. and Paul Werstine, eds., *Henry IV Part I: The New Folger Library Shakespeare* (New York: Washington Square Press, 1994)

Nye, Robert, *Falstaff* (Boston: Little Brown, 1976)

O'Brien, Peggy, et al., *Shakespeare Set Free: Teaching* Hamlet *and* Henry IV Part 1 (New York: Washington Square Press, 1994)

Pargeter, Edith, *A Bloody Field by Shrewsbury* (1972; rpt, London: Headline Book Publishing, 1989)

Rozett, Martha Tuck, 'Book review of *The Norton Shakespeare, The Riverside Shakespeare*, 2nd edition, and *The Complete Works of Shakespeare*, ed. David Bevington (4th edition)', *Shakespeare Quarterly*, 48:4 (Winter 1997), 465–72

— *Constructing a World: Shakespeare's England and the New Historical Fiction* (Albany, NY: State University of New York Press, 2003)

— *Talking Back to Shakespeare* (Newark, DE: University of Delaware Press, 1994. Urbana, IL, NCTE, 1995)

Saccio, Peter, *Shakespeare's English Kings: History, Chronicle and Drama* (New York: Oxford University Press, 1977)

Segar, Sir William, *Honor Military and Civil* (London: R. Barker, 1602)

Sprague, Arthur C., 'Gadshill Revisited', *Shakespeare Quarterly* 4:2 (1953), 125–37

Weil, Herbert and Judith Weil, eds, *The First Part of King Henry IV* (Cambridge: Cambridge University Press, 1997)

Welsford, Enid, *The Fool: His Social and Literary History* (London: Faber & Faber, 1935)

Bibliography

Adamson, John, *The Princely Courts of Europe: Rituals, Politics and Culture under the Ancien Regime 1500–1750* (London: Weidenfeld and Nicholson, 1999)

Ainger, Alfred, *Lectures and Essays, Volume I* (London: Macmillan, 1905)

Akrigg, G. P. V., *Jacobean Pageant: The Court of James I* (London: Hamish Hamilton, 1962)

Alexander, Franz, 'A Note on Falstaff', *Psychoanalytic Quarterly*, 3 (1933), 592–606

Anon, *A Student's Lamentation* (1595)

Appleby, Andrew, *Famine in Tudor and Stuart England* (Stanford, CA: Stanford University Press, 1978)

Archer, Ian, *The Pursuit of Stability: Social Relations in Elizabethan London* (Cambridge: Cambridge University Press: 1991)

Armstrong, William, ed., *Shakespeare's Histories: An Anthology of Modern Criticism* (London: Penguin, 1972)

Astington, John H., *English Court Theatre 1558–1642* (Cambridge: Cambridge University Press, 1999)

Auden, W. H., 'The Prince's Dog' (1948), in *Henry the Fourth Parts I and II: Critical Essays*, ed. David Bevington (New York and London: Garland Publishing Inc., 1986), pp. 157–80

Austin, J. L., *How to Do Things with Words* (Cambridge: Harvard University Press, 1975)

Avery, Bruce, 'Gelded Continents and Plenteous Rivers: Cartography as Rhetoric in Shakespeare', in *Playing the Globe: Genre and Geography in English Renaissance Drama*, ed. John Gillies and Virginia Mason Vaughan (London: Associated University Presses, 1998), pp. 46–62

Barasch, Frances K., 'Harlequin/Harlotry in *Henry IV, Part One*', in *Italian Culture in the Drama of Shakespeare and His Contemporaries: Rewriting, Remaking, Refashioning*, ed. Michele Marrapodi (Aldershot: Ashgate, 2007), pp. 27–37

Barber, C. L., *Shakespeare's Festive Comedy: A Study of Dramatic Form and Its Relation to Social Custom* (Princeton, NJ: Princeton University Press, 1959)

Barker, Roberta, 'Tragical-Comical-Historical Hotspur', *Shakespeare Quarterly*, 54 (2003), 288–307

Bate, Jonathan and Rasmussen, Eric, *Complete Works of William Shakespeare* (Basingstoke: Macmillan, 2007)

Bate, Jonathan, 'Shakespeare Nationalised, Shakespeare Privatised', *English*, 42 (1993), 1–18

Beaumont, Francis, and John Fletcher, *Comedies and Tragedies* (London: Humphrey Robinson and Humphrey Moseley, 1647)

Beck, Ervin, 'Terence Improved: The Paradigm of the Prodigal Son in Early English Renaissance Comedy', *Renaissance Drama*, 6 (1973), 107–22

Bednarz, James P., 'Biographical Politics: Shakespeare, Jonson, and the Oldcastle Controversy', *Ben Jonson Journal*, 11 (2004), 1–20

Behn, Aphra, 'An Epistle to the Reader' (1673), in *More Seventeenth-Century Allusions to Shakespeare and his Works*, ed. George Thorn-Drury (London: P. J. and A. E. Dobell, 1924) p. 10

Bell, Robert H., 'The Anatomy of Folly in Shakespeare's Henriad', *Humor*, 14 (2001), 181–201

Berg, James E., ' "This dear, dear Land": "Dearth" and the Fantasy of the Land-Grab in Richard II and Henry IV', *English Literary Renaissance*, 29 (1999), 225–45

Berger, Harry Jr., *Making Trifles of Terrors: Redistributing Complicities in Shakespeare*, ed. Peter Erickson (Stanford.,CA Stanford University Press, 1997)

— 'The Prince's Dog: Falstaff and the Perils of Speech-Prefixity', *Shakespeare Quarterly*, 49 (1998), 40–73

— 'A Horse Named Cut: *1 Henry IV*, 2.1', in *Renaissance Historicisms: Essays in Honor of Arthur F. Kinney*, ed. James M. Dutcher and Anne Lake Prescott (Newark, DE: University of Delaware Press, 2008), pp. 193–205

Bevington, David, ed., *Henry the Fourth Parts I and II: Critical Essays* (New York and London: Garland Publishing Inc., 1986)

— ed., *Henry IV, Part One* (Oxford: Oxford University Press, 1987–1994).

Billing, Christian M., *Masculinity, Corporality, and the English Stage 1580–1635* (Aldershot: Ashgate, 2008)

Blau, Herbert, *Sails of the Herring Fleet: Essays on Beckett* (Ann Arbor, MI: University of Michigan Press, 2000)

Bloom, Harold, ed., *Modern Critical Interpretations: William Shakespeare's Henry IV, Part 1*, (New York: Chelsea House Publishers, 1987)

— *Ruin the Sacred Truths: Poetry and Belief from the Bible to the Present* (Cambridge: Harvard University Press, 1989)

— *Shakespeare and the Invention of the Human* (New York: Riverhead Books, 1998)

— *Sir John Falstaff* (Broomall, PA: Chelsea House, 2004)

Bradley, A. C., 'The Rejection of Falstaff' (1902), in *Henry the Fourth Parts I and II: Critical Essays*, ed. David Bevington (New York and London: Garland Publishing Inc., 1986), pp. 77–98

— 'The Rejection of Falstaff', in *Oxford Lectures on Poetry* (London: Macmillan, 1909)

Breight, Curtis C., *Surveillance, Militarism and Drama in the Elizabethan Era* (London and New York: Macmillan and St Martins, 1996)

Brigden, Susan, 'Youth and the English Reformation', in *The Impact of the English Reformation 1500–1640*, ed. Peter Marshall (London: Arnold, 1997), pp. 55–84

Brooks, Cleanth and Robert Heilman, *Understanding Drama* (London: George G. Harrap & Co Ltd., 1946)

Brooks, Douglas A., *From Playhouse to Printing House: Drama and Authorship in Early Modern England* (Cambridge: Cambridge University Press, 2000)

Browne, Thomas, *Christian Morals* (London: Rivingtons, 1863)

Buland, Mable, *The Presentation of Time in the Elizabethan Drama* (New York: Henry Holt, 1912)

Bullough, Geoffrey, ed., *Narrative and Dramatic Sources of Shakespeare Volume Two: The Comedies 1597–1603* (London: Routledge and Kegan Paul, 1958)

Bullough, Geoffrey, ed., *Narrative and Dramatic Sources of Shakespeare Volume Four: Later English History Plays* (London: Routledge and Kegan Paul; New York: Columbia University Press, 1962)

Burckhardt, Sigurd, 'Shakespearean Meanings' (1968), in *Henry the Fourth Parts I and II: Critical Essays*, ed. David Bevington (New York and London: Garland Publishing Inc., 1986), pp. 289–314

Cahill, Patricia A., *Unto the Breach: Martial Formations, Historical Trauma, and the Early Modern Stage* (Oxford: Oxford University Press, 2008)

Calderwood, James L., *Metadrama in Shakespeare's Henriad: 'Richard II' to 'Henry V'* (Berkeley, CA: University of California Press, 1979)

Caldwell, Ellen M., ' "Banish all the wor(l)d": Falstaff's Iconoclastic Threat to Kingship in *1 Henry IV*', *Renascence*, 59 (2006–2007), 219–45

Campbell, Lily B., *Shakespeare's 'Histories': Mirrors of Elizabethan Policy* (1947) (San Marino: The Huntington Library, 1963)

Canino, Catherin Grace, *Shakespeare and the Nobility: The Negotiation of Lineage* (Cambridge: Cambridge University Press, 2007)

Cardullo, Bert, 'One Dramatic Character, Two Artistic Media: Shakespeare's Falstaff in Drama and Film', *Lamar Journal of the Humanities*, 31:2 (2006), 43–68

Carlton, Charles, *Charles I: The Personal Monarch* (London: Ark Paperbacks, 1983)

Carlson, Eric, 'The Origin, Function, and Status of the Office of Churchwarden', in *The World of Rural Dissenters 1520–1725* ed. Margaret Spufford (Cambridge: Cambridge University Press, 1995), pp. 164–207

Casellas, Jesús López-Peláez, ' "And dressed myself in such humility": Honour and Disguising in Shakespeare's *1 Henry IV*', in *Masquerades: Disguise in Literature in English from the Middle Ages to the Present*, ed. Jesús López-Peláez Casellas, David Malcolm, Pilar Sánchez Calle (Gdansk: Wydawnictwo Uniwersytetu Gdanskiego, 2004), pp. 38–54

Cavendish, Margaret, 'Letter CXIII' (1664), in *Women Reading Shakespeare 1660–1900: An Anthology of Criticism*, ed. Ann Thompson and Sasha Roberts (Manchester: Manchester University Press, 1997), pp. 12–13

Chambers, E. K., *The Elizabethan Stage Volume Four* (Oxford: Oxford University Press, 1923)

Chardin, Philippe, 'De la grandeur du désastre à l'héroï-comique du désastruex', *Littératures*, 45 (2001), 267–77

Charlton, H. B., *Shakespearian Comedy* (London: Methuen & Co., 1938)

— 'Shakespeare, Politics and Politicians' (1929), in *Shakespeare: Henry IV Parts I and II: A Casebook*, ed. G. K. Hunter (London: Macmillan, 1970), pp. 81–91

Chedgzoy, Kate, 'The Civility of Early Modern Welsh Women', in *Early Modern Civil Discourses*, ed. Jennifer Richards (Basingstoke: Palgrave Macmillan, 2003), pp. 162–82

Chimes At Midnight, dir. Orson Welles (Suevia Films, 1965)

Claret, Jean-Louis, 'Aveu et redemption dans le théâtre de Shakespeare', in *Cultures de la confession: Formes de l'aveu dans le monde anglophone*, ed. Sylvie Mathé and Gilles Teulié (Aix-en-Provence: Publications de l'Université de Provence, 2006), pp. 27–38

— 'La prise de croix n'aura pas lieu: L'idée de croisade dans *Henry IV* de Shakespeare', in *Religious Writings and War/Les discourse religieux et la guerre*, ed. Gilles Teulié (Montpellier: Université Paul-Valéry, 2006), pp. 103–24

Clark, Peter, *The English Alehouse: A Social History 1200–1830* (London: Longman, 1983)

Cobb, Barbara Mather, ' "Suppose that you have seen the well-appointed king": Imagining Succession in the Henriad', *Cahiers Élisabéthains* 70 (2006), 33–38

Cohen, Derek, 'The Rites of Violence in *1 Henry IV*', *Shakespeare Survey*, 38 (1985), 77–84 – *Searching Shakespeare: Studies in Culture and Authority* (Toronto: University of Toronto Press, 2003)

Coleridge, Samuel Taylor, '*Henry IV*: The Character of Falstaff' (1811), in *Henry the Fourth Parts I and II: Critical Essays*, ed. David Bevington (New York and London: Garland Publishing Inc., 1986), p. 53

Collinson, Patrick, *From Iconoclasm to Iconophobia: the Cultural Impact of the Second Reformation* (Reading: University of Reading, 1986)

Colvin, Daniel L., '(Re)covering the Self: Hal and the Psychology of Disguise', in *Staging Shakespeare: Essays in Honor of Alan C. Dessen*, ed. Lena Cowen Orlin and Miranda Johnson-Haddad (Newark, DE: University of Delaware Press, 2007), pp. 45–59

Conrad, Peter, *Orson Welles: The Stories of His Life* (London: Faber and Faber, 2003)

Corbin, Peter and Douglas Sedge, eds, *The Oldcastle Controversy*, (Manchester: Manchester University Press, 1991)

Costa de Beauregard, Raphaëlle, *Silent Elizabethans: The Language of Colour in the Miniatures of Nicholas Hilliard and Isaac Oliver* (Montpellier: Centre d'Etudes et de Recherches sur la Renaissance Anglaise, Université Paul Valéry – Montpellier III, 2000)

Council, Norman, *When Honour's at the Stake: Ideas of honour in Shakespeare's plays* (London: George Allen and Unwin Ltd, 1973)

Courtenay, Thomas, *Commentaries on the Historical Plays of Shakespeare* (London: Henry Colbourn, 1840)

Coussement-Boillot, Laetitia, *Copia et cornucopia: La poétique shakespearienne de l'abondance* (Bern: Lang, 2008)

Cox, Nick, 'The Great Enlargement: The Uses of Delinquency in *Henry IV Part One*', *Literature and History*, 8 (1999), 1–19

Crawford, John W., 'Secondary Wisdom: The Role of Women as Mentors in Shakespeare's Plays', *The Learning, Wit, and Wisdom of Shakespeare's Renaissance Women*, ed. John W. Crawford (Lewiston, NY: Mellen, 1997), pp. 63–93

Crosby, David, 'Examination and Mockery in *Henry IV, Part One*', *Journal of the Wooden O Symposium*, 4 (2004), 24–34

Cumberland, Richard, 'Remarks Upon the Characters of Falstaff and his Group' (1786), in *Henry the Fourth Parts I and II: Critical Essays*, ed. David Bevington (New York and London: Garland Publishing Inc., 1986), pp. 49–52

Daniel, Samuel, *The first fovvre bookes of the ciuile wars between the two houses of Lancaster and Yorke* (London: Simon Waterson, 1595)

Danson, Lawrence, 'Shakespeare and the Misrecognition of Fathers and Sons', in *Paternity and Fatherhood: Myths and Realities*, ed. Lieve Spaas, (Basingstoke: Macmillan, 1998), 236–45

David, Richard, 'Shakespeare's History Plays: Epic or Drama?', *Shakespeare Survey*, 6, 1953, 129–39

Davidson, Clifford, 'The Coventry Mysteries and Shakespeare's Histories', *Shakespeare's Second Historical Tetralogy: Some Christian Features,* ed. Beatrice Batson (West Cornwall, CT: Locust Hill Press, 2004), pp. 3–25

Davies, Anthony, 'Falstaff's Shadow', in *Shakespeare on Screen: The Henriad,* ed. Sarah Hatchuel and Nathalie Vienne-Guerrin, (Mont-Saint-Aignan: Publications des Universités de Rouen and du Havre, 2008), pp. 99–117

Davies, Michael, 'Falstaff's Lateness: Calvinism and the Protestant Hero in *Henry IV*', *Review of English Studies*, 56 (2005), 351–78

Davies, Thomas, *Dramatic Micellanies: Consisting of Critical Observations on Several Plays of Shakespeare* (London: Thomas Davies, 1783)

Davies, Rees, 'Shakespeare's Glendower and Owain Glym Dwr', *Historian*, 66 (2000), 22–25

Dawson, Anthony B. and Paul Yachnin, *The Culture of Playgoing in Shakespeare's England* (Cambridge: Cambridge University Press, 2001)

De Carles, Nathalie Rivère, 'Tenture et théâtre, de Minerve à Thespis', *Anglophonia*, 13 (2003), 83–96

Dean, Paul, 'Forms of Time: Some Elizabethan Two-Part History Plays', *Renaissance Studies*, 4:4 (1990), 410–30

— 'Shakespeare's Historical Imagination', *Renaissance Studies*, 11:1 (1997) 27–40

Dekker, Thomas, *The Shoemaker's Holiday*, ed. Robert Smallwood and Stanley Wells (Manchester: Manchester University Press, 1979)

Desmet, Christy, *Reading Shakespeare's Characters: Rhetorics, Ethics and Identity* (Amherst, MA: University of Massachusetts Press, 1992)

Di Michele, Laura, 'Shakespeare's History Plays as a "Scene" of the Disappearance of Popular Discourse', in *Italian Studies in Shakespeare and His Contemporaries*, ed. Michele Marrapodi and Giorgio Melchiori (Newark, DE: University of Delaware Press, 1999), 128–51

Dickey, Stephen, 'The Crown and the Pillow: Royal Properties in *Henry IV*', *Shakespeare Survey*, 60 (2007), 102–17

Dobson, Michael, 'Falstaff after John Bull: Shakespearean History, Britishness, and the Former United Kingdom', *Shakespeare Jahrbuch,* 136 (2000), 40–55

Dorius, R. J. 'A Little More than a Little', *Shakespeare Quarterly*, 11 (1960), 13–26

Dowden, Edward, from *Shakespeare: A Critical Study of his Mind and Art* (1875), in *Henry the Fourth Parts I and II: Critical Essays*, ed. David Bevington (New York and London: Garland Publishing Inc., 1986), pp. 65–71

Driver, Tom F., *The Sense of History in Greek and Shakespearean Drama* (New York: Columbia University Press, 1960)

Drouet, Pascale, 'Répétitions et différenciations à Eastcheap dans *1 Henry IV* de Shakespeare', *Imaginaires: Revue du Centre de recherche sur l'imaginaire dans les littératures de langue anglaise*, 9 (2003), 9–20

Dryden, John, *Of Dramatick Poesy, An Essay* (1668) (London: Jacob Tonson, 1735)

Dubrow, Heather, *Shakespeare and Domestic Loss: Forms of Deprivation, Mourning, and Recuperation* (Cambridge: Cambridge University Press, 1999

Dunlop, Fiona S. *The Late Medieval Interlude: The Drama of Youth and Aristocratic Masculinity* (Woodbridge, Suffolk: York Medieval Press in association with Boydell and Brewer, 2007)

Earnshaw, Steven, *The Pub in Literature: England's Altered State* (Manchester: Manchester University Press, 2000)

Edelman, Charles, 'Shakespeare and the Invention of the Epic Theatre: Working with Brecht', *Shakespeare Survey*, 58 (2005), 130–36

Ellis, David, 'Falstaff and the Problems of Comedy', *Cambridge Quarterly*, 34 (2005), 95–108

— *Shakespeare's Practical Jokes: An Introduction to the Comic in His Work* (Lewisburg, WV: Bucknell University Press, 2007)

Empson, William, 'Falstaff and Mr Dover Wilson' (1953), in *Shakespeare: Henry IV Parts I and II: A Casebook*, ed. G. K. Hunter (London: Macmillan, 1970), pp. 135–54

Erickson, Carolly, *The First Elizabeth* (1983; rpt. New York: St Martin's Griffin, 1997)

Fehrenbach, Robert, '"When Lord Cobham and Edmund Tilney were at odds": Oldcastle, Falstaff and the date of *1 Henry IV*', *Shakespeare Studies*, 18 (1986), 87–101

Feuillerat, Albert, 'An Unknown Protestant Morality Play', *Modern Language Review*, 9 (1914), 94–96

— ed., *Documents Relating to the Revels at Court in the Time of King Edward VI and Queen Mary* (Louvain, 1914)

Fiehler, Rudolph, 'How Oldcastle became Falstaff', *Modern Language Quarterly*, 16.1 (1955), 16–28

Firth, Richard, *Tikopia Ritual and Belief* (Boston: Beacon Press, 1967)

Fitter, Chris, 'The quarrel is between our masters and us their men: *Romeo and Juliet*, dearth, and the London riots', *English Literary Renaissance*, 30:2 (2000), 154–83

— '"Your captain is brave and vows reformation": Jack Cade, the Hacket rising, and Shakespeare's vision of popular rebellion in *2 Henry VI*', *Shakespeare Studies*, 32 (2004), 173–216

— *Radical Shakespeare: Politics and Stagecraft in the Early Career*, forthcoming.

Fitzpatrick, Joan, *Shakespeare, Spenser, and the Contours of Britain: Reshaping the Atlantic Archipelago* (Hatfield: University of Hertfordshire Press, 2004)

Flachmann, Michael, 'Parrot, Parody, and Paronomasia: Damnable Iteration in *Henry IV, Part I'*, *Journal of the Wooden O Symposium*, 4 (2004), 45–52

Flügel, Edwald, ed., *Ralph Roister Doister*, in *Representative English Comedies*, gen. ed., C. M. Gayley (New York: Macmillan, 1903)

Forker, Charles R., 'The State of the Soul and the Soul of the State: Reconciliation in the Two Parts of Shakespeare's *Henry IV'*, *Studies in Medieval and Renaissance History*, 4 (2007), 289–313

Frenk, Joachim, 'Falstaff erzählen und zeigen', *Wissenschaftliches Seminar Online* 3 (2005), 16–23 (www.shakespeare-gesellschaft.de/publikationen/seminar/ausgabe2005.html, accessed 24 March 2011)

Frye, Northrop, 'The Argument of Comedy' (1949), in *Henry the Fourth Parts I and II: Critical Essays*, ed. David Bevington (New York and London: Garland Publishing Inc., 1986), pp. 181–86

George, David, 'Sons without Fathers: Shakespeare's Second tetralogy', in *Shakespeare's Second Historical Tetralogy: Some Christian Feature*, ed. Beatrice Batson (West Cornwall, CT: Locust Hill Press, 2004), 27–55

Gildon, Charles, 'Remarks on the Plays of Shakespeare' (1710), in *William Shakespeare: The Critical Heritage, 1693–1733 (Volume 2)*, ed. Brian Vickers (London: Routledge, 1996), p. 183

Goldberg, Jonathan, 'The Commodity of Names: "Falstaff" and "Oldcastle" in *1 Henry IV'*, in *Reconfiguring the Renaissance: Essays in Critical Materialism*, ed. Jonathan Crewe (London: Associated University Presses, 1992), pp. 76–88

Gluckman, Max, and Mary Gluckman, 'On Drama, Games and Athletic Contests', in *Secular Ritual*, ed. Sally F. Moore and Barbara Meyerhoff (Amsterdam: Van Gorcum, 1977), pp. 227–43

Grady, Hugh, 'Falstaff: Subjectivity between the Carnival and the Aesthetic', *Modern Language Review*, 96: 3 (2001), pp. 609–623

Greenburg, Bradley, 'Romancing the Chronicles: *1 Henry IV* and the Rewriting of Medieval History', *Quidditas*, 26–27 (2005–2006), 34–50

Greenblatt, Stephen, 'Invisible Bullets: Renaissance Authority and its Subversion, *Henry IV* and *Henry V'*, in *Political Shakespeare: New Essays in Cultural Materialism*, ed. Jonathan Dollimore and Alan Sinfield (Ithaca, NY: Cornell University Press, 1985), pp. 18–47

Greenfield, Matthew, '*I Henry IV*: Metatheatrical Britain', in *British Identities and English Renaissance Literature*, ed. David J. Baker and Wily Maley (Cambridge: Cambridge University Press, 2002), pp. 71–80

Griffin, Benjamin, 'Marring and Mending: Treacherous Likeness in Two Renaissance Controversies', *Huntington Library Quarterly*, 60 (1998), 363–80

— *Playing the Past: Approaches to English Historical Drama, 1385–1600* (Woodbridge: D.S. Brewer, 2001)

Griffith, Elizabeth, *The Morality of Shakespeare's Drama Illustrated* (1775) (London: Frank Cass & Co. Ltd., 1971)

Griffiths, Huw, '"O, I am ignorance itself in this!": Listening to Welsh in Shakespeare and Armin', in *Shakespeare and Wales: From the Marches to the*

Assembly, ed. Willy Maley and Philip Schwyzer (Farnham: Ashgate, 2010), pp. 111–26

Grinnell, Richard W., 'Witchcraft, Race, and the Rhetoric of Barbarism in *Othello* and *1 Henry IV*', *Upstart Crow*, 24 (2004), 72–80

Groves, Beatrice, 'Hal as Self-Styled Redeemer: The Harrowing of Hell and *Henry IV Part 1*', *Shakespeare Survey*, 57 (2004), 236–48

Gurr, Andrew, *Playgoing in Shakespeare's London* (Cambridge: Cambridge University Press, 1987)

Hall, Jonathan, *Anxious Pleasures: Shakespearean Comedy and the Nation-State* (Madison, NJ: Fairleigh Dickinson University Press, 1995)

— 'The Evacuations of Falstaff', in *Shakespeare and Carnival: After Bakhtin*, ed. Ronald Knowles (New York: St Martin's Press, 1998), pp. 123–51

Hamilton, Gary D., 'Mocking Oldcastle: Notes toward Exploring a Possible Catholic Presence in Shakespeare's Henriad', in *Shakespeare and the Culture of Christianity in Early Modern England*, ed. Dennis Taylor and David N. Beauregard (New York: Fordham University Press, 2003), 141–58

Hammer, Paul, *Elizabeth's Wars: War, Government and Society in Tudor England* (Basingstoke: Palgrave Macmillan, 2003)

Harding, John, *The Chronicle of Iohn Hardyng*, ed. Sir Henry Ellis (London: Rivington, 1812)

Hardin, Richard F., *Civil Idolatry: Desacralizing and Monarchy in Spenser, Shakespeare, and Milton* (Newark, DE: University of Delaware Press, 1992)

Hart, Alfred, 'The Time Allotted for Representation of Elizabethan and Jacobean Plays', *Review of English Studies*, 8 (1932) 395–413

— *Shakespeare and the Homilies* (London: Oxford University Press, 1934)

Hart, Jonathan, *Theater and World: The Problematics of Shakespeare's History* (Boston: Northeastern University Press, 1992)

— *Shakespeare: Poetry, History, and Culture* (New York: Palgrave Macmillan, 2009)

Hartley, T. E., ed., *Proceedings in the Parliament of Elizabeth I, Vol. 1, 1558–1581* (Leicester: Leicester University Press, 1981)

Hartwig, Joan, ' "Mine honor's pawn": Gage-Throwing and Word-Play in Shakespeare's Second tetralogy', *CEA Critic* 68, (2006), 3–11

Hawkes, Terence, 'Bryn Glas', *European Journal of English Studies*, 1 (1997), 269–90

Hawkins, Sherman, '*Henry IV*: The Structural Problem Revisited', *Shakespeare Quarterly*, 33 (1982), 278–301

Hayes, Douglas W., *Rhetorical Subversion in Early English Drama* (New York: Peter Lang, 2004)

Hazlitt, William, from*Characters of Shakespeare's Plays* (1817), in *Henry the Fourth Parts I and II: Critical Essays*, ed. David Bevington (New York and London: Garland Publishing Inc., 1986), pp. 55–64

Hedrick, Donald K., 'Male Surplus Value', *Renaissance Drama*, 31 (2002), 85–124

Henry IV Part 1, dir. Michael Bogdanove (London: Portman Classics, 1990)

Henry IV, Part One, dir. David Giles (London: BBC, 1979)

Highley, Christopher, *Shakespeare, Spenser, and the Crisis in Ireland* (Cambridge: Cambridge University Press, 1997)

Hill, Christopher, *Society and Puritanism in Pre-Revolutionary England* (London: Secker and Warburg, 1964)

Hirsh, James, *Shakespeare and the History of Soliloquies* (Madison, NJ: Fairleigh Dickinson University Press, 2003)

Helgerson, Richard, *Forms of Nationhood: The Elizabethan Writing of England* (Chicago: University of Chicago Press, 1992)

Hodgdon, Barbara, The End Crowns All: Closure and Contradiction in Shakespeare's History (Princeton, NJ: Princeton University Press, 1991)

Höfele, Andreas, ' "The great image of authority": Königsbilder in Shakespeare's Theatre', *Shakespeare Jahrbuch*, 133 (1997), 77–97

Holderness, Graham, *Shakespeare's History* (Dublin: Gill and Macmillan, 1985)
— *Shakespeare Recycled: The Making of Historical Drama* (Hemel Hempstead: Harvester Wheatsheaf, 1992)
— ed., *Shakespeare's History Plays: Richard II to Henry V*, (New York: St. Martin's Press, 1992)

Holland, Norman M., ' "The barge she sat in": Psychoanalysis and Diction', *PsyArt: An Online Journal for the Psychological Study of the Arts* (2005) (www.clas.ufl.edu/ipsa/journal/2005_holland09.shtml#holland09, accessed 24 March 2011)

Holland, Peter, 'Mapping Shakespeare's Britain', in *Spectacle and Public Performance in the Late Middle Ages and the Renaissance*, ed. Robert E. Stillman (Leiden and Boston: Brill, 2006), pp. 157–81

Holliday, Shawn, ' "Now for our Irish wars": Shakespeare's Warning against England's Usurpation of Ireland in the Lancastrian Tetralogy', *Pennsylvania English*, 20:2 (1996), 12–23

Hopkins, Lisa, 'New Historicism and History Plays', *Shakespeare Yearbook*, 6 (1996), 53–73
— 'The Iliad and the Henriad: Epics and Brothers', *Classical and Modern Literature*, 19 (1999–2000), 149–71
— 'Welshness in Shakespeare's English Histories', in *Shakespeare's History Plays: Performance, Translation and Adaptation in Britain and Abroad*, ed. A. J. Hoenselaars (Cambridge: Cambridge University Press, 2004), pp. 60–74

Howard, Jean E. and Phyllis Rackin, *Engendering a Nation: A Feminist Account of Shakespeare's English Histories* (London: Routledge, 1997)

Huang, Bikang, *Politics in Form: Imagery and Ideology in Shakespeare's History Plays* (Beijing: Peking University Press, 2000)

Hughes, P. L. and J. F. Larkin, eds, *Tudor Royal Proclamations*, (New Haven, CT: Yale, 1969)

Hunt, Alice, The Drama of Coronation: Medieval Ceremony in Early Modern England (Cambridge: Cambridge University Press, 2008)

Hunter, G. K., 'Henry IV and the Elizabethan Two part Play', *Review of English Studies*, 5 (1954), 236–48
— *Shakespeare: Henry IV Parts I and II: A Casebook*, (London: Macmillan, 1970)

Hunter, Robert G., 'Shakespeare, Pattern of Excelling Nature' (1978), in *Henry the Fourth Parts I and II: Critical Essays*, ed. David Bevington (New York and London: Garland Publishing Inc., 1986), pp. 349–58

Hutson, Lorna, ' "Our old storehouse": Plowden's Commentaries and Political Consciousness in Shakespeare', *Shakespeare Yearbook*, 7 (1996), 249–73

— 'Not the King's Two Bodies: Reading the 'Body Politic' in Shakespeare's *Henry IV*, Parts 1 and 2', in *Rhetoric and Law in Early Modern Europe*, ed. Victoria Kahn, and Lorna Hutson (New Haven, CT: Yale University Press, 2001), pp. 166–98

— *The Invention of Suspicion: Law and Mimesis in Shakespeare and Renaissance Drama* (Oxford: Oxford University Press, 2007)

Inchbald, Elizabeth, *King Henry IV, The First Part . . . With Remarks* (1806–1809) (New York: Scholars' Facsimiles and Reprints, 1990)

Iselin, Pierre, ' "Thou hast damnable iteration!": Anatomie de la citation dans *Henry IV, part 1*', in *Le grotesque au theatre* (special issue of *Cercles*, October 1992), ed. Jean-Pierre Maquerlot (Mont-Saint-Aignan: Centre d'Etudes en Littérature, Linguistique et Civilisation de Langue Anglaise and Centre d'Etudes du Théâtre Anglo-Saxon, 1992), pp. 25–36

Ivic, Christopher, 'Reassuring Fratricide in *1 Henry IV*', in *Forgetting in Early Modern English Literature and Culture: Lethe's Legacies*, ed. Christopher Ivic and Grant Williams, (London: Routledge, 2004), pp. 99–109

Jenkins, Harold, 'Shakespeare's History Plays: 1900–1951', *Shakespeare Survey*, 6 (1953), 1–15

— *The Structural Problem in Shakespeare's 'Henry The Fourth'* (London: Methuen, 1956), and excerpted in *Shakespeare: Henry IV Parts I and II: A Casebook*, ed. G. K. Hunter (London: Macmillan, 1970), pp. 155–73

Jensen, Phebe, *Religion and Revelry in Shakespeare's Festive World* (Cambridge: Cambridge University Press, 2008)

Johnson, Samuel, 'The Plays of William Shakespeare' (1765), in *Henry the Fourth Parts I and II: Critical Essays*, ed. David Bevington (New York and London: Garland Publishing Inc., 1986), pp. 7–8

Jones, Robert C., *These Valiant Dead: Renewing the Past in Shakespeare's Histories* (Iowa City, IA: University of Iowa Press, 1991)

Jorgensen, Paul, *Redeeming Shakespeare's Words* (Berkeley, CA: University of California Press, 1962)

Karremann, Isabel, ' "Drinking of the wyne of forgetfulnesse": The Ambivalent Blessings of Oblivion and the Early Modern Stage', *Wissenschaftliches Seminar Online* 6 (2008), (www.shakespeare-gesellschaft.de/publikationen/seminar/ausgabe2008/karremann.html, accessed 24 March 2011)

Kastan, David Scott, ed., *Shakespeare and the Shapes of Time* (Basingstoke: Macmillan, 1982)

— ' "The King Hath Many Marching in his Coats", or, What did you do in the War, Daddy?', in *Shakespeare Left and Right*, ed. Ivo Kamps (London: Routledge, 1991), pp. 241–58.

— *King Henry IV Part 1* (London: Arden Shakespeare, Thomson Learning, 2002)

— *Understanding Falstaff* (San Diego: San Diego State University, 2003)

Kendrick, Christopher, *Utopia, Carnival, and Commonwealth in Renaissance England* (Toronto: University of Toronto Press, 2004)

Kennedy, Michael, *The Life of Elgar* (Cambridge: Cambridge University Press, 2004)

Kermode, Lloyd, *Aliens and Englishness in Elizabethan Drama* (Cambridge: Cambridge University Press, 2009)

Kerrigan, John, '*Henry IV* and the Death of Old Double', *Essays in Criticism*, 40:1 (1990), 24–53

King, Pamela M., 'Minority Plays: Two Interludes For Edward VI,' *Medieval English Theatre*, 15 (1993), 87–102

Kingsley-Smith, Jane, *Shakespeare's Drama of Exile* (Basingstoke: Palgrave Macmillan, 2003)

Kirby, J. L., *Henry IV of England* (London: Constable, 1970)

Kisby, Fiona, '"When a King Goeth a Procession": Chapel Ceremonies and Services, the Ritual Year and Religious Reforms at the Early Tudor Court', *Journal of British Studies*, 40:1 (2001), 44–75

— ed., 'Religious Ceremonial at the Tudor Court: Extracts from Royal Household Regulations', in *Religion, Politics and Society in Sixteenth Century England*, ed. Ian W. Archer with Simon Adams, G. W. Bernard, Mark Greengrass, Paul E. J. Hammer and Fiona Kisby, Camden Fifth Series, Vol. 22 (London: Royal Historical Society Publications, 2003), pp. 1–34

Klawitter, Uwe, *Die Darstellung des einfachen Volkes in Shakespeares Dramen: Eine ideologiekritische Studie* (Trier: Wissenschaftlicher Verlag Trier, 2004)

Klooss, Wolfgang, 'Feasting with Falstaff: Luxus und Verschwendung im kulinarischen Diskurs von Shakespeares England', in *Texting Culture – Culturing Texts: Essays in Honor of Horst Breuer*, ed. Anja Müller-Wood (Trier: Wissenschaftlicher Verlag, 2008), pp. 71–91

Knowles, James, '*1 Henry IV*', in *A Companion to Shakespeare's Works Volume Two*, ed. Richard Dutton and Jean E. Howard (Oxford: Blackwell, 2003), pp. 412–31

Knowles, Ronald, *The Critics Debate: Henry IV Parts I and II* (Basingstoke: Macmillan, 1992)

— *Shakespeare's Arguments with History* (Basingstoke: Palgrave, 2002)

Kreps, Barbara, 'Power, Authority, and Rhetoric in Shakespeare's Lancastrians', in *The Complete Consort: Saggi di anglistica in onore di Francesco Gozzi*, ed. Roberta Ferrari and Laura Giovannelli (Pisa: Pisa University Press, 2005), pp. 63–76

Krieger, Elliott, '"To Demand the Time of Day": Prince Hal', in *Modern Critical Interpretations: William Shakespeare's Henry IV, Part 1*, ed. Harold Bloom (New York: Chelsea House Publishers, 1987), pp. 101–08

Krims, Marvin B., 'Hotspur's Antifeminine Prejudice in Shakespeare's *1 Henry IV*', *Literature and Psychology*, 40 (1994), 118–32

— 'Prince Hal's Play as Prelude to His Invasion of France', *Psychoanalytic Review*, 88 (2001), 495–510

— 'Prince Hal's Aggression', *PsyArt: A Hyperlink Journal for Psychological Study of the Arts*, (2002), 1–21

— *The Mind According to Shakespeare: Psychoanalysis in the Bard's Writing* (Westport, CT: Praeger, 2006)

Kris, Ernst, 'Prince Hal's Conflict', *Psychoanalytic Quarterly*, 17 (1948), 487–506

Lamont, Claire, 'Shakespeare's Henry IV and "the old song of Percy and Douglas"', in *Shakespearean Continuities: Essays in Honour of E. A. J. Honigmann*, ed. John Batchelor, Tom Cain, and Claire Lamont (Basingstoke: Macmillan, 1997), pp. 56–73

Lander, Jesse M., '"Crack'd crowns" and Counterfeit Sovereigns: The Crisis of Value in *1 Henry IV*', *Shakespeare Studies*, 30 (2002), 137–61

Langbaine, Gerard, 'An Account of the English Dramatick Poets' (1691), in *William Shakespeare: The Critical Heritage, 1623–1692 (Volume 1)*, ed. Brian Vickers (London: Routledge, 1974), p. 419

Langbaum, Robert, 'The Poetry of Experience' (1957), in *Henry the Fourth Parts I and II: Critical Essays*, ed. David Bevington (New York and London: Garland Publishing Inc., 1986), pp. 207–22

Laroque, François, 'Shakespeare's "Battle of Carnival and Lent": The Falstaff Scenes Reconsidered (*1 and 2 Henry IV*)', in *Shakespeare and Carnival: After Bakhtin*, ed. Ronald Knowles (New York: St Martin's, 1998), pp. 83–96

— 'Les rois de carnaval dans le théâtre de Shakespeare: Le cas de *Jules César* et d'*Hamlet*', in *Figures de la royauté en Angleterre de Shakespeare à la Glorieuse Révolution*, ed. François Laroque, and Franck Lessay (Paris: Presses de la Sorbonne Nouvelle, 1999), 49–60

Larsen, Darl, *Monty Python, Shakespeare and English Renaissance Drama* (London: McFarland, 2003)

Larue, Anne, *A la guerre comme au théâtre: Les Perses, Henry IV, Les Paravents* (Paris: Editions du Temps, 2000)

__ 'La fantasme de la terre-mère dans trois pièces de guerre: *Les Perses, 1 Henry IV, Les Paravents*', in *Théâtres de la guerre: La mise en scène de la guerre dans Les Perses d'Eschyle, la première partie de Henry IV de Shakespeare, Les Paravents de Genet* (Paris: Klincksieck, 2001), pp. 79–103

Law, Robert Adger, 'Structural Unity in the Two Parts of *Henry the Fourth*', *Studies in Philology*, 24:2 (April, 1927), 223–42

Leahy, William, ' "Thy hunger-starved men": Shakespeare's *Henry* Plays and the contemporary Lot of the Common Soldier', *Parergon*, 20 (2003), 119–34

Lecercle, Ann, 'Of Benches and Wenches: Subversion de l'espace et topologie de la tyrannie dans *I Henry IV*', in *L'espace littéraire dans la littérature et la culture anglo-saxonnes*, ed. Bernard Brugière (Paris: Presses de la Sorbonne Nouvelle, 1995), pp. 33–40

— 'Epics and Ethics in *1 Henry IV*', in *French Essays on Shakespeare and His Contemporaries: "What would France with us?"* ed. Jean-Marie Maguin and Michèle Willems (Newark, DE: University of Delaware Press, 1995), pp. 175–88

François Lecercle, 'La croisade avortée: Shakespeare, Henry IV, première partie, acte I, scène 1', in *Théâtres de la guerre: La mise en scène de la guerre dans Les Perses d'Eschyle, la première partie de Henry IV de Shakespeare, Les Paravents de Genet*, ed. François Lecercle (Paris: Klincksieck, 2001), pp. 211–19

— ' "Ne'er seen but wonder'd at": La mise en scène politique dans *Henry IV* de Shakespeare', in *Cité des hommes, cité de Dieu: Travaux sur la littérature de la Renaissance en l'honneur de Daniel Ménager* (Geneva: Droz, 2003), pp. 163–76

Lennox, Charlotte, *Shakespear Illustrated: Or, the Novels and Histories, on which the Plays of Shakespear are Founded, Collected and Translated from the Original Authors* (London: A. Millar, 1754)

Lescot, David, 'La mise en drame de la guerre', in *Théâtres de la guerre: La mise en scène de la guerre dans Les Perses d'Eschyle, la première partie de Henry*

IV de Shakespeare, Les Paravents de Genet, ed. François Lecercle (Paris: Klincksieck, 2001), pp. 67–77

Levine, Nina S., 'Extending Credit in the Henry IV Plays', *Shakespeare Quarterly*, 51 (2000), 403–31

Levy-Navarro, Elena, *The Culture of Obesity in Early and Late Modernity: Body Image in Shakespeare, Jonson, Middleton, and Skelton* (New York: Palgrave Macmillan, 2008)

Lloyd, Megan, *'Speak it in Welsh': Wales and the Welsh Language in Shakespeare* (Lanham, MD: Lexington Books-Rowman and Littlefield, 2007)

— 'Rhymer, Minstrel Lady Mortimer, and the Power of Welsh Words', in *Shakespeare and Wales: From the Marches to the Assembly*, ed. Willy Maley and Philip Schwyzer (Farnham: Ashgate, 2010), pp. 59–73

Loades, David, 'Dudley, John, duke of Northumberland (1504–1553)', *Oxford Dictionary of National Biography*, (Oxford: Oxford University Press, 2004); online edn, May 2005 (www.oxforddnb.com/view/printable/8156, accessed 20 December 2007).

Loehlin, James N., *The Shakespeare Handbooks. Henry IV: Parts I and II* (Basingstoke: Palgrave Macmillan, 2008)

Love, Karen, *Lies before Our Eyes: The Denial of Gender from the Bible to Shakespeare and Beyond* (Oxford: Lang, 2005)

Low, Jennifer, *Manhood and the Duel: Masculinity in Early Modern Drama and Culture* (New York: Palgrave Macmillan, 2003)

Lutkus, Alan, 'Sir John Falstaff', in *Fools and Jesters in Literature, Art, and History: A Bio-Bibliographical Sourcebook*, ed. Vicki K. Janik (Westport, CT: Greenwood, 1998), pp. 176–84

MacDonald, Ronald R., 'Uneasy Lies: Language and History in Shakespeare's Lancastrian Tetralogy', *Shakespeare Quarterly*, 35 (1984), 22–39

Mackenzie, Henry, 'The Lounger' (1786), in *William Shakespeare: The Critical Heritage, 1774–1801 (Volume 6)*, ed. Brian Vickers (London: Routledge, 1981), pp. 440–46

Maestro, Jesús G., 'Cervantes y Shakespeare: El nacimiento de la literatura metateatral', *Bulletin of Spanish Studies* 81 (2004), 599–611

Mangan, Michael, *Staging Masculinities: History, Gender, Performance* (Basingstoke: Palgrave Macmillan, 2003)

Manning, Roger B., *Village Revolts* (Oxford: Oxford University Press, 1988)

— *Hunters and Poachers: A Social and Cultural History of Unlawful Hunting 1485–1640* (Oxford: Clarendon Press, 1993)

Marchant, Alicia, 'Cosmos and History: Shakespeare's Representation of Nature and Rebellion in *Henry IV Part One*', in *Renaissance Poetry and Drama in Context: Essays for Christopher Wortham*, ed. Andrew Lynch and Anne M. Scott (Newcastle: Cambridge Scholars, 2008), pp. 41–59

Marotti, Arthur F., 'Shakespeare and Catholicism', in *Theatre and Religion: Lancastrian Shakespeare*, ed. Richard Dutton, Alison Findlay and Richard Wilson (Manchester: Manchester University Press, 2003), pp. 218–41

Marsalek, Karen, 'Marvels and Counterfeits: False Resurrection in the Chester *Antichrist* and *1 Henry IV*', in *Shakespeare and the Middle Ages*, ed. Curtis Perry and John Watkins (Oxford: Oxford University Press, 2009), pp. 217–40

Martella, Giuseppe, 'Henry IV: The Frame of History', in Mnema per Lino Falzon Santucci, ed. Paola Pugliatti, (Messina: Siciliano, 1997), pp. 55–85

Maxwell, James, The Laudable Life and Deplorable Death of our late peerless Prince Henry (London: Thomas Pavier, 1612)

Mayer, Jean-Cristophe, 'Pro Patria Mori: War and Power in the Henriad', Cahiers élisabéthains, 51 (1997), 29–46

McAlindon, Tom, 'Pilgrims of Grace: Henry IV Historicized', Shakespeare Survey 48 (1995), 69–84

— Shakespeare's Tudor History: A Study of Henry IV, Parts 1 and 2 (Aldershot: Ashgate, 2001)

McDonough, Christopher M., ' "A mere scutcheon": Falstaff as Rhipsaspis', Notes and Queries, 55 (2008), 181–83

McLoughlin, Cathleen T., Shakespeare, Rabelais, and the Comical-Historical (New York: Lang, 2000)

McMillin, Scott and MacLean, Sally-Beth, The Queen's Men and Their Plays (Cambridge: Cambridge University Press, 1998)

McMillin, Scott, Shakespeare in Performance: Henry IV Part One (Manchester: Manchester University Press, 1991)

McMullan, Gordon, ed., 1 Henry IV: A Norton Critical Edition, 3rd edition (New York: W. W. Norton & Co., 2003)

Melchiori, Giorgio, 'Falstaff mediterráneo', Contrastes: Revista cultural 12 (2000), 24–29

— 'Hal's Unrestrained Loose Companions', Memoria di Shakespeare, 1 (2000), 19–32

— ed., The Merry Wives of Windsor, (Walton-on-Thames: Thomas Nelson and son, 2000)

— ed., The Second Part of King Henry IV, (1989; rpt.: Cambridge: Cambridge University Press, 2007)

Meres, Francis, Palladis Tamia, Wits Treasury Being the Second Part of Wits Commonwealth (London: Cuthbert Burbie, 1598)

Middleton, Thomas, Civitatis Amor (London: Thomas Archer, 1612)

Miller, Lesley Ellis, 'Dress to Impress: Prince Charles Plays Madrid, March-September 1623', in The Spanish Match: Prince Charles's Journey to Madrid, 1623, ed. Alexander Samson (Aldershot: Ashgate, 2006), pp. 27–50

Milward, Peter, 'Shakespeare's Sacred Fools', Renaissance Bulletin, 29 (2002), 19–28

Monod, Paul Kleber, The Power of Kings: Monarchy and Religion in Europe 1589–1715 (New Haven, CT: Yale University Press, 1999)

Montagu, Elizabeth, 'An Essay on the Writings and Genius of Shakespeare, Compared with the Greek and French Dramatic Poets' (1769), in Henry the Fourth Parts I and II: Critical Essays, ed. David Bevington (New York and London: Garland Publishing Inc., 1986), pp. 9–14

Montrose, Louis, The Purpose of Playing: Shakespeare and the Cultural Politics of the Elizabethan Theatre (Chicago: Chicago University, 1996)

More, St Thomas, The Confutation of Tyndale's Answer, in The Complete Works of St Thomas More, ed. L. A. Schuster, et al. (New Haven, CT: Yale University Press, 1973), 8: 42

Morgann, Maurice, 'An Essay on the Dramatic Character of Sir John Falstaff' (1777), in *Henry the Fourth Parts I and II: Critical Essays*, ed. David Bevington (New York and London: Garland Publishing Inc., 1986), pp. 15–40

Morris, Corbyn, 'An essay Towards Fixing the True Standards of Wit, Humour, Raillery, Satire and Ridicule' (1744), in *Henry the Fourth Parts I and II: Critical Essays*, ed. David Bevington (New York and London: Garland Publishing Inc., 1986), pp. 1–5

Mortier, Daniel, 'Le théâtre de la guerre', in *Théâtres de la guerre: La mise en scène de la guerre dans Les Perses d'Eschyle, la première partie de Henry IV de Shakespeare, Les Paravents de Genet*, ed. François Lecercle (Paris: Klincksieck, 2001), pp. 47–65

Mortimer, Ian, *The Fears of Henry IV: The Life of England's Self-Made King* (London: Vintage, 2008)

Mossman, Judith, 'Plutarch and Shakespeare's Henry IV Parts 1 and 2', *Poetica: An International Journal of Linguistic-Literary Studies*, 48 (1997), 99–117

Muir, Kenneth, *The Sources of Shakespeare's Plays* (New Haven, CT: Yale University Press, 1978)

Mullaney, Steven, *The Place of the Stage: Liberty, Play and Power in Renaissance England* (Ann Arbor, MI: University of Michigan, 1988)

Murphy, Andrew, 'Ireland as Foreign and Familiar in Shakespeare's Histories', in *Shakespeare's History Plays: Performance, Translation and Adaptation in Britain and Abroad*, ed. A. J. Hoenselaars (Cambridge: Cambridge University Press, 2004), pp. 42–59

Mynott, Glen, 'Chivalry, Monarchy, and Rebellion in Shakespeare's Henry IV, Parts One and Two', in *The Iconography of Power: Ideas and Images of Rulership on the English Renaissance Stage*, ed. György Endre Szonyi and Rowland Wymer (Szeged: IATE Press, 2000), pp. 147–60

My Own Private Idaho, dir. Gus Van Sant (New Line Cinema, 1991)

Nardizzi, Vin, 'Grafted to Falstaff and Compounded with Catherine: Mingling Hal in the Second tetralogy', in *Queer Renaissance Historiography: Backward Gaze*, ed. Vin Nardizzi, Stephen Guy-Bray and Will Stockton (Farnham: Ashgate, 2009), pp. 149–69

Nelson, Alan H., ed., *REED: Cambridge* (Toronto: University of Toronto Press, 1989)

Nicolaescu, Madalina, ' "What is honour?": Falstaff's Deconstruction of Chivalric Values in *1 Henry IV*', *Studii de limbi si literaturi moderne*, (2000), 287–96

— *Meanings of Violence in Shakespeare's Plays* (Bucharest: Editura Universitatii Bucuresti, 2002)

Nichol, Charles, *The Reckoning: the Murder of Christopher Marlowe* (London: Picador, 1993)

Nichols, John Gough, ed., *The Diary of Henry Machyn, Citizen and Merchant-Taylor of London, From A.D. 1550 to A.D. 1563* (London: British Library, 1848)

Novy, Marianne, 'Women's Re-visions of Shakespeare 664-1988', in *Women's Re-visions of Shakespeare: On the Responses of Dickinson, Woolf, Rich, H. D., George Eliot, and Others*, ed. Marianne Novy (Chicago: University of Illinois Press, 1990), pp. 1–15

O'Brien, Peggy, et al., *Shakespeare Set Free: Teaching* Hamlet and Henry IV Part 1 (New York: Washington Square Press, 1994)

O'Connor, John and Katharine, Goodland, eds, *A Directory of Shakespeare in Performance, 1970 – 2005* (Basingstoke: Macmillan, 2006)

Ornstein, Robert, *A Kingdom for a Stage: The Achievement of Shakespeare's History Plays* (Cambridge: Harvard University Press, 1972)

Outhwaite, R. B., 'Dearth, the English Crown and the Crisis of the 1590s' in *The European Crisis of the 1590s* ed. Peter Clark (London: George Allen & Unwin, 1985), pp. 23–43

Oz, Avraham, 'Nation and Place in Shakespeare: The Case of Jerusalem as a National Desire in Early Modern English Drama', in *Post-Colonial Shakespeares*, ed. Ania Loomba and Martin Orkin (London: Routledge, 1998), pp. 98–116

Oxford Dictionary of National Biography (Oxford: Oxford University Press, 2004)

Palmer, D. J., 'Casting off the Old Man: History and St. Paul in *Henry IV*' (1970), in *Henry The Fourth Parts I and II. Critical Essays*, ed. David Bevington (New York and London: Garland Publishing Inc., 1986), pp. 315–35

Palmer, Henrietta Lee, *The Stratford Gallery; or, the Shakespeare Sisterhood: Comprising Forty-Five Ideal Portraits* (New York: Appletin and Co., 1859)

Peat, Derek, 'Falstaff Gets the Sack', *Shakespeare Quarterly* 53 (2002), 379–85

Penberthy, Susan, 'Falstaff's Reformation: Virtue in Idleness', in *The Touch of the Real: Essays in Early Modern Culture in Honour of Stephen Greenblatt* ed. Philippa Kelly (Crawley: University of Western Australia, 2002), pp. 143–58

Pendleton, Thomas, ' "This is not the man": On Calling Falstaff Falstaff', *Analytical and Enumerative Bibliography*, 4 (1990), 59–71

Pepys, Samuel, *The Diary of Samuel Pepys Volume VII*, ed. Henry B. Wheatley (London: G Bell, 1926), pp. 183–84

— 'Diary' (1667), in *William Shakespeare: The Critical Heritage, 1623–1692 (Volume 1)*, ed. Brian Vickers (London: Routledge, 1974)

Perrinchief, Richard, *The Royal Martyr, or, The History of the Life and Death of King Charles I* (London: R. Royston, 1676)

Plaw, Avery, 'Prince Harry: Shakespeare's Critique of Machiavelli', *Interpretation: A Journal of Political Philosophy*, 33 (2005), 19–43

Pollnitz, Aysha, 'Educating Hamlet and Prince Hal', in *Shakespeare and Early Modern Political Thought*, ed. David Armitage, Conal Condren and Andrew Fitzmaurice Andrew (Cambridge: Cambridge University Press, 2009), pp. 119–38

Poole, Kristen, 'Saints Alive! Falstaff, Martin Marprelate, and the Staging of Puritanism', *Shakespeare Quarterly*, 46.1 (1995), 47–75

— *Radical Religion from Shakespeare to Milton: Figures of Nonconformity in Early Modern England* (Cambridge: Cambridge University Press, 2000)

Quinn, Dennis, 'Pastimes and the Prince: Hal and *Eutrapelia*', *Ben Jonson Journal*, 4 (1997), 103–14

Quinones, Ricardo, *The Renaissance Discovery of Time* (Cambridge: Harvard University Press, 1972)

Quint, David, 'Bragging Rights: Honor and Courtesy in Shakespeare and Spenser', in *Creative Imitation: New Essays on Renaissance Literature in Honor of Thomas M. Greene*, ed. David Quint, Margaret W. Ferguson, G.W. Pigman III, Wayne A. Rebhorn (Binghamton, NY: Medieval and Renaissance Texts and Studies, 1992), pp. 405–14

— 'The Tragedy of Nobility on the Seventeenth-Century Stage', *Modern Language Quarterly*, 67 (2006), 7–29

Rabkin, Norman, *Shakespeare and the Problem of Meaning* (Chicago: University of Chicago Press, 1981)

Rackin, Phyllis, *Stages of History: Shakespeare's English Chronicles* (Ithaca, NY: Cornell University Press, 1990)

— 'Historical Difference/Sexual Difference', in *Privileging Gender in Early Modern England*, ed. Brink, Jean R. (Kirksville, MO: Sixteenth Century Journal Publishers, 1993), pp. 37–63

Rallo, Élisabeth, 'Tel père, tel fils? Paternité et filiation dans *Henry IV* de Shakespeare', in *Femmes, familles, filiations: Société et histoire*, ed. Marcel Bernos and Bitton, Michèle Bitton, (Aix-en-Provence: Publications de l'Université de Provence, 2004), pp. 205–14

Rauchut, E. A., 'Hotspur's Prisoners and the Laws of War in *1 Henry IV*', *Shakespeare Quarterly*, 45 (1994), 96–97

Read, David, 'Losing the Map: Topographical Understanding in the Henriad', *Modern Philology*, 94 (1996–1997), 475–95

Rebhorn, Wayne A., *The Emperor of Men's Minds: Literature and the Discourse of Rhetoric* (Ithaca, NY and London: Cornell University Press, 1995)

Redondo, Augustin, 'En torno a dos personajes festivos: El shakesperiano Falstaff y el cervantino Sancho Panza', in *Entre Cervantes y Shakespeare: Sendas del Renacimiento/Between Shakespeare and Cervantes: Trails along the Renaissance*, ed. Zenón Luis Martínez,; Luis Gómez Canseco (Newark, DE: Juan de la Cuesta, 2006), pp. 161–82

Reid, Robert L., 'Humoral Psychology in Shakespeare's Henriad', *Comparative Drama*, 30 (1996–1997), 471–502

Ribner, Irving, 'The English History Play in the Age of Shakespeare' (1957), in *Shakespeare's Histories: An Anthology of Modern Criticism*, ed. William Armstrong (London: Penguin, 1972), pp. 29–59

Richardson, William, *Essay on Shakespeare's Dramatic Character of Sir John Falstaff* (London: J. Murray, 1788)

Robinson, Benedict, 'Harry and Amurath', *Shakespeare Quarterly*, 60: 4 (2009), 399–424

Rolls, Albert, *The Theory of the King's Two Bodies in the Age of Shakespeare* (Lewiston, ID: Mellen, 2000)

Rosendale, Timothy, 'Sacral and Sacramental Kingship in the Lancastrian Tetralogy', in *Shakespeare and the Culture of Christianity in Early Modern England*, ed. Dennis Taylor and David N. Beauregard (New York: Fordham University Press, 2003), pp. 121–40

Rossiter, A. P., 'Angel with Horns: The Unity of *Richard III*' (1961), in *Shakespeare's Histories: An Anthology of Modern Criticism*, ed. William Armstrong (London: Penguin, 1972), pp. 123–44

Ruiter, David, *Shakespeare's Festive History: Feasting, Festivity, Fasting, and Lent in the Second Henriad* (Aldershot: Ashgate, 2003)

— 'Harry's (In)Human Face', *Spiritual Shakespeares*, ed. Ewan Fernie (London: Routledge, 2005), pp. 50–72

Ryan, Kiernan, 'The Future of History in *Henry IV*', in *Henry IV Parts 1 and 2*, ed. Nigel Wood (Buckingham: Open University Press, 1995), pp. 92–125

Salgado, Gamini, *Eyewitnesses of Shakespeare* (London: Sussex University Press, 1975)

Sanderson, William, *A Compleat History of the Lives and Reigns of Mary, Queen of Scotland, and of Her Son and Successor, James the Sixth, King of Scotland* (1656)

— *A Compleat History of the Life and Raigne of King Charles from His Cradle to His Grave* (London: H. Meseley, R. Tomlins and G.Sawbridge, 1658)

Schamp, Jutta, *Repräsentation von Zeit bei Shakespeare: Richard II, Henry IV, Macbeth* (Tübingen: Niemeyer, 1997)

Schelling, Felix E., *The English Chronicle Play: A Study in the Popular Historical Literature Environing Shakespeare* (London: Macmillan, 1902)

Schlegel, A. W., *A Course of Lectures on Dramatic Art and Literature*, translated by John Black (London: Bohn, 1846)

Scoufos, Alice-Lyle, *Shakespeare's Typological Satire: A Study of the Falstaff-Oldcastle Problem* (Ohio: Ohio University Press, 1979)

Scragg, Leah, *Shakespeare's Alternative Tales* (London: Longman, 1996)

Severgnini, Silvestro, 'Shakespeare da Oldcastle a Falstaff, per predenza', *La rivista illustrata del Museo teatrale alla Scala*, 7 (Autumn 1994), 31, 34–35

Shaaber, Matthias, 'The Unity of *Henry IV*', in *Joseph Quincy Adams Memorial Studies*, ed. J. G. McManaway (Washington: Folger Library, 1948), pp. 217–27

Shaheen, Naseeb, *Biblical References in Shakespeare's History Plays* (Newark, DE: University of Delaware Press, 1989)

Shakespeare, William, *Poems* (Tho. Cotes, 1640)

— *The Riverside Shakespeare*, 2nd edition, ed. G. Blakemore Evans, et al. (Boston: Houghton-Mifflin, 1997)

Sharpe, Jim, 'Social strain and social dislocation, 1585–1603' in *The Reign of Elizabeth: Court and Culture in the Last Decade*, ed. John Guy (Cambridge: Cambridge University Press, 1995), pp. 192–211

Shaughnessy, Robert, ' "I do, I will": Hal, Falstaff, and the Performative', in *Alternative Shakespeares 3*, ed. Diana E. Henderson (London: Routledge, 2008), 14–33

Shaw, Jonathan Samuel, *History Plays of Shakespeare: A Revaluation* (Allahabad: Kitab Mahal, 1999)

Shurgot, Michael W., *Stages of Play: Shakespeare's Theatrical Energies in Elizabethan Performance* (Newark, DE: University of Delaware Press, 1998)

Shusterman, Richard, *Surface and Depth: Dialectics of Criticism and Culture* (Ithaca, NY: Cornell University Press, 2002)

Sidney, Philip, *A Defence of Poetry*, ed. J. A. Van Dorsten (Oxford: Oxford University Press, 1966)

Simmons, J. L., 'Masculine Negotiations in Shakespeare's History Plays: Hal, Hotspur, and "the foolish Mortimer"', *Shakespeare Quarterly*, 44 (1993), 440–63

Simon, Richard Keller, *Trash Culture: Popular Culture and the Great Tradition* (Berkeley, CA: University of California Press, 1999)

Simpson, Richard, 'The Politics of Shakespeare's Historical Plays', *The New Shakespeare Society Transactions*, 1 (1874), pp. 396–441

Smith, Irwin, 'Dramatic Time versus Clock Time in Shakespeare', *Shakespeare Quarterly*, 20:1 (1969) 65–69

Sohmer, Steve, *Shakespeare and the Wiser Sort* (Manchester: Manchester University Press, 2007)

Spencer, Janet M.,'Violence and the Sacred: Holy Fragments, Shakespeare, and the Postmodern', *Christianity and Literature*, 50 (2000–2001), 613–29

Spiekerman, Tim J., 'The Education of Hal: *Henry IV, Parts One and Two*', in *Shakespeare's Political Pageant: Essays in Literature and Politics*, ed. Joseph Alulis and Vickie Sullivan (Lanham, MD: Rowman and Littlefield, 1996), pp. 103–24

— *Shakespeare's Political Realism: The English History Plays* (Albany, NY: State University of New York Press, 2001)

Spivack, Bernard, 'Shakespeare and the Allegory of Evil' (1958), in *Henry the Fourth Parts I and II: Critical Essays*, ed. David Bevington (New York and London: Garland Publishing Inc., 1986), pp. 221–22

Stack, Richard,'An Examination of an Essay on the Dramatick Character of Sir John Falstaff' (1788), in *William Shakespeare: The Critical Heritage, 1693–1733 (Volume 2)*, ed. Brian Vickers (London: Routledge, 1974), pp. 469–79

Stanco, Michele, 'Historico-Tragico-Comical Kings: Genre Conventions and/as Emblems of Power in Shakespeare's Histories', in *The Iconography of Power: Ideas and Images of Rulership on the English Renaissance Stage*, ed. György Endre Szonyi and Rowland Wymer (Szeged: IATE Press, 2000), pp. 117–45

— 'Le sette vite di Falstaff: Giustizia penale e giustizia poetica in *Henry IV (1 e 2)* e *Henry V*', in *Shakespeare e Verdi*, ed. Giovanna Silvani and Claudio Gallico, (Parma: Facoltà di Lettere e Filosofia, Università degli Studi de Parma, 2000), pp. 99–117

Steppat, Michael, 'Globe of Sinful Continents: Desires in the Henriad', in *Anglistentag: 2005 Bamberg Proceedings*, ed. Christoph Houswitschka, Gabriele Knappe and Anja Müller, (Trier:Wissenschaftlicher Verlag Trier, 2006), pp. 145–58

Stewart, Alan, *Shakespeare's Letters* (Oxford: Oxford University Press, 2008)

Stewart, J. I. M., 'Character and Motive in Shakespeare' (1949), in *Shakespeare: Henry IV Parts I and II: A Casebook*, edited by G. K. Hunter (London: Macmillan, 1970), pp. 127–33

Strong, Roy, *Henry Prince of Wales and England's Lost Renaissance* (London: Pimlico, 2000)

Stříbrný, Zdeněk, *The Whirligig of Time: Essays on Shakespeare and Czechoslovakia*, ed. Lois Potter (Newark, DE: University of Delaware Press, 2007)

Stoll, Elmer Edgar, 'Falstaff', *Modern Philology*, 12.4 (1914), 197–240

Stubbes, Philip, *Anatomy of Abuses in England in Shakspere's Youth AD 1583*, ed. F. J. Furnivall (New Shakespeare Society, n.s.s. iv, vi, xii. 1877–1882)

Summers, Ellen, ' "Judge, my masters": Playing Hal's Audience', in *Shakespeare's Second Historical Tetralogy: Some Christian Features,* ed. Beatrice Batson (West Cornwall, CT: Locust Hill Press, 2004), pp. 165–78

Szczekalla, Michael, 'Shakespeare als gutter Europäer', *Anglistik,* 16 (2005), 25–34

Tawney, R. H. and Eileen Power, eds, *Tudor Economic Documents* (London: Longman, 1924)

Taylor, Gary, 'The Fortunes of Oldcastle', *Shakespeare Survey* 38 (1985), 85–100

Taylor, Gary, Stanley Wells, John Jowett and William Montgomery, eds, *William Shakespeare: The Complete Works* (Oxford: Clarendon Press, 1986)

Taylor, Mark, 'Falstaff and the Origins of Private Life', *Shakespeare Yearbook,* 3, (1992), 63–85

Taylor, Michael, *Shakespeare and Criticism in the Twentieth Century* (Oxford: Oxford University Press, 2001)

Theobald, Lewis, 'The Works of Shakespeare' (1733), in *William Shakespeare: The Critical Heritage, 1693–1733 (Volume 2),* ed. Brian Vickers (London: Routledge, 1974), pp. 475–528

Thorn-Drury, George, *Some Seventeenth-Century Allusions to Shakespeare and his Works* (London: P. J. and A. E. Dobell, 1920)

Tiffany, Grace, 'Puritanism in Comic History: Exposing Royalty in the Henry Plays', *Shakespeare Studies,* 26 (1998), 256–87

Tillyard, E. M. W., *Shakespeare's History Plays* (1944) (London: Penguin Books, 1991)

Time, Victoria M., *Shakespeare's Criminals: Criminology, Fiction, and Drama* (Westport, CT: Greenwood, 1999)

Toliver, Harold, 'Falstaff, the Prince and the History Play', *Shakespeare Quarterly,* 16.1 (1965), 63–80

Trawick, Buckner B, *Shakespeare and Alcohol* (Amsterdam: Rodopi, 1978)

Traub, Valerie, 'Prince Hal's Falstaff: Positioning Psychoanalysis and the Female Reproductive Body', *Shakespeare Quarterly,* 40 (1989), 456–74

— *Desire and Anxiety: Circulations of Sexuality in Shakespearean Drama* (London: Routledge, 1992)

Traversi, Derek, *Shakespeare: From Richard II to Henry V* (Stanford, CA: Stanford University Press, 1957)

Trewin, J. C., *Shakespeare on the English Stage 1900–1964* (London: Barrie and Rockliff, 1964)

Turner, Walt, 'Coins, Cons, and the Caduceus: The Making of a Sovereign in Shakespeare's *Henry* Plays', *Shakespeare and Renaissance Association of West Virginia: Selected Papers,* 27 (2004), 1–10

Tyler, Royall, ed., *Calendar of Letters, Despatches, and State Papers. Relating to the Negotiations between England and Spain* (London: David Nutt, 1914)

Ulrici, Hermann, *Shakespeare's Dramatic Art,* translated by L. Dora Schmitz (London: George Bell and Sons, 1876)

Underdown, David, *Revel, Riot and Rebellion: Popular Politics and Culture in England 1603–1660* (Oxford: Oxford University Press, 1985)

Ungerer, Gustav, 'Prostitution in Late Elizabethan London: The Case of Mary Newborough', *Medieval and Renaissance Drama in England,* 15 (2002), pp. 138–223

Upton, John, *Critical Observations on Shakespeare* (London: G. Hawkins, 1748)

Van Doren, Mark, 'Shakespeare' (1939), in *Henry the Fourth Parts I and II: Critical Essays*, ed. David Bevington (New York and London: Garland Publishing Inc., 1986), pp. 99–116

Vescovi, Alessandro, 'A journeyman to grief: L'idea di viaggio in *Enrico IV* ed *Enrico V*', in *Shakespeare Days – I edizione Milano, 16–23–30 maggio 2002: Atti del convegno* ed. Luisa Camaiora (Milan:Università Cattolica, 2004), pp. 245–55

Videbaek, Bente A., *The Stage Clown in Shakespeare's Theatre* (Westport, CT: Greenwood, 1996)

Vienne-Guerrin, Nathalie, 'L'anatomie de l'insulte dans *1 Henry IV*', *Bulletin de la Société de stylistique anglaise*, 17 (1996), 21–35

— 'Les jeux de l'injure dans *Henry IV*', in *Shakespeare et le jeu*, ed. Pierre Kapitaniak and Yves Peyré (Paris: Société Française Shakespeare, 2005), pp. 185–99

— 'Flyting on Screen: Insults in Film Versions of *Henry IV*', in *Shakespeare on Screen: The Henriad*, ed. Sarah Hatchuel and Nathalie Vienne-Guerrin (Mont-Saint-Aignan: Publications des Universités de Rouen and du Havre, 2008), pp. 119–45

Vignaux, Michèle, *L'invention de la responsabilité. La deuxième tétralogie de Shakespeare* (Paris: Presses de l'École Normale Supérieure, 1995)

Wai-fong, Cheang, 'Laughter, Play, and Irony: Rereading the Comic Space in Shakespeare's Second tetralogy', *NTU Studies in Language and Literature*, 10 (2001), 51–74

Wall, Alison, *Power and Protest in England 1525–1640* (London: Arnold, 2000)

Walsh, Brian, *Shakespeare, The Queen's Men, and the Elizabethan Performance of History* (Cambridge: Cambridge University Press, 2009)

Walter, John and Keith Wrightson, 'Dearth and the Social Order in Early Modern England' in *Rebellion, Popular Protest and the Social Order in Early Modern England*, ed. Paul Slack (Cambridge: Cambridge University Press, 1984), pp. 108–28

Ward, Ian, 'Shakespeare, the Narrative Community, and the Legal Imagination', in *Law and Literature*, ed. Michael Freeman and Andrew D. E. Lewis (Oxford: Oxford University Press, 1999), pp. 117–48

Watson, Robert, *Shakespeare and the Hazards of Ambition* (Cambridge: Harvard University Press, 1984)

Weil, Herbert, 'Montaigne and Falstaff', *Shakespeare Newsletter*, 58 (2008), 49, 54, 60, 70

Weil, Herbert and Judith Weil, eds, *The First Part of King Henry IV* (Cambridge: Cambridge University Press, 1997)

Weimann, Robert, *Shakespeare and the Popular Tradition in the Theatre: Studies in the Social Dimension of Dramatic Form and Function*, ed. Robert Schwartz (Baltimore, MD: John Hopkins University Press, 1978)

— *Author's Pen and Actor's Voice: Playing and Writing in Shakespeare's Theatre* (Cambridge: Cambridge University Press, 2000)

Welsh, Alexander, *What Is Honor: A Question of Moral Imperatives* (New Haven, CT and London: Yale University Press, 2008)

Wharton, T. F., *Text and Performance: Henry the Fourth Parts 1 and 2* (London: Macmillan, 1983)

Wheatley, Henry B, ed., *The Diary of Samuel Pepys Volume VII* (London: G. Bell and Sons Ltd, 1929)

White, Paul Whitfield, 'Patronage, Protestantism, and Stage Propaganda in Early Elizabethan England', in *Patronage, Politics, and Literary Tradition in England 1558-1658*, ed. Cedric C. Brown (Detroit, MI: Wayne State University Press, 1991), pp. 111–24 (p. 123).

— 'Shakespeare, the Cobhams, and the Dynamics of Theatrical Patronage', in *Shakespeare and Theatrical Patronage in Early Modern England*, ed. Paul Whitfield White and Suzanne R. Westfall (Cambridge: Cambridge University Press, 2002), pp. 64–89

— 'Shakespeare and Religious Polemic: Revisiting *1 Henry IV* and the Oldcastle Controversy', in *Shakespeare's Second Historical Tetralogy: Some Christian Features*, ed. Beatrice Batson (West Cornwall, CT: Locust Hill Press, 2004), pp. 147–64

Whitney, Charles, Festivity and Topicality in the Coventry Scene of *1 Henry IV*', *English Literary Renaissance*, 24 (1994), 410–48

— *Early Responses to Renaissance Drama* (Cambridge: Cambridge University Press, 2006)

Winter, Guillaume, ' "In the suburbs of your good pleasure": Les lieux de plaisir à Londres à la fin du XVIe et au début du XVIIe siècles', in *Enfers et délices à la Renaissance*, ed. François Laroque and Franck Lessay (Paris: Presses Sorbonne Nouvelle, 2003), pp. 31–41

Wilkinson, Kate, 'Review of Shakespeare's Richard II, Henry IV Part 1, Henry IV Part 2, and Henry V (directed by Michael Boyd and Richard Twyman for the Royal Shakespeare Company) at the Courtyard Theatre, Stratford-upon-Avon 2007' in *Shakespeare* 4, Nos. 1–4, March – December 2008, 181–87

Wilson, John, 'Dies Boreales', *Blackwood's Edinburgh Magazine*, 66:409 (1849) pp. 620–54, and 67:414 (1850) pp. 481–512

Wilson, John Dover, 'The Origins and Development of Shakespeare's *Henry IV*' *Library*, new series XXIV 1: 2 (1945), pp. 9–10

— *The Fortunes of Falstaff* (Cambridge: Cambridge University Press, 1943)

Wilson, J. D. and T. C. Worsley, *Shakespeare's Histories at Stratford 1951* (London: Max Reinhardt Stellar Press, 1952)

Wilson, Richard, 'A Sea of Troubles: The Thought of the Outside in Shakespeare's Histories', in *Shakespeare's Histories and Counter-Histories*, ed. Dermot Cavanagh, Stuart Hampton-Reeves and Stephen Longstaffe (Manchester: Manchester University Press, 2006), pp. 101–34

Winstanley, William, 'The Lives of the Most Famous English Poets' (1687), in *More Seventeenth-Century Allusions to Shakespeare and his Works*, ed. George Thorn-Drury (London: P. J. and A. E. Dobell, 1924), p. 25

Wood, Andy, 'Poore Men woll speke one daye: Plebeian Languages of Deference and Defiance in England c. 1520–1640' in *The Politics of the Excluded, c.1500–1850*, ed. Tim Harris (New York: Palgrave, 2001), pp. 67–98

— 'Fear, hatred and the hidden injuries of class in early modern England' in *Journal of Social History*, 39:1 (2006), pp. 803–26

Wotton, Henry, *Reliquiae Wottonianae*, 4th ed. (London: B. Tooke & T. Sawbridge, 1685)

Wrightson, Keith, 'Alehouses, order and reformation in rural England, 1590–1660' in *Popular Culture and Class Conflict 1590–1914: Explorations in the History of Labour and Leisure* ed. Eileen Yeo and Stephen Yeo (Brighton, Sussex: Harvester, 1981), pp. 1–27

— 'Estates, Degrees and Sorts in Tudor and Stuart England', *History Today* 37 (1987), 17–22

Yachnin, Paul, '"The Perfection of Ten": Populuxe Art and Artisanal Value in *Troilus and Cressida*', *Shakespeare Quarterly*, 56 (2005), 306–27

Yeandle, Laetitia, 'The Dating of Sir Edward Dering's Copy of "The History of Henry King the Fourth," *Shakespeare Quarterly*, 37 (1986), 224–26

Youings, Joyce, *Sixteenth Century England* (Harmondsworth: Penguin, 1984)

Young, R. V., 'Juliet and Shakespeare's Other Nominalists: Variations on a Theme by Richard Weaver', *Intercollegiate Review*, 33 (1997), 18–29

Notes on Contributors

Graham Atkin is a Senior Lecturer in the Department of English at the University of Chester. He has published *Studying Literature: A Practical Introduction* (1995, with Chris Walsh and Susan Watkins) and *Studying Shakespeare: A Practical Guide* (1998, with Katherine Armstrong). He has also published an essay on Edmund Spenser's *The Faerie Queene* in a collection of essays edited by Julian Lethbridge. His book on *Twelfth Night* in the Character Studies series from Continuum Press was published in 2008.

Alison Findlay is Professor of Renaissance Drama and Director of the Shakespeare Programme at Lancaster University (UK). She specialises in sixteenth- and seventeenth-century drama, gender issues and performance practices. She is the author of *Illegitimate Power: Bastards in Renaissance Drama* (Manchester University Press, 1994), *A Feminist Perspective on Renaissance Drama* (Blackwell Publishers, 1998) and *Playing Spaces in Early Women's Drama* (Cambridge University Press, 2006). Most recently she has published *Women in Shakespeare* (Continuum, 2010). She is co-author of *Women and Dramatic Production 1550–1700* (Longman's Medieval and Renaissance Library, Pearson, 2000) based on a research project using practical workshops and productions. She has published essays on Shakespeare and his contemporaries and is currently a General Editor of the Revels Plays (Manchester University Press). She is currently working on *Much Ado About Nothing: A Text and Its Theatrical Life*, to be published by Palgrave.

Chris Fitter is Associate Professor of English at Rutgers University at Camden. He is the author of *Poetry, Space, Landscape: Toward a New*

Theory (Cambridge University Press, 1995), and of *Radical Shakespeare: Politics and Stagecraft in the Early Career* (forthcoming). He has published some 20 articles and book chapters on Renaissance literature, the journal essays appearing in *Shakespeare Studies, Milton Studies, English Literary Renaissance, English Literary History, Essays in Criticism, Medieval and Renaissance Drama in English,* and elsewhere. His current work in progress is on Shakespeare and the Essex Crisis, 1595–1601.

Jonathan Hart, Director of Comparative Literature, Professor of English and Adjunct Professor of History at University of Alberta, has held visiting appointments at Harvard, Cambridge, Princeton, Toronto, Nouvelle-Sorbonne and elsewhere and has published widely, including books and collections such as *Theater and World: the Problematics of Shakespeare's History* (1992); *Northrop Frye: The Theoretical Imagination* (1994): *Reading the Renaissance : Culture, Poetics, and Drama* (1996); *Imagining Culture: Essays in Early Modern History and Literature* (1996); *Representing the New World: Example of Spain, 1492–1713* (2001); *Columbus, Shakespeare, and the Interpretation of the New World* (2003); *Comparing Empires: European Colonialism from Portuguese Expansion to the Spanish-American War* (2003); *Contesting Empires: Promotion, Opposition and Slavery* (2005); *Interpreting Culture: Literature, Religion, and the Human Sciences* (2006); *Empires and Colonies* (2008); *City of the End of Things: Lectures on Civilization and Empire* (2009); *Shakespeare: Poetry, History, and Culture* (2009), and *Shakespeare and His Contemporaries* (2010). His books of poetry include *Breath and Dust* (2000); *Dream China* (2002); *Dream Salvage* (2003); *Dreamwork* (2010) and, a book of sonnets, *Musing* (forthcoming 2011). His poetry has been translated into French, Greek, Estonian, Russian and other languages, including the volume, *Souffle et poussière* (forthcoming 2011).

Robert Hornback, Associate Professor of English and Theatre at Oglethorpe University in Atlanta, GA, has authored several articles focused on the comic in journals including *Shakespeare Stud*ies, *Medieval and Renaissance Drama in England, English Literary Renaissance, Shakespeare International Yearbook, Early Theatre, Studies in English Literature, Comparative Drama, Research Opportunities in Medieval and Renaissance Drama, Exemplaria,* and *Notes & Queries,* and in collections such as *The Blackwell Companion to Tudor Literature, as well as* reviews in *Shakespeare Quarterly, Renaissance Quarterly, and Sixteenth Century Journal.* Having published *The English Clown Tradition from the Middle Ages to Shakespeare* (Boydell & Brewer, 2009), he is currently at work on a book unearthing long overlooked medieval and Renaissance blackface fool traditions and their proto-racist legacy.

Edel Lamb is an Australian Research Council Fellow at the University of Sydney, and previously held an Irish Research Council Fellowship at University College Dublin. She is the author of *Performing Childhood in the Early Modern Theatre: The Children's Playing Companies (1599–1613)* (Palgrave Macmillan, 2008) and of various essays on early modern drama. Her current research focuses on early modern representations of children as readers.

Martha Tuck Rozett is a Professor of English at the University at Albany in the State University of New York system. She is the author of *The Doctrine of Election and the Emergence of Elizabethan Tragedy, Talking Back to Shakespeare*, and *Constructing a World: Shakespeare's England and the New Historical Fiction*. She has also written about and offered workshops on the teaching of Shakespeare and takes an active interest in arts-in-education programs in Albany and New York City.

Brian Walsh is an Assistant Professor in the English Department at Yale University, and is the author of *Shakespeare, The Queen's Men, and the Elizabethan Performance of History* (Cambridge University Press, 2009).

Index

SHAKESPEARE NOW

Series Editors: **Ewan Fernie, The Shakespeare Institute, Universit** of Birmingham, UK and **Simon Palfrey, University of Oxford, U**

'An innovative new series . . . Series editors Simon Palfrey and Ewan Fernie have rejected the notion of business as usual in order to pursue a distinctive strategy that aims to put "cutting-edge scholarship" in front of a broad audience. With its insistent appeal to the contemporary, this is fresh Shakespeare for readers turned off by the prospect of dry-as-dust scholarship' - Shakespeare Quarterly

Shakespeare Now! is a series of short books that engage imaginatively and often provocatively with the possibilities of Shakespeare's plays. It goes back to the source - the most living language imaginable - and recaptures the excitement, audacity and surprise of Shakespeare. It will return you to the plays with opened eyes.

 continuum

For further details visit
www.continuumbooks.com